ECONOMIC DEVELOPMENT IN AFRICA

ECONOMIC DEVELOPMENT IN AFRICA

GODFREY MWAKIKAGILE

Nova Science Publishers, Inc.
Commack, New York

Editorial Production: Susan Boriotti
Office Manager: Annette Hellinger
Graphics: Frank Grucci and Jennifer Lucas
Information Editor: Tatiana Shohov
Book Production: Donna Dennis, Patrick Davin, Christine Mathosian, Tammy Sauter and Lynette Van Helden
Circulation: Maryanne Schmidt
Marketing/Sales: Cathy DeGregory

Library of Congress Cataloging-in-Publication Data
Economic Development in Africa / Godfrey Mwakikagile
p. cm.
Includes bibliographical references and index.
ISBN 1-56072-708-X.
1. Africa--Economic conditions--1960- 2. Africa--Economic policy.
I. Title.
HC800.M854 1999 99-41866
338.96--dc21 CIP

6080 Jericho Turnpike, Suite 207
Commack, New York 11725
Tele. 516-499-3103 Fax 516-499-3146
e-mail: Novascience@earthlink.net
e-mail: Novascil@aol.com
Web Site: http://www.nexusworld.com/nova

Printed in the United States of America

CONTENTS

Acknowledgment vii
Introduction ix
Chapter One: Africa's New Strategy for Economic Development: Capitalism Versus Socialism - Case Studies 1
Chapter Two: Tanzania: Union of Two Independent States: Challenge to Unity and Ideology 31
Free-Market Approach Towards Tanzania's Economic Growth 57
Chapter Three: Africa's Potential for Economic Growth: Basis for Regional Integration and Viable States 95
Chapter Four: The State as a Fundamental Dynamic in Africa's Economic Performance 171
Africa's Economic Success 207
Map of Africa 253
About the Author 255
Index 257

ACKNOWLEDGMENT

I CANNOT ADEQUATELY express my profound gratitude to every individual who has helped to make this work possible. I can only thank them collectively, hoping that such acknowledgment will convey the depth of my indebtedness to them all in a way I would not have been able to, had I attempted to thank them individually even if I had been given ample space to do so.

Each of them has contributed to the success of this book in a very special way which could not have been duplicated by any of the others. And that means a lot in terms of how I pursued this project. I will always be grateful to them. But while I am humbled by them all, I exalt none above the rest. They have all contributed to the success of my work, and their contribution is fully acknowledged in the text and in the chapter notes.

But it is to Africa to whom I must express my deepest gratitude for obvious reasons: She is the subject of this book, she inspired it, and deserves it more than anybody else including myself. Without her, this book could not have been written. And without her, I wouldn't be what I am today. And that says it all.

While all credit is due to Africa and to all those who have contributed to the success of this project, any mistakes my readers may be able to find here and there are entirely my fault. I did my best, but we are all mere mortals, with human frailties. Yet in pursuit of dispassionate analysis, I have tried to make this work as independent as scholarship is transcendent.

INTRODUCTION

PROBABLY MORE THAN anything else, Africa is known by the stereotypes many people around the world have about the "Dark Continent." But Africa is also a strange paradox. It is the richest continent in the world. Yet it is also the poorest. Its potential wealth is enormous, unrivaled anywhere else in the world. As David Lamb states in his book *The Africans*: "There is not another continent blessed with such abundance and diversity."[1]

So why so much poverty in the midst of such abundance? The answer lies in the wrong policies and imported ideologies, good intentions notwithstanding, African countries pursued since independence during the sixties. However, with the collapse of communism during the late eighties and early nineties, came a rude awakening. The impoverished African nations were forced to re-evaluate their policies and ideological underpinnings which had failed to sustain one of their ideological "mentors": the Soviet Union and her satellites.

More than any other ideology, socialism had the strongest appeal among the newly independent African countries as the most dynamic tool in their quest for unity and progress. With its centralized planning, it was adopted by most of them as the best strategy not only for rapid economic transformation, as exemplified by the Soviet Union which became an industrial nation and a superpower within 40 years after the Russian Revolution; but also as an efficient mechanism for mobilizing different tribes into a cohesive bloc under strong one-party leadership not much different from the communist party in terms of mobilization tactics although not ideology. Only a few African countries, during the seventies, declared themselves Marxist-Leninist: Benin,

---

[1] David Lamb, *The Africans* (New York: Random House, 1982), p. 20.

formerly Dahomey; Guinea-Bissau, Mozambique, Angola, Ethiopia, Congo-Brazzaville. And during the sixties, Ghana under Dr. Kwame Nkrumah, Guinea under Sekou Toure, and Mali under Modibo Keita also embraced Marxism-Leninsim, although they did not officially adopt it as a state ideology in the same way Benin or Ethiopia, for example, did during the seventies. However, all these countries were no more regimented than the rest. It was a continental phenomenon.

But such mass regimentation proved to be counterproductive. It stifled individual initiative, leading to lower productivity, although the logic behind it was compelling: scarcity of resources in the young impoverished nations demanded full mobilization at the national level in order to be able to invest in development projects. It was the government which had the money and access to foreign capital for investment, not the peasants. Unfortunately, the system in most African countries - even if not deliberately - did not encourage the people to exploit their full potential. This lack of incentives and an environment conducive to both domestic and foreign investment is one of the biggest reasons African economies collapsed during the seventies and the eighties.

Most of them are still in tatters today; a legacy of socialism which has never been very good at providing incentives to production, despite its laudable goals of social equality and equitable distribution of wealth which could have been pursued more realistically had there been more wealth to redistribute. But such wealth could have been produced only if socialism did not rob the people of the incentive to work.

Practically in all African countries, workers did not earn enough - they still don't - even to support themselves or their families, let alone accumulate savings so critical to building domestic capital vital to long-term national investment and development; foreign capital is an unreliable catalyst for economic development: it can stop anytime or be used to manipulate recipient nations, compromising their national interests. The only alternative to that is domestic capital accumulation through national savings which can be used to fuel economic growth. But because African workers did not earn enough money even for themselves, they were robbed of the incentive to production which could have led to greater savings and economic growth. Also, the peasants, the backbone of the economy, were grossly underpaid for their agricultural commodities, thus discouraging them from producing more. They are still not rewarded accordingly for the fruits of their labor.

Africa has lost an entire generation. The result is what we see today, 40 years after independence: shattered economies, demoralized populations, and crumbling state institutions under the heavy-handed rule of corrupt dictatorship which has none of the redeeming qualities of benevolence claimed by some of the continent's most notorious autocrats. And with the exception of very few African leaders such as Julius Nyerere, none of the other leaders lived as true socialists. Yet their clarion call for socialism resonated across the continent for very good reasons especially soon after independence during the sixties; so did the ideal of one-party democracy.[2]

---

[2] Julius Nyerere, *Freedom and Socialism* (Dar es Salaam, Tanzania: Oxford University Press, 1969); William H. Friedland and Carl G. Rosberg, Jr., editors, *African Socialism* (Stanford, California: Stanford University Press, 1964). For the prevalent view that under present conditions (soon after independence during the sixties, and presumably, the seventies) there is no alternative to one-party rule in Africa, see Immanuel Wallerstein, *Africa: The Politics of Independence* (New York: Random House, 1961); Julius Nyerere, *One-Party Rule*, in *Spearhead*, Dar es Salaam, Tanganyika, November 1961, reprinted in Paul E. Sigmund, Jr., editor, *The Ideologies of the Developing Nations* (New York: Frederick A. Praeger, 1963), pp. 197-202. See also Gwendolen M. Carter, editor, *African One-Party States* (Ithaca, New York: Cornell University Press, 1962).

But while capitalism has been denounced for being exploitative, which it is by nature since it capitalizes on man's greed, it has proved to be more productive because it rewards the producers of wealth - peasants and workers - more than socialism does. Africans have learned the hard way, and, after an entire generation, have now turned to capitalism as their new strategy for economic development after socialism failed to develop their economies.

See also Thomas Hodgkin, *African Political Parties* (Baltimore, Maryland: Penguin Books, 1961). For a contrasting view on the one-party system in Africa, see Obafemi Awolowo, "A Critique of One-Party Systems", in *Awo: The Autobiography of Chief Obefemi Awolowo* (New York: Cambridge University Press, 1961); James S. Wunsch and Dele Olowu, editors, *The Failure of the Centralized State: Institutions and Self-Governance in Africa* (Boulder, Colorado: Westview Press, 1996).

CHAPTER ONE

AFRICA'S NEW STRATEGY FOR ECONOMIC DEVELOPMENT: CAPITALISM VERSUS SOCIALISM - CASE STUDIES

THE DEATH OF Somalia has brought into sharp focus the problem of the modern African state as a fragile institution incapable of forging national unity based on African realities. But even fore she died as a nation, her economy was already dead, because of her attempt to implement an imported ideology: Marxism-Leninism. Other African countries which adopted Marxism-Leninism renounced the ideology during the late eighties and early nineties as their economies faced imminent collapse after years of trying to make it work in an alien environment - and against human nature.

Others which adopted different versions of socialism, including Tanzania which tried to elevate African traditional communal values to the national level as a national ethos and an indigenous form of socialism, abandoned that ideological pursuit because it wrecked their economies. Socialism collided with the individual pursuit of profit, robbing the people of the incentive to work. Because they could not make profit for themselves, productivity declined, and the economies collapsed.

Now all African countries are trying to achieve economic development through what most of them once considered to be their nemesis: capitalism. We are going to look at some of those countries as case studies whose relevance is continental in scope. Their success in implementing their new economic policies will help strengthen the modern African state and give it credibility as a legitimate institution responsive to the needs of the people.

Since independence, African governments tried to meet those needs mainly through foreign aid which they have depended on for decades to achieve economic development. Yet even they themselves, as well as the foreign donors, have through the decades neglected the development of rural areas, resulting in huge urban problems across Africa because of the magnetic pull of urban centers drawing people from rural areas to the cities and towns in search of a better life; several African cities now have millions of people each. One way to make sure aid reaches its intended recipients is for foreign donors to take it directly to the people in the villages and towns instead of channeling it through African governments, only to be stolen by corrupt officials.

But Africans cannot rely on foreign aid to develop their countries or fulfill their basic needs. Now that the Cold War is over, and economic aid from the industrialized nations - especially Western ones - is in decline, African governments realize that the era of dependency on foreign aid is over. They have also come to realize that only the private sector - with opportunities for both local and foreign investors - can fuel economic development. But they can attract foreign investors, who are the only ones capable of providing the largest share of investment far more than local African investors can, only when they liberalize and privatize their economies and help entrepreneurship flourish. Admittedly, Africa's prospects for economic development in the short-term are bleak. But in the long-run they are bright because of new economic policies and the continent's abundant natural resources, most of which remains unexploited. As Malcolm Rifkind, Britain's foreign secretary during that time, stated in November 1996:

> "While many are dazzled by the tigers of Asia, the farsighted are recognizing that Africa could be a boom-region of the 21st century."[3]

---

[3] Malcolm Rifkind, in a statement at the end of November 1996, quoted by Reginald Dale, "Finally, Some Good News From Africa," in the *International Herald Tribune*, December 13, 1996, p. 15.

Growth-rate statistics have been impressive in a number of countries such as Uganda, which has one of the highest economic growth rates in Africa under the leadership of President Yoweri Museveni, a former socialist who is now pursuing free-market policies; and Ghana where another former socialist leader, President Jerry Rwalings, adopted austerity measures and capitalist methods to revive the economy. The shift towards the private sector as the engine of progress has been remarkable in several countries on the continent during the past few years, with commendable results in economic development and emphasis on liberalization of the economy.

Yet Africa still faces formidable problems in her quest for progress because she already lags far behind other continents. She has 20 percent of the world's population but accounts for only 2 percent of world trade. And that share has been falling,[4] because of her inability to compete on the world market due to lack of skills in a technologically-oriented globalized market. Africa is also a paradox: it is potentially one of the richest continents - some claim it is the richest - yet it is the poorest. Since independence, Africa has fallen so far behind other developing regions of the world that the gap sometimes seems to have no rational explanation - besides the crackpot pseudoscientific theory about the congenital idiocy of Africans based on some mysterious genetic logic.

But there is an explanation for Africa's poor performance: bad policies pursued by African countries through the decades, and rampant corruption. And the contrast between the performance of African countries and that of other developing nations is glaring. For example, in 1965, Nigeria was richer than Indonesia, and Ghana richer than Thailand. Today Indonesia is three times as rich as Nigeria, and Thailand five times richer than Ghana.[5] In 1967, just three years after Zambia won independence, her per capita income was higher than that of South Korea: $200 for Zambia as opposed to $120 for South Korea. After 30 years, South Korea's Gross Domestic Product (GDP) per person was over $10,000 in 1998, compared with less than $400 for Zambia,[6] one of the richest countries in Africa - by African standards. And it

[4] Michael Samuels, a Washington trade and investment consultant, cited by Reginald Dale, ibid.
[5] R. Dale, ibid.
[6] "Africa's Democratic Despots," in *The Economist*, January 3, 1998, p. 15.

is not going to be easy for Africa to catch up, if at all. A lot of that has to do with the African governments themselves.

Many of the African leaders are not only corrupt - but demand kickbacks whenever investors, both local and foreign, invest in the economy. Yet, in spite of their appetite for kickbacks, they also discourage foreign investment by setting tough requirements for doing business in Africa which many foreign investors find to be too rigid to comply with. There is also red tape. It is suffocating because the bureaucracy is slow in making and implementing decisions regarding investment. And that discourages both local and foreign investors.

There is also the problem of infrastructure: bad transportation, poor communications, lack of storage facilities, among other things. In many places, there aren't even any roads at all - let alone good roads; no vehicles or petrol, and no spare parts. A lot of times there is no electricity, and sometimes even water - let alone clean water. Even telephones in major cities don't always work, cutting off all links to the outside world. Most of those operations were nationalized after African countries won independence, as governments assumed control of the economy to implement socialist policies. The intentions were good, but no substitute for sound policy. For decades, African economies were run with well-meaning incompetence - mostly along socialist lines - until they came to a grinding halt. State-owned enterprises have, in most cases, proved to be a total failure, forcing African governments to sell them to private owners. Privatization has now replaced nationalization everywhere across the continent, although in varying degrees of success, sometimes due to the reluctance of some leaders to relinquish state control of the levers of the economy.

In Zambia, one of the world's five largest producers of copper, the government launched efforts during the early and mid-nineties to privatize the country's assets including copper mines and other state-owned industries as the only way to rejuvenate her sagging economy. When the country won independence in 1964, her Consolidated Copper Mines was the pride of the new nation and its biggest foreign-exchange earner. But lack of investment through the years, and poor management, crippled production. However, the biggest problem - and from that flowed all the rest - was government ownership and control of the major means of the economy, as was the case in practically all African countries most of which adopted socialist policies soon after they won independence. Zambia was one of the countries in the forefront of socialist transformation in Africa, as was neighboring Tanzania, Ghana under Nkrumah, Guinea under Sekou Toure, Mali under Modibo Keita, Benin under Kerekou, Congo-Brazzaville, Angola, Mozambique, Ethiopia, and Somalia. Today, Zambia is again one of those in the lead who have chosen to go exactly in the opposite direction. As Lynne Duke stated from Zambia in a report in *The Washington Post*, in August 1996:

> "With copper still the major asset on which Zambia's economy is based, and with more high-grade copper still to be tapped, the mines are the biggest prize among 202 state-owned companies that are being sold to rejuvenate a hobble economy. Zambia's privatization program, with 140 sales in the last 18 months, is being called the most aggressive in Africa... On a continent where many countries established centrally controlled economic systems soon after independence in the 1950s and 60s, state-run enterprises have proven to be inefficient, deficit-producing drags on developing economies."[7]

Many African countries still control much of their economies in varying degrees. They are slow to privatize state-owned enterprises, a reluctance which leaves them marginalized in the global economy by discouraging investors, and international lenders and donors who - because of their leverage with loans and grants - strongly urge African governments to privatize their economies and adopt other free-market devices such as lifting exchange controls and liberalizing trade in order to attract foreign investment and encourage local entrepreneurship. As Professor Jeffrey Sachs, director of the Harvard Institute for International Development which advises several African governments on economic policy, bluntly states:

> "The important thing right now (in Africa) is a general reorientation of economic policy from one based on government and internal markets to one based on the private sector and export growth.

[7] Lynne Duke, "Putting an Economy on the Block: Zambia is Moving to Privatize its Copper Mines and Other Government-Owned Industries," in *The Washington Post*, National Weekly Edition, August 19, 1995, p. 16.

(Privatization has) got to be part of an overall strategy. Privatization without opportunities for growth is not going to succeed."[8]

And such opportunities are impossible without privatization, a lesson which is now being learned in several African countries, although sometimes unwillingly by politicians and bureaucrats. Zambia is one of the countries where there has been such reluctance, although it has not compromised the privatization program.

In 1997 state-owned enterprises in Zambia constituted 80 percent of the country's economy.[9] Businesses being privatized included not only obvious ones like the copper industry but rock crushers, sugar mills, hotels, supermarkets - and even dry cleaners and bakeries all of which had been nationalized when President Kenneth Kaunda and his ruling United National Independence Party (UNIP) instituted socialist policies and the one-party system shortly after independence. Besides stimulating economic growth, the privatization process is also intended to attract investors, create jobs and increase exports, enabling the country to reduce its huge external debt of $6.3 billion - which is more than 200 percent of the annual gross domestic product,[10]making Zambia one of the most indebted countries in Africa. Some African countries are even worse off. They are saddled with more debts per capita, and are far less endowed than Zambia in terms of natural resources, painting a gloomy picture of the continent's economic performance. Yet the situation is not hopeless.

But even with Zambia's abundant copper, the country has not benefited as much as it could have from its mineral wealth. Copper production fell through the years - from 700,000 tons in 1965 down to 300,000 tons in 1995.[11] Much of that had to do with bad economic policies, but also with the government's refusal to reinvest in the copper industry and in exploration for more mines. And that includes the government of Frederick Chiluba, a trade unionist who won the presidential election on October 31, 1991, against the long-serving

[8] Jeffrey Sachs, quoted ibid. See also Jeffrey Sachs, "The Limits of Convergence: Nature, Nurture and Growth," in *The Economist*, June 14, 1997, pp. 19-22.
[9] L. Duke, ibid.
[10] Ibid.
[11] Ibid.

President Kenneth Kaunda, after waging a vigorous campaign for economic reforms including privatization and the establishment of a stock market. He also campaigned against the one-party system instituted by Dr. Kaunda and coasted to victory by vehemently denouncing one-partyism and centralization of power, only to become an autocrat himself. He went on amend the constitution to bar Kaunda from running for office again, and even jailed him in December 1997 on spurious charges of being involved in an abortive coup attempt in October. However, there seems to be no turning back against the privatization policies he introduced when he won the presidency in what was probably the most stunning defeat for one of Africa's most respected elder statesmen and a hero of the African independence movement.

When Chiluba assumed the presidency many people believed he was going to revive the economy with his free-market approach, although that has yet to be proven. Zambia's copper production is still low, for a number of reasons of course, but it accounts for 90 percent of the country's export earnings and 40 percent of Africa's entire copper production. And the country still has substantial reserves of the mineral. As Edwin Koloko, director of the mines privatization program, put it:

> "Because of the richness and vastness of the reserve, people can mine here for the coming 100 years. The future of Zambia is here."[12]

But it is not easy to get there. Success or failure depends on how the privatization program is implemented, not just on the blueprint itself. Some African countries have not done well, in spite of all the enthusiasm for the new free-market policies adopted across the continent during the early nineties. One such country which has not been very successful is Guinea, ruled by Sekou Toure as a socialist state from 1958 until 1984 when he died, after which the army executed a coup. Between 1985 and 1992, Guinea privatized or liquidated 158 companies, selling many of them far below their market value. By 1991, according to a report by the World Bank, only four of the companies were making profit.[13]

---

[12] Edwin Koloko, quoted ibid.

[13] Guinea's Privatization Program, in *World Bank Report*, 1995.

However, Zambia's commitment to privatization is unwavered and may even be pursued with religious zeal to rejuvenate the economy and create jobs in a country where industrial output is low and with many factories operating at only 15 percent capacity even as late as 1998.

Besides copper, Zambia's other major exports include lead, zinc, cobalt, and tobacco. Gold, silver and gemstones are also mined. In addition to tobacco, other leading crops are maize, sorghum, millet, beans, groundnuts, and cotton. Large numbers of poultry are also raised. Unfortunately, tsetse flies hinder livestock raising. Although the world's copper prices have declined since the 1970s, Zambia has enough minerals and cash crops to achieve economic growth by concentrating on the private sector as the engine of progress and substitute for foreign aid.

In Zimbabwe also, economic deregulation has increased foreign investment which has been further encouraged by the country's educated and low-cost work force. In fact, Zimbabwe has one of the largest numbers of educated people in black Africa, together with other countries such as Nigeria, Ghana, Ivory Coast, Senegal, Kenya, Uganda, Tanzania, Ethiopia, Zambia, and South Africa. And her economic growth has been impressive, with the help of mother nature and uniqueness of the country. According to a report by the *International Herald Tribune*:

> "The heavens opened in the 1995 - 96 rainy season, spurring economic growth on to a forecast 8 percent, the strongest recovery since independence in 1980... Zimbabwe is unique in Africa. A small nation of 11 million people, it has infrastructure and a diverse economy that set it apart from the rest of the continent. Only South Africa, with its vastly greater resources, stands ahead of it...Zimbabwe boasts a high standard of education, low production costs, relatively cheap labor, a benign climate and the absence of any serious security problems."[14]

In a move towards privatization, Zimbabwe has slowly abandoned its price controls, wage setting, high taxes, rigid exchange controls, stringent

[14] Ibid., p. 21.

import and labor restrictions, enabling more foreign investment to flow in what is already one of the richest countries in Africa with an abundance of natural resources.

In terms of minerals, Zimbabwe's Great Dyke, the geological rupture running diagonally through the center of the country, holds a dazzling array of minerals and is about to yield its richest treasure yet: platinum. Full-scale production began in October 1997, with an output of 150,000 ounces of platinum per year. The volume, a modest 3 percent of global output, will make Zimbabwe the world's second-largest producer of platinum. Yet that is only the beginning. Zimbabwe is going to triple production to 450,000 ounces per annum.

In addition to platinum, the mine will also produce the platinum group metals - palladium and rhodium; precious metals - gold and silver; and base metals - copper, cobalt and nickel. When the production is tripled to 450,000 ounces of platinum, the value of all the metals from that mine which went into operation in 1997 is expected to be equivalent to 73 percent more than the value of the country's entire output of gold. Other platinum mines and those of other minerals were also scheduled to go into production after 1997, boosting the total mineral output even further. Already, Zimbabwe is Africa's third-largest gold producer and is a world-leading producer of nickel, lithium, graphite, natural corundum and a variety of other minerals including chrome, coal, asbestos, copper, tin and iron. As Peter Simpson, director of an engineering firm Peacocke and Simpson in the country's capital Harare, said about the projected output of the entire mineral wealth in Zimbabwe:

> "These all have the potential to outstrip South Africa."[15]

In fact, the Great Dyke in Zimbabwe is the second largest platinum deposit outside South Africa's Bushveld Complex. After manufacturing and agriculture, mining is the third-largest contributor to Zimbabwe's gross domestic product (GDP). Besides minerals, Zimbabwe is well-endowed in terms of agricultural potential far more than several other African countries. Her crops include tobacco, which is the principal cash crop; maize, sugarcane,

[15] Peter Simpson, quoted ibid.

cotton, wheat, tea, millet, sorghum, livestock, vegetables, fruits, groundnuts and cassava.

Coffee is increasingly becoming a major agricultural product which is going to earn the country even more foreign exchange. There are also numerous tea plantations in Zimbabwe, and in the middle veld is an excellent ranching land. Also the country's forests yield valuable hardwoods. Zimbabwe is also one of the few African countries with significant industry. Major industrial products include iron and steel, gold, copper, machinery, vehicles, cement, food products, textiles, chemicals, and petroleum products. And unlike most African countries, Zimbabwe has good road and rail networks and internal air service.[16]

But in order to forge ahead, Zimbabwe needs to privatize her economy which was nationalized after the country won independence in 1980 and went socialist:

> "About half of the country's GDP of $2.5 billion until recently comprised parastatal companies directly answerable to civil servants, state-owned private businesses and large chunks of equity in blue-chip corporations on the Zimbabwe Stock Market."[17]

Zimbabwe began, cautiously, to privatize her state-owned businesses during the mid-eighties and still has a long way to go. The first step she took was what the government called "commercialization", which means that 100 percent state ownership is retained while the parastatal status of most companies is eliminated, abolishing restrictive marketing laws and providing companies with boards of directors composed of individuals from the private sector to replace civil servants and politicians. As Cephas Msipa, Minister without Portfolio and head of the newly formed Department of Privatization and Indigenization, stated:

---

[16] *Columbia Encyclopedia* (New York: Columbia University Press, 1993), p. 3041; *1997 Almanac* (New York: Houghton Mifflin, 1996), pp. 296-297; and *1986 Reader's Digest Almanac and Yearbook* (Pleasantville, New York: Reader's Digest Association, 1985), p. 686.

[17] "Southern Africa: Zimbabwe Trade," in the *International Herald Tribune*, ibid., p. 22.

"We don't want foreigners buying all the shares. We want to keep them in trust of our people."[18]

Even the foremost capitalist country in the world, the United States, does not allow foreigners to buy just any business they want to buy on American soil; nor do most countries. That is simply economic nationalism which is neither socialist nor capitalist. But African countries must still find ways to attract foreign investment by allowing foreign investors to reap enough profits for them to reinvest in the local economy. Unfortunately, because of lack of capital, many Africans cannot buy most of the state assets which are up for sale. And that slows privatization since most countries on the continent are not going to allow foreigners to grab anything they want. But privatization must go on if African countries are not to remain marginalized in the global economy. And Zimbabwe, however slowly and cautiously, set out in that direction in the mid-nineties. One way to enable ordinary Africans participate in privatization is through corporate ownership, making it possible for them to buy lost-cost shares in state companies, for example those floated on the stock exchange in Zimbabwe. Compared to most countries in black Africa, Zimbabwe is in a better position to achieve that goal because of her relative wealth in a country where "whites have enjoyed a standard of living comparable to that of (white) Americans.[19]

Neighboring Botswana, formerly the British protectorate of Bechuanaland, is also endowed with an abundance of minerals and a climate conducive to livestock raising. With about the same area and climate as Texas and only about 1.5 million people, Botswana has specialized in cattle raising on a large scale for many years, helping the country earn foreign exchange besides the substantial portion which was already coming from other sources. The discovery of substantial mineral deposits in the 1970s boosted Botswana's economy in a country which had already been producing minerals. British and American companies opened a large diamond mine at Orapa which turned out to be a treasure-trove for the country. And a large copper-nickel mine began production at Selbi-Pikwe in 1975. After the

[18] Cephas Msipa, quoted ibid.

[19] *1986 Reader's Digest Almanac and Yearbook*, op. cit., p. 686.

discovery of all those minerals, Botswana's gross national product (GNP) grew at an annual rate of about 20 percent.[20]

Unlike most countries on the continent, except those in southern Africa, Botswana's climate Is subtropical. Cattle raising and the export of beef and other cattle products are among the chief economic activities. Cotton, groundnuts, and sunflowers are the main crops; while sorghuam, maize, millet and beans are the principal subsistence crops. But only a small percentage of the land is arable. Yet the country's vast mineral wealth compensates for lack of agricultural potential in terms of contribution to her gross national product.

Botswana's bleak economic outlook was dramatically brightened during the 1960s with the discovery of significant quantities of several minerals. The only known minerals in the country at the time of independence in 1966 were manganese and some gold and asbestos. Then during the seventies came the discovery of diamonds, large nickel and copper deposits, salt and soda ash. Antimony and sulfur are also known to exist. Vast coal deposits are also being exploited. Deposits of plutonium and platinum have also been found. Three diamond mines - at Orapa, Lethlakane, and Jwaneng - collectively constitute one of the largest diamond reserves in the world. Botswana's mineral wealth has made it one of the wealthiest countries in Africa. The country also has one of Africa's largest natural game reserves, making tourism one of Botswana's major industries and foreign-exchange earners. And the country is also one of the best places on the entire continent for investment because of its wealth and stability.

Throughout the entire generation since independence, Botswana remained and still is one of the most peaceful countries in Africa, a critical factor in the country's economic development in a country which is already potentially rich. How rich the country is in the African context is probably best determined by contrast:

> "Botswana's per capita gross domestic product of $3,050 a year is one of the highest in Africa and is about 10 times higher than that of

[20] Ibid., p. 504; and *Columbia Encyclopedia*, op. cit., p. 341.

some of its neighbors. The government maintained a budget surplus for 10 years, until 1994."[21]

With only 1.5 million people in an area of 227,028 square miles, Botswana is one of the least populated countries in the world, and one of the wealthiest in the entire Third World. And her growth has been phenomenal. Real economic growth was about 10 percent a year from 1982 to 1992, and the country's foreign exchange reserves of about $4.4 billion in 1996 were enough to cover imports for 25 months,[22] a capacity few countries in the world achieve even during the best of times.

Botswana's substantial wealth comes mainly from diamonds, which account for 78 percent of the country's export earnings and about 50 percent of government revenues. In fact, Botswana is the world's largest producer of gem-quality diamonds. And the government has used diamond revenues to build one of the best infrastructures on the African continent, with some of the best state schools at all levels of education – from the primary to the university level; and also some of the best housing.

However, in 1993, the country's economic growth slowed down for the first time in 10 years, mainly because of reduced production in diamonds due to low demand on the world market. Production fell by 15 percent, which led to the contraction of the economy by 0.2 percent during that year. But the economy bounced back in 1994, growing up 4.5 percent in 1995.[23] The decline in the demand for diamonds on the international market did, however, have one positive effect: it encouraged Botswana to go even further in her efforts to diversify her economy instead of relying on a single commodity to earn foreign exchange and finance development projects. In fact such dependence, on a single crop or mineral as the primary source of national income, has been one of the main obstacles to economic growth in most African countries.

Agriculture is eclipsed by minerals, its share of gross domestic product having dropped from 40 percent in 1966 down to 5 percent during the 1990s

[21] "Botswana: Celebrating 30 Years of Independence," in the *International Herald Tribune*, September 28, 1996, p. 20.
[22] Ibid.
[23] Ibid.

mainly because of the dramatic increase in diamond production, a shift unprecedented in sub-Saharan Africa. In spite of such decline in agricultural contribution to gross domestic product, livestock accounts for 80 percent of Botswana's output in the agricultural sector, and beef exports alone more than cover the cost of the country's food imports.[24]

Botswana has also made significant strides towards privatization. Attractive incentives for investors and the elimination of bureaucratic obstacles have drawn into the country substantial investment in industries such as textile manufacture and automobile assembly. Most of the industrial products, including cars, are geared to the export market. And because of the country's extensive livestock, Botswana also - in addition to beef exports - has an excellent chance through privatization and foreign investment of developing a major industry in leather products for both domestic and foreign markets. Besides its extensive mineral wealth, foreign investors are also attracted to Botswana because the country has been able to liberalize trade far more than most African countries, including neighboring mineral-rich Zimbabwe, have been able to do:

> "Industrialists in Botswana... can export duty free to fellow members of the five-nation Southern African Customs Union, to which South Africa also belongs. They get preferential tariffs in Europe under the Lomé Convention and have various quota-free preferential pacts with North America. Company tax is only 25 percent, and foreign investors are free to repatriate their profits. Moreover, the government actually pays businesses to create jobs. Under the Financial Assistance Policy (FAP), foreign-owned companies receive 1,000 pula ($292) a year for each unskilled worker they employ; Botswana-owned companies receive $438. To encourage industrial decentralization, total payments of these allowances to companies in urban areas are restricted to 40 percent of the value of their fixed investment, and in rural areas up to 85 percent of their fixed

[24] Ibid.

investment. The state also pays half the costs of training unskilled employees."[25]

These arrangements point to two goals targeted by the government's industrial policy: to create jobs, and to enable the people of Botswana to participate directly in business enterprises involving local and foreign investors. And that explains why many joint ventures have been launched involving both domestic and foreign capital. In many African countries, it is not very common for local businessmen to team up with foreign investors to start businesses. Botswana is one of the few leading the way. And its FAP was intended to play a critical role in that area. As Monty Letshwiti, a spokesman for the Department of Trade and Investments Promotion (TIPA), put it:

> "The FAP was designed primarily to create employment through diversification away from mining. We are encouraging secondary industries, such as textiles, to establish themselves to ensure that employment grows even after the mines have been worked out. (For example), in Selebi Pikwe (a nickel-mining town in eastern Botswana), three factories have been closed, but 11 new ones have opened. All are aimed primarily at export market either in Southern Africa or Europe and North America. The investors are either Asian or South African. Some are in joint ventures with the government's Botswana Development Corporation, and some have come in as sole shareholders."[26]

But even with diversification, mining remains - at least for now and may be for several years to come - a mainstay of the country's economy. Diamonds are, of course, the best known mineral coming out of Botswana. But it is not the only important mineral, although diamonds account for the largest share of the country's exports. However, the mineral's contribution to the economy is unrivaled. For example in 1994, Botswana's diamond exports

---

[25] Ibid.

[26] Monty Letshwiti, quoted ibid.

amounted to $1.4 billion, equivalent to nearly $1,400 per head of population.[27] And the country is guaranteed many more years of wealth from diamonds. Orapa alone, one of Botswana's three major diamond mines, is one of the lowest-cost major diamond producers in the world whose life span will outlast the current lease which expires in 2017. Botswana's diamond business is operated by Debswana Diamond Company, a 50-50 joint venture owned by De Beers Centenary and the government of Botswana. Debswana will spend more than $370 million to more than double Orapa's output by the year 2000.[28]

Other minerals which bring in significant earnings into Botswana include copper and nickel which account for 8 percent of the country's exports, making them the second-biggest foreign-exchange earner; beef is third and accounts for 4 percent of the exports; and soda ash is fourth, accounting for 2 percent. Botswana also has one coal mine, which has 12 billion tons of easily exploitable coal reserves more than enough to meet the country's power and industrial needs. The rest of the coal is going to be exported as soon as transportation links to the coast have been established in neighboring countries.[29] So far, South Africa is the only country which provides main access to the sea for landlocked Botswana. The other countries with major potential sea outlets are Mozambique and Namibia.

Unlike most African countries, Botswana also assembles and exports cars. By 1998, automobiles assembled in Botswana were expected to account for 10 percent of the passenger car market in South Africa. The automobile plant is Gaborone, the country's capital, which is the only such plant in the country, has a minimum production capacity of 30,000 passenger cars per year.[30] It builds Korean Hyundai cars. Trucks made by Swedish companies Volvo and Scania and the Russian company Kamaz are also being assembled in Botswana. And car-component manufacturers were also expected to build manufacturing plants in the country, joining the automobile assemblers already established in Botswana to make the prosperous African nation a full

[27] "Botswana: Celebrating 30 Years of Independence," in *International Herald Tribune*, ibid., p. 21.
[28] Ibid.
[29] Ibid.
[30] Ibid.

manufacturer and assembler of cars and trucks; an achievement usually associated only with industrialized nations. As Les Watson, projects manager of Hyundai Motor Distributors which operates the plant in Botswana, said about the country:

> "Business climate here is friendly, and the government is pragmatic. There are no foreign exchange restrictions on us, and we are benefiting from a tax holiday. There has been a stable political environment since independence 30 years ago, and we have a stable and dependable work force that is not as prone to strikes as those of South Africa. There is very little crime."[31]

But Botswana's wealth does not come only from her minerals and livestock. Tourism is also a significant source of income, and is expected to grow. As Curt von Keyserlingk, business editor of "Sake-Beeld," a daily business newspaper published in Johannesburg, South Africa, put it:

> "The Okavango Delta (in Botswana) is one of the wonders of Africa. It is the world's largest delta and acts as a giant sponge that provides sustenance to a rich profusion of African game in an otherwise arid region."[32]

The Okavango Delta may be the best known tourist attraction in Botswana, but there are others. As Mtetoh Gaseitsiwe, a senior tourism officer in the Ministry of Tourism, explained:

> "To take the pressure off Okavango, we are developing the Chobe National Park, Central Kalahari Game Reserve, Khutse Game Reserve and Makgadigkadi Game Reserve."[33]

And the government is doing that through the private sector in what is widely acknowledged as a new era for Africa: most countries across the

---

[31] Les Watson, quoted ibid.
[32] Curt von Keyserlingk, quoted ibid.
[33] Mtetoh Gaseitsiwe, quoted ibid.

continent have opted for privatization as the best way to achieve economic development and become active participants in the global market where state-owned enterprises have never been very competitive. Botswana allocated concessions to foreign markets to develop the parks and opportunities for investment in the tourist industry, as in the rest of the economy, were expected to expand through the years - facilitated by the government's Financial Assistance Policy (FAP).

As we noted earlier, immediately after independence, most African countries adopted a socialist strategy for development. Most did not declare themselves socialist, for example like Ghana and Tanzania or Guinea and Mali under Modibo Keita did. But they acted as if they were, in different areas, especially in controlling the major means of production, although in varying degrees. As Professor Ali Mazrui states in his penetrating analytical work *Towards a Pax Africana*:

> "No ideology commands respect so widely in Africa as the ideology of 'socialism' ... In Guinea and Mali a Marxist framework of reasoning is evident. In Ghana Leninism was wedded to notions of traditional collectivism. In Tanzania the concept of Ujamaa, derived from the sense of community of tribal life, is being radicalized into an assertion of modern socialism. In Kenya there is a dilemma between establishing socialism and Africanizing the capitalism which already exists. In Nigeria, Senegal and Uganda some kind of allegiance is being paid to the ideal of social justice in situations with a multi-party background. There are places, of course, where no school of socialism is propagated at all. But outside the Ivory Coast there is little defiant rejection of the idea of 'socialism' in former colonial Africa."[34]

---

[34] Ali A. Mazrui, *Towards A Pax Africana* (London: Weidenfeld & Nicolson, 1968), p. 97; See also William H. Friedland and Carl G. Rosberg, Jr., editors, *African Socialism* (Stanford: Stanford University Press, 1964); Kenneth W. Grundy, "Marxism-Leninism: The Mali Approach," in the *International Journal*, Vol XVII, No. 3, Summer 1962; L. Gray Cowan, "Guinea," in Gwendolen M. Carter, editor, *African One-Party State* (Ithaca, New York: Cornell University Press, 1962); Kenneth W. Grundy, "Nkrumah's Theory of Underdevelopment: An Analysis of Recurrent Themes," in *World Politics*, Vol XV, No. 3, April 1963; Kenya Government Paper, "African Socialism and its Application to Planning in Kenya," 1965;

Among the African countries which sought to undergo radical socialist transformation was, of course, Ghana under the leadership of Dr. Kwame Nkrumah as we have just noted. After President Nkrumah was overthrown in 1966, all successive Ghanaian governments no longer pursued that goal. The exception was Jerry Rawlings who was wary of capitalism from the time - and even before - he seized power in June 1979 and talked in populist rhetoric about the well-being of the common man being sacrificed by businessmen to accumulate wealth at the expense of the masses. He remained a socialist-oriented fire-breathing populist until the early 1990s when he mellowed somewhat after the World Bank and the International Monetary Fund as well as other donors demanded implementation of austerity measures - as a condition for financial assistance - to restructure and rejuvenate Ghana's economy along capitalist lines. Ghana, the first socialist country in black Africa also became the first to be the most successful in achieving economic growth on capitalist basis under President Rawlings. The key to Ghana's success was foreign investment and privatization of state-owned enterprises, a strategy populist Rawlings and his firebrand compatriots grudgingly accepted. But it worked for the economy.

Even after Nkrumah was overthrown and socialism renounced, successive governments did not entirely - or even to a large degree - pull out of the economy and let laissez-faire to take its course all the way. They still continued to play a dominant role in the management of the economy even though they were capitalist-oriented. But such continued involvement was also for understandable reasons, considering the fact that the government in all African countries had always been - since independence - the biggest institution with the largest amount of capital for investment and development; and it has played a similar role in every society, including the foremost capitalist country in the world, the United States, where the federal government continues to play a big role in the American economy. As Adebayo Adedeji, the distinguished Nigerian economist who was Executive Secretary of the UN Economic Commission for Africa (ECA), pointed out in

African Report, Special issue on African Socialism, VIII, May 1963; Julius Nyerere, *Freedom and Socialism* (Dar es Salaam, Tanzania: Oxford University Press, 1968); Kwame Nkrumah, *Class Struggle in Africa* (New York: Monthly Review Press, 1967).

1983 in response to the World Bank's *Agenda for Action* - also known as the Berg Report - critical of Africa's economic performance:

> "Where we do not agree is the argument in the report that African countries are not doing well because they are not increasing their production of commodities for export. How can you increase export production in a situation where the demand for your exports is diminishing and prices are going down? Second, the report says we are not doing well because of public enterprises and government involvement in economic activities. Compared to the proportion of the gross domestic product adsorbed by the government of the United States at the federal, state and local levels, that of the most so-called socialist state in Africa is only a small fraction."[35]

African governments undoubtedly have had a negative impact on their economies in many areas through the decades since independence. But that has mainly been due to mismanagement, in spite of the positive role they have sometimes played in economic development. That kind of government involvement is not unique or peculiar to Africa, a point underscored by Adedeji:

> "Right from the very beginning, government has played a very important role in the development process in every society; and we in Africa in particular, given our limited entrepreneurial capacity and the lack of capital, cannot begrudge governments getting involved in pushing development. Our governments have a catalytic role to play in this area. There is no proof of inherent weakness in public enterprise vis-a-vis private enterprise. However, that does not mean that many of the public enterprises in Africa are not being mismanaged. But that should not lead us to the conclusion that we should privatize our economies. This is an area of important difference between us and the Berg report."[36]

---

[35] Adebayo Adedeji, interviewed by Margaret A. Novicki, in *Africa Report*, September-October 1983, p. 16.
[36] Ibid.

And privatization, if unregulated, could also mean that foreigners are going to own Africa lock, stock and barrel - if they are allowed to buy and invest in everything they want to. Africans themselves must therefore own the largest share, or African governments must have a controlling interest in all business ventures if Africa is to belong to Africans - just as America belongs to Americans in spite of investment by foreigners in the American economy. That is because the American federal government restricts, within prescribed limits, their involvement in the American economy.

However, African governments ignored two important things when they assumed state ownership of a number of enterprises or nationalized the economy as a way to develop their countries. They ignored human weakness for self-interest - call it greed or selfishness or what have you. In short, they ignored human nature. The second thing they ignored or overlooked was finding the source of wealth which they wanted redistributed on an egalitarian basis to achieve social equality.

People are not going to work hard if they don't reap profit directly for themselves of if they are not remunerated accordingly. That is why communal farms failed; it is also one of the reasons why most state-owned enterprises failed. A person who works for himself - be it as a peasant, a vendor, or a shop owner or whatever - works harder, and even puts in extra hours and weekends, than he would if he worked for the state or for somebody else. That is because he knows most of the profit he generates from his labor goes to him directly, besides paying mandatory taxes and meeting business expenses.

The other big failure for socialist-oriented economies, such as those in Africa, was that they did not fully address the question: Who is going to produce the wealth we want to redistribute? The simple answer was, of course, the people. But how?

That is the question - and it is a fundamental one - even Karl Marx himself was never able to answer in his magnum opus, *Das Kapital*, or anywhere else. The answer is incentive. Without incentive, no one is going to produce enough wealth the government wants to redistribute in order to build a socialist society. And that incentive is profit – going directly to the people who produce the wealth, and produce it for themselves – not for the state. Tell them to produce it for the state; they are not going to produce enough - even if they have to starve under mass regimentation.

Although many African countries were slow to abandon their dream for a socialist utopia, realism - and human nature - dictated otherwise even to an anti-capitalist leader like Jerry Rawlings. It was the dawn of a new era, of privatization, of what South African Vice President Thabo Mbeki calls the African Renaissance, an African rebirth and awakening spanning the entire socioeconomic political spectrum.

In Ghana privatization now ranges from farms and quarries to strategic assets such as the national airline and telecommunications facilities, after the government decided to pull out of a number of major economic enterprises. As Emmanuel Agbodo, executive secretary of Ghana's Divestiture Implementation Committee, put it, one of the primary aims of Ghana's divestiture program is to mobilize private-sector management and capital. And that involves a lot of foreign investment to facilitate joint ownership of ventures in which Ghana is in partnership with foreign investors. Thus, after years of preparation, Ghana during the mid-1990s entered a new era of investment with the backing of international and domestic private-sector investors who collectively constitute a potent force as the locomotive of fundamental economic transformation to achieve prosperity in what once was one of the richest countries in Africa.

Both the government and the private sector have played a critical role in trying to transform Ghana from a predominantly state-run economy into a free-enterprise system for her agricultural, mineral, industrial and financial operations. Most of the investors in Ghana's economy by the mid-1990s were expected to come from Europe, Asia - mainly from the Orient, but mainly from Southern Africa. New interest in Ghana's investment opportunities has been generated since late 1995 when the government declared the "Ghana Trade and Investment Gateway" program to be a national economic development priority and launched a new "free zone" initiative, whereby exporters will benefit from an array of tax and duty exemptions. As George Yankey, a senior director in the Ministry of Finance, explained:

> "Privatization will not only revitalize state-owned enterprises but will increase the participation of the private sector in the running of the economy. We also see the need for the private sector to be involved in

the provision of services at the airport, the harbors and the free zone, and thereby generate an even greater level of investment."[37]

Among the groups interested in Ghana's privatization program to acquire existing assets and capitalize on the country's domestic and export potential were a major South African construction group, and a consortium of horticultural firms in Zimbabwe attracted by Ghana's relative proximity to markets in Europe and North America for tropical fruit, vegetables and flowers; Zimbabwe is much further from those markets for her perishable goods.

In spite of Ghana's serious economic problems in many areas - including inflation and unemployment, perennial problems in most African countries, and a weak infrastructure - the people in the private sector believe, and rightly so, that the solution to all those problems lies in a total re-orientation of the economy. As one business consultant in Accra put it:

"The government has found itself sustaining a large and unproductive payroll in public-sector businesses that have become stagnant, or have even ceased production, simply because they have failed to attract new investment."[38]

Therefore many of those public-sector enterprises had to be sold, a task assigned to the Divestiture Implementation Committee (DCI). As the committee's executive secretary, Emmanuel Agbodo, states:

"Divestiture is a complex task and a sensitive one, too. It has a major impact on people in different ways, be they managers, employees, investors or consumers."[39]

In spite of the difficulties, the committee had by the end of 1995 seen the divestiture of 159 state-owned businesses, no mean accomplishment in a

---

[37] George Yankey, quoted by Richard Synge, "Privatization in Ghana: Greater Private-Sector Role is Key Plans for Growth," in the *International Herald Tribune*, July 30, 1996, p. 18.

[38] Quoted in *Privatization in Ghana*, ibid.

[39] Emmanuel Agbodo, quoted ibid.

country where the government was firmly entrenched in the economy like in all the other African countries. The largest state-owned enterprises which were up for sale in 1996 included Ghana Telecommunications, the State Insurance Company and the State Housing Corporation; while those in the middle rank included Tema Oil Refinery, Ghana Oil Company, Precious Minerals Marketing Company, Aluworks, Ghana Bauxite Company, trading and transport firms, a major hotel, and a pharmaceutical company. Smaller businesses also being handled by the divestiture committee included quarries, ranches, rice farms, and agro-industries. The privatization program went on as planned and Ghana's most strategic assets such as telecommunications facilities and the national airline were sold within months.

In the infrastructural area, Ghana's Civil Aviation sought to modernize Accra's international airport and encourage private-sector participation in the provision of services, with the intention of making the airport the most modern and efficient in West Africa. The Ghana Ports and Harbors Authority also sought to privatize its operations and facilities to make the country's ports more competitive. European and Far Eastern investors expressed great interest in participating in a duty-free zone at Ghana's main port of Tema, as did others in the country's other port facilities. As Daniel Kwagbenu, secretary general of the Ghana Free Zones Board, stated about the investors' interest in the Trade and Investment Gateway concept:

> "This will be the flagship industrial park. We have serious inquiries and letters of intent from companies wishing to acquire free-zone status in activities ranging from food processing and cosmetics to data processing. Any company exporting more than 70 percent of its production can qualify.'[40]

Ghana is one of the few African countries where the private sector has had great success in reinvigorating the economy. Several formerly state-owned companies which had been privatized were by 1996 generating substantial profit. Following the spectacular performance in 1994-95 by Ghana's principal gold mining group, Ashanti Goldfields Corporation (AGC),

---

[40] Daniel Kwagbenu, quoted ibid.

which greatly impressed international investors, there were other impressive signs showing Ghana emerging as a business center in West Africa. The disposition of government assets or share holdings in a number of enterprises which were acquired by entrepreneurs in the private sector helped revitalize businesses such as brewing, vegetable-oil milling, and steel rolling. But nowhere was such economic performance as impressive as in the mining industry. As Richard Synge explains:

> "The performance of the mining sector has clearly outshone all others. The 1994 sale on the Ghana and London stock exchanges of 30 percent of AGC not only raised $450 million for the government but also launched the company on an acquisition trail that has made it a gold producer and explorer throughout West Africa and further afield in Tanzania and Zimbabwe."[41]

In Ghana itself, the Ashanti Goldfields Corporation's (AGCs) mine at Obuasi is one of the world's largest, producing one million ounces of fine gold per year. Besides Ashanti Goldfields, there are other gold corporations in Ghana. The sale of shares in the former State Gold Mining Corporation properties at Tarkwa, Dunkwa and Prestea helped Ghana acquire mining expertise which is greatly needed. Goldfields Ghana, a subsidiary of Goldfields South Africa, had already increased its output at its mine in Tarkwa from 26,000 ounces to 40,000 in 1996, and expects to produce 200,000 ounces by the year 2000.[42]

Privatization of ABC Brewery in 1992 was also a significant success. By 1995 the brewery had more than doubled its production to 1.6 million carton units; and during the same period, its share of the domestic market rose from 8 percent to 15 percent. The year 1996 saw another success in privatization and economic performance. A joint venture, known as Ghana Agro-Food Company (GAFCO), was formed out of the former state-owned Tema Food Complex Corporation. The government still owns 25 percent of the shares. But the majority are held by a Swiss company, Industrie Bau Nord, which has

[41] Richard Synge, *Privatization in Ghana*, ibid.
[42] Ibid.

been doing business in Africa for more than 30 years. The company also intends to actively participate in the country's agricultural sector which has the potential of making Ghana one of the continent's major food producers. As Michael Zetzsche, GAFCO managing director, put it:

> "Having brought the four main mills and food factories in Tema back into production, we are now working on developing Ghana's potential as a valuable source of cassava chips for the world animal-feed market."[43]

Other companies which have also been restored to vitality or have increased production after they were privatized include West African Mills Company in Takoradi, a joint venture between the Ghanaian government and Germany's Walter Schroeder which exports cocoa butter and cake; Tropical Glass, which, after privatization, became one of the leading producers of beer bottles in West Africa; and Tema Steel Company, a joint venture between the government and investors from Britain, India and Kenya, which increased its production dramatically from negligible levels in 1991, when it was privatized, up to 25,000 tons of assorted steel products in 1995.[44]

In all those privatized businesses, the number of jobs created also increased dramatically, something state-run enterprises had never been able to achieve; they had large numbers of employees getting inflated wages on padded payrolls while generating no profit. That is because they impeded economic progress. Divestiture changed all that.

Further divestitures included those of vehicle distributor Ghamot and Ghana Rubber Estates, in both of which foreign and local investors took 75 percent of the shares. Since the overthrow of President Nkrumah in 1996 in a CIA-inspired coup, Ghana turned West in terms of ideological orientation, except during Rawlings' tenure. Yet it was not until during the 1990s, ironically again under Rawlings, that the country successfully implemented free-market policies in a number of areas.

---

[43] Michael Zetzsche, quoted ibid.

[44] R. Synge, ibid.

Privatization in Ghana was advanced much further with the expansion of the Ghana Stock Exchange whose market capitalization soared in value from a mere $76 million in 1991 to $1.7 billion in 1995. Market flotations on the stock exchange include the financial sector as well as leading mining and industrial companies, chief among them being the Ashanti Goldfields Corporation and other heavyweights, and many second-level ventures. And Ghana's liberal approach to privatization has paid good dividends. As one South African entrepreneur who acquired one of the state-owned enterprises in Ghana stated:

> "What we appreciate about the Divestiture Implementation Committee is their flexibility."[45]

This multi-faceted approach to privatization has been shown in the way the divestiture committee disposes of state enterprises for acquisition. As Emmanuel Agbodo explains, the divestiture process includes trade sales of assets; the direct sale of shares; a public offering combined with a listing on the Ghana Stock Exchange; joint venture with the state by establishing a new company; lease or management agreements; or liquidation. He goes on to say:

> "The mode of divestiture chosen for a particular enterprise necessarily depends on a blend of political, commercial and strategic objectives... Enterprise-specific factors need to be considered."[46]

They include the state of the enterprise; the level of capitalization that the enterprise might need to be revitalized; and the degree of state intervention demanded by the government, especially when it wishes to retain a controlling interest.

Other state enterprises scheduled for sale after 1996 included sugar estates and factories, timber operations, a modern tire factory, and transportation and construction companies. Sugar companies were among the worst, having fallen into disuse following breakdowns of machinery which

[45] Quoted, ibid.

[46] E. Abdodo, quoted ibid.

resulted in the abandonment of the sugar fields. One of the best state-owned companies up for sale was the State Transport Corporation (STC), operating a fleet of 100 buses and about 30 fuel tankers, and with a good reputation in Ghana for sound management, reliability and safety. The company also had another great attraction for investors: the potential for expanding its routes to and between Ghana's neighboring countries such as the Ivory Coast, Togo, and Burkina Faso and possibly beyond.

Yet another attractive asset for sale was the GIHOC Fibre Products Company, founded during the 1960s to manufacture jute sacks for agricultural products including Ghana's chief export crop, cocoa beans. The state-owned company acquired new equipment, including modern looms and sewing machines in the 1980s, but was closed in 1991. It remained closed in 1996, yet was able to attract a number of potential investors. Once privatized, chances are excellent that it will stay open and generate profit as most of the companies sold by the state have been doing. As Agbodo stated:

> "Many of the enterprises divested have been modernized and, where applicable, brought back into production."[47]

Ghana today is very different in terms of economic orientation from the Ghana Dr. Nkrumah left behind.[48]

Besides Ghana under Nkrumah, and Guinea under Sekou Toure, probably no other African country was more committed to socialist transformation than Tanzania under the leadership of Julius Nyerere. As in all the other African countries which had gone "socialist", the goal was laudable but the results lamentable; there was nothing wrong with trying to achieve social equality.

---

[47] Ibid.

[48] Nyerere, *Freedom and Socialism*, Nkrumah, *Class Struggle in Africa*, op. cit., Sekou Toure, *African Emancipation*, and Kofi Baako, "Nkrumaism - Its Theory and Practice," in Paul E. Sigmund, Jr., editor, *The Ideologies of the Developing Nations* (New York: Frederick A. Praeger, 1963), pp. 155-169, and 188-196. As Nkrumah says in his autobiographical work: "Capitalism is too complicated a system for a newly independent nation. Hence the need for a socialistic society." See Kwame Nkrumah, *Ghana: The Autobiography of Kwame Nkrumah* (New York: Thomas Nelson and Sons, 1957). See also James S. Wunsch and Dele Olowu, *The Failure of the Centralized State: Institutions and Self-Governance in Africa* (Boulder, Colorado: Westview Press, 1994).

Even capitalists talk about that; they admit it is a noble objective. But again like Ghana, Guinea and other socialist-oriented countries on the continent, Tanzania failed to achieve that goal, although due to a number of factors some of them beyond Africa's control: mainly her peripheral role in conducting international trade. Africa has no say in setting prices for her commodities on the world market; she has no bargaining strength to lower prices for her imports - oil, heavy-duty equipment and other machinery as well as a variety manufactured goods - all of which drain her foreign exchange; she is economically underdeveloped, and technologically backward in a global economy which is becoming more and more capital-intensive requiring high technical skills to achieve development. Tanzania being an integral part of Africa, is handicapped by all those problems and is even worse off than many other countries on the continent because it is one of the poorest.

But Tanzania's failure to achieve her goals was also, probably more than anything else, due to the wrong approach to solving the country's economic problems. There was nothing wrong with the overall objective of achieving social equality by narrowing the gap between the rich and the poor and promoting an equitable distribution of wealth. The problem was how to generate enough wealth to achieve that goal. She spread herself too thin, trying to provide free service to everybody in many areas, even to people who could afford to pay for it.

And as a union of two independent states, Tanzania has also faced other challenges through the years countries which have never been united have never faced. She still faces them today, and continues to pursue new economic policies like other African countries are doing as we have learned from the case studies presented in this chapter. The case studies are applicable in other African contexts, not just in the countries focused on, and they give us a better understanding of the role of the modern African state as an indispensable institution if it is adapted to respond to the needs and aspirations of its people. We continue with that examination of the role of the modern African state as we look at the challenges to unity and ideology in Tanzania in the next chapter.

CHAPTER TWO

TANZANIA: UNION OF TWO INDEPENDENT STATES: CHALLENGE TO UNITY AND IDEOLOGY

THE UNION OF Tanganyika and Zanzibar which led to the creation of Tanzania in 1964 is the only union of two independent states that has ever been formed on the African continent.

There have been other mergers in Africa, but not between independent states to form one country. British Togoland, made up of western Togoland - the eastern part was French Togoland - was administered as part of the British Gold Coast colony and protectorate. In 1957 it became part of the independent state of Ghana. In 1961, the people of the northern part of British Cameroons voted to unite with Nigeria (which won independence in 1960) in a UN-supervised plebiscite, while those in the southern part voted to join the former French Cameroons which became independent in 1960 as the Republic of Cameroon.

But unlike Tanganyika and Zanzibar, neither British Togoland, nor the northern part of British Cameroons which united with Nigeria, was a whole country - let alone an independent one. Therefore the union of Tanganyika and Zanzibar is the only union of two independent countries - which also won independence on different dates and in different years - that exists in Africa today as the United Republic of Tanzania. Tanganyika won independence on December 9, 1961, and Zanzibar on December 10, 1963. But the union has also faced some problems because of the union itself; separatist tendencies on the former island nation of Zanzibar have surfaced off and on through the years, although they have never posed a serious threat to the union itself.

There was another union in East Africa, of Eritrea and Ethiopia. But it was not really a union between two independent countries since Eritrea was simply absorbed by Ethiopia. The situation would be analogous to Zanzibar simply becoming part of Tanganyika without even changing the name of the new country from Tanganyika to Tanzania - or Tangazibar or any other name - to reflect the new status of a union of two truly independent countries. Eritrea was not such country when it merged with Ethiopia - its independence was conditional.

Britain occupied Eritrea - an Italian colony - after the Second World War in which Italy was defeated. Beginning in 1949, the country was administered by the British as a UN trust territory. In 1950 the United Nations decided that Eritrea was to be made independent as a federated part of Ethiopia. That decision was implemented in late 1952, and Eritrea ceased to exist as a separate country, although not according to Eritrean nationalists. In 1962 they launched guerrilla warfare to fight for independence from Ethiopia. In 1991, the United Nations scheduled a referendum on Eritrean independence for 1993. It wouldn't have scheduled such a vote if Eritrea had willingly united with Ethiopia. In fact it was the United Nations itself - not the people of Eritrea - which decided to merge Eritrea with Ethiopia as a condition of her independence. It was not until May 3, 1993, that Eritrea became truly independent. Within a few days, Ethiopia accepted and recognized Eritrea as an independent state.

There was also the Mali Federation in West Africa formed in 1960. But it was not a complete merger. It was formed by two former French colonies: the French Soudan which was renamed the Sudanese Republic in 1959 although it was still a colony, yet was called a republic; and Senegal. The federation was formed on June 20, 1960, the same day the two countries emerged from colonial rule supposedly as a single political entity. The merger was no more than symbolic and collapsed shortly thereafter when Senegal withdrew and declared independence on August 20. A few months later on September 22, the former French Soudan proclaimed itself the Republic of Mali.

And in 1982, Gambia and Senegal formed a confederation known as Senegambia. The two countries agreed to consolidate their defense by integrating their armed forces; form a monetary and economic union; and harmonize their foreign policies. But each country retained its sovereign status, making the union more apparent than real. By 1989, popular opposition to the confederation in both countries led to its dissolution. And that left Tanzania as the only union on the continent; a complete merger which obliterated the distinctions between Tanganyika and Zanzibar as two independent countries. Tanganyika is no longer a country, nor is Zanzibar, but integral parts of one.

Therefore, despite all the professions for African unity which ring across the continent, little has been accomplished in terms of mergers of different African countries into one here and there. However, the fact that Tanzania has existed as a union for 35 years now, shows that a merger of African countries under one government is possible, although that is not to downplay the problem which inherently exist in any such union. Separatism is probably the greatest threat, not only to African unions and federations but also to countries which were once single entities during colonial rule and which remained as such after independence. For example, in the West African country of Equatorial Guinea, the only former Spanish colony in sub-Saharan Africa, secessionist demands on the island of Bioko, formerly Fernando Po, have flared up through the years, threatening the nation's territorial integrity. Equatorial Guinea comprises two widely separated provinces: the mainland area of Rio Muni, a forested region with about 75 percent of the population; and the island of Bioko which lies about 20 miles off the cost of Cameroon. The island also controls the smaller island of Pagalu, formerly Annobion, over 200 miles to the southwest of Bioko. The farms and plantations of the offshore island of Bioko grow cocoa, while exports of coffee and okume wood used in the production of plywood, come from Rio Muni.

In 1998, fighting erupted between the secessionist forces and government troops on Bioko island which has always resented control from the mainland preferring, instead, its own independence along with the smaller island of Pagalu it controls:

> "Four soldiers of Equatorial Guinea's army were killed yesterday (January 21, 1998) in the first reported attack by a group demanding independence for the island of Bioko, state radio said. The radio said

the soldiers were killed in an early morning attack on the port of Luba."[49]

And in the East African nation of the Comoros in the Indian Ocean, two of its islands - out of three - declared independence in 1997:

"More than 30 (other reports said 56) people, including soldiers and secessionists, died in the Comoros during a failed attempt to crush separatist rebellion in Nzwani island, also known as Anjouan... The separatists in Nzwani, a tiny tropical island wracked by poverty and unemployment, declared independence on August 3 (1997) from the Comoros chain, which also includes the islands of Njazidja, also known as GrandeComore, and Moheli. Nzwani separatists want a return to the French fold and the benefits provided by Paris - as enjoyed on Mayotte, which voted to remain French in 1974... Separatists on the Indian Ocean island of Anjouan declared that their independence from Comoros was irrevocable and empowered their self-proclaimed president to rule by decree. A spokesman for the separatists, Mohammed Abdou, said a political council had 'established the state of Anjouan' and entitled Abdallah Ibrahim to make laws... Anjouan separatists declared independence asserting that their economic and political interests were being ignored... Anjouan, the second-largest of the three islands that make up Comoros, seceded after months of civil unrest and clashes between protestors and security forces... The smallest of the three islands, Moheli, followed suit, leaving (Comoroan) President Mohamed Taki's government in control only on Grand-Comore... Political leaders on the two secessionist islands... are unanimous in their assertions that the Comoros federation, formed after independence from France in 1975, has brought only poverty, political instability and a series of coups to the country of 670,000 people."[50]

---

[49] "Equatorial Guinea Soldiers Attacked," in *The Boston Globe*, January 22, 1998, p. A-15.

[50] "30 Said to Die in battle for Comoro Isle," in the *International Herald Tribune*, September 8, 1997, p. 14; "Separatists Establish Indian Ocean State," in the *International Herald Tribune*, September 9, 1997, p. 7; "Comoro Lands Troops on a Secessionist Island," in the *International*

The secessionists did not achieve their goal of independence, but they remain a threat to the territorial integrity of the two countries: Equatorial Guinea and the Comoros. Short of total independence, the only other solution to the crisis is to grant greater autonomy to the different regions which constitute the two African countries; a strategy which can also help to neutralize secessionist demands in other African countries, although not always. Tanzania has done that, yet there are still some people in Zanzibar, especially on Pemba island, who want to dissolve the union. However, they are a minority. The secessionist sentiment has not found full acceptance on the two islands which constitute the former island nation of Zanzibar: Pemba, and Zanzibar which is also the larger of the two. Yet the challenge to unity continues. So does the challenge to ideology, as Tanzania undergoes transformation from a one-party state to a multi-party democracy, and from a socialist state to a capitalist-oriented one. The country is still going through fundamental change because it will take some time for the new political parties, formed only during the early 1990s, to establish themselves and constitute a formidable challenge to the old ruling party which is basically the same one that led the country to independence, a stature not easy to match. It will also take quite some time for Tanzania to build a strong private sector to replace the public sector which dominated the country's socialist-oriented economy for decades almost since independence.

But the opening up of the economy to private ownership in most areas especially during the 1990s - which entails disposition of state assets for acquisition by local and foreign investors - has also fueled opposition to the union in Zanzibar and created even more problems for the united republic. So has the adoption of the multi-party system which has emboldened opponents of the union, especially on Pemba island, to pursue their goal even more diligently, however surreptitiously.

The former island nation has played a critical role in the history of East Africa because of its strategic location. For centuries, outsiders, especially from Asia and the Arabian peninsula, used Zanzibar as a launching pad from

Herald Tribune, September 4, 1997, p. 2. See also "Small War in the Comoros: Freedom Follies," in *The Economist*, September 13, 1997, pp. 47-48.

which to penetrate the East African mainland. In fact, even the Western world acknowledged the island nation's significance in its relations with America and West European countries. It was in Zanzibar that the United States opened its first diplomatic mission in sub-Saharan Africa. As Professor Robert Rotberg states in "Africa-U.S. Relations":

> "After the slave trade was outlawed by Congress (in January 1808), the mills of Massachusetts continued to supply parts of Africa as distant as Kenya and Tanzania with the rough cotton cloth that is still known, in upcountry East Africa, as *amerikani*. The first U.S. consulate south of the Sahara was established in Zanzibar in 1837 to foster trade. It was followed by consulates in Cape Town, Gabon, and Liberia."[51]

Explorers penetrated East Africa through Zanzibar. Christian missionaries, such as Dr. David Livingstone, also entered the East African mainland through Zanzibar. So did European and Asian and Arab traders, including those engaged in the diabolical traffic in human beings: the last slave market on the African continent was on Zanzibar island, closed only in 1873 long after the slave trade had been abolished. But slavery remained legal on the island until 1909, and continued for many years even after it was declared illegal. The law meant nothing, morality meant nothing.

After the Zanzibar revolution in 1964 which ousted the Arab minority rulers from power, there were some people who feared that communists - some of whom supported the revolution - would use the island as a base from which they could launch their communist onslaught into Africa. And more recently, Zanzibar again has some people worried. They fear that the island is becoming a hotbed of militant Islamic fundamentalism which in Africa now dominates Sudan, and threatens to overtake Algeria where militant Moslems

---

[51] Robert I. Rotberg, *Africa-U.S. Relations*, in Eric Foner and John A. Garraty, editors, *The Reader's Companion to American History* (Boston: Houghton Mifflin, 1991), p. 17. See also Peter Duignan and Lewis H. Gann, *The United States and Africa: A History* (1984); Roland Oliver and Gervase Mathew, editors, *History of East Africa*, Vol. I (Oxford: Oxford University Press, 1963); and Vincent Harlow, E.M. Chilver, and Alison Smith, editors, *History of East Africa*, Vol. II (Oxford: Oxford University Press, 1967).

have wreaked havoc killing tens of thousands of people since 1992 when the election they were poised to win was cancelled by Algeria's military government - fearing that the militants would establish a theocracy run by fanatical clerics similar to the one instituted by Ayatollah Khomeini in Iran.

But there is yet another fear, concerning Zanzibar, especially with regard to the union. As *The Economist* states:

> "Meantime, it is mammon rather than God or political ideology that Zanzibar is exporting to Africa. And its sharp traders, most of them from Pemba, its smaller sister island to the north, are creating havoc for Tanzania's revenues... The economy has been gradually freed over the past 13 years, (and) Zanzibar's semiautonomous government recently used its ambiguous status to make tariffs lower than on the mainland, opening the 'Zanzibar loophole.' Traders would buy goods in the Gulf, ship them to Zanzibar, paying duty there, and then on to the mainland and wider markets in east and Southern Africa. Zanzibar began to boom and was planning an export-processing zone called Star City. The mainland government meanwhile lost millions in tariffs, and its manufacturers were being put out of business by cheap imports."[52]

That is something which is not supposed to happen in a union, which is one country, one part undermining the other. But that is what has been happening. Differences between the two sides surfaced even more after the Tanzania National Assembly voted almost unanimously to introduce a multi-party system of democracy. When the country held its first multi-party election in October 1995, a political party in Zanzibar known as the Civic United Front (CUF), with its strongest support coming from Pemba island and from traders in Zanzibar, opposed Tanzania's national ruling party in the electoral contest on both islands and demanded renegotiation of the union. Tanzania's ruling party is known in Swahili as Chama Cha Mapinduzi (CCM), meaning Revolutionary Party.

---

52 "Zanzibar Angers the Mainland: East Africa's Offshore Entrepot," in *The Economist*, October 5, 1996, p. 45.

In fact the CUF leadership and other islanders even talked about demanding independence for the former island nation, thus dissolving the union. A return to the status quo ante is preferred not only by some Pemba islanders but also by some people on the main Zanzibar island. For example, there have some leaders in Zanzibar - who are already in the union government - who say the two islands should build their own university, institute an independent revenue service, and even establish their own foreign affairs department.[53] Yet constitutionally, all those areas fall under the jurisdiction of the union government - not Zanzibar's semiautonomous government. So do tariffs. Yet Zanzibar - that's collectively including Pemba, instituted its own, circumventing the union constitution by using its semiautonomous status to make its tariffs lower than those on the mainland. Therefore any suggestion by some Zanzibaris to go their own way in any of those areas is an attempt to undermine the union.

They do, of course, have the constitutional right to do so - free speech as well as the right to mobilize support for their cause within the bounds of the law - if they place the matter on a plebiscite and let the people of the two islands decide whether or not they want to remain part of the union. As President Julius Nyerere stated during the Nigerian civil war following the secession of Eastern Nigeria which declared independence as the Republic of Biafra:

> "Leaders of Tanzania have probably talked more about the need for African unity than those of any other country. Giving formal recognition to even greater disunity in Africa was therefore a very difficult decision to make. Our reluctance to do so was compounded by our understanding of the problems of unity - of which we have some experience - and of the problems of Nigeria. For we have had very good relations with the Federation of Nigeria, even to the extent that when we needed help from Africa we asked it of the Federation.
>
> But unity can only be based on the general consent of the people involved. The people must feel that this State, or this Union, is theirs... Once a large number of the people of any such political unit

[53] Ibid.

stop believing that the State is theirs, and that the Government is their instrument, then the unit is no longer viable. It will not continue to receive the loyalty of its citizens...

In Nigeria this consciousness of a common citizenship was destroyed by the events of 1966, and in particular by the pograms in which 30,000 Eastern Nigerians were murdered, many more injured, and about two million forced to flee from the North of their country. It is these pogroms, and the apparent inability or unwillingness of the authorities to protect the victims, which underlies the Easterners' conviction that they have been rejected by other Nigerians and abandoned by the Federal Government.

Whether the Easterners are correct in their belief that they have been rejected is a matter for argument. But they do have this belief. And if they are wrong they have to be convinced that they are wrong. They will not be convinced by being shot. Nor will their acceptance as part of the Federation be demonstrated by the use of Federal power to bomb schools and hospitals in the areas to which people fled from persecution...

As president of Tanzania it is my duty to safeguard the integrity of the United Republic. But if the mass of the people of Zanzibar should, without external manipulation, and for some reason of their own, decide that the Union was prejudicial to their existence, I could not advocate bombing them into submission. To do so would not be to defend the Union. The Union would have ceased to exist when the consent of its constituent members was withdrawn. I would certainly be one of those working hard to prevent secession, or to reduce its disintegrating effects. But I could not support a war on the people whom I have sworn to serve - especially not if the secession is preceded by a rejection of Zanzibaris by Tanganyikans.

Similarly, if we had succeeded in the 1963 attempt to form an East African Federation, or if we should do so in the future, Tanzania would be overjoyed. But if at some time thereafter the vast majority of the people of any one of the countries should decide – and persist in a decision - to withdraw from the Federation, the other two countries could not wage war against the people who wished to secede. Such a decision would mark a failure by the Federation. That would be tragic; but it would not justify mass killings."[54]

It has, of course, not been determined in a plebiscite that the majority of the Zanzibaris want to secede from the union. Therefore secession - hence dissolution of the union - cannot be justified, although some Zanzibari leaders want the islanders to go their own way in a number of areas which fall under the jurisdiction of the union government, as we have shown.

Those have not been the only attempts to weaken and preferably end the union, even if indirectly. Zanzibari leaders threatened the union even further when they secretly made the former island nation a member of the Organization of the Islamic Conference in January 1993 - thus implicitly declaring Zanzibar's independence - officially making Zanzibar part of the Islamic group of nations, as if it were an independent country and not just part of Tanzania, without even consulting the national government on the mainland. The leaders on the isles maintained that Zanzibar's membership in the Islamic organization did not affect the two islands' union with mainland Tanzania. But some members of the national parliament from the mainland said Zanzibar's action was unconstitutional and demanded a separate government for Tanganyika, thus effectively ending the union. The matter was resolved when Zanzibar agreed to withdraw its membership from the conference of Islamic nations, and maintained its allegiance to the union although probably with some reservations.

But that does not mean the United Republic of Tanzania is about to collapse. Its resilience during the past 35 years, and as the only merger of two independent countries on the continent both of which renounced their sovereignty upon consummation of the union, points exactly in the opposite direction. However, this is not to downplay the problems which inherently exist in the union, just like they do in any other, although in varying degrees.

---

[54] Julius Nyerere, "Why We Recognized Biafra," in *The Observer*, London, April 28, 1968; reprinted in Colin Legum and John Drysdale, *Africa Contemporary Record: Annual Survey and Documents 1968-1969* (London: Africa Research Ltd., 1969), pp. 651-652. Tanzania was the first country to recognize Biafra, on April 13, 1968. See also Tanzania's ruling party's daily newspaper, *The Nationalist*, Dar es Salaam, April 13-14, 1968; and *The Standard*, Dar es Salaam, April 13-14, 1968.

The question is not only how to resolve differences but also how to harmonize them through coexistence in order to accommodate conflicting interests for the transcendent good, especially through devolution of power.

Unfortunately, Tanzania's success in maintaining the union has not been matched in the economic field. Self-reliance and social equality remain distant goals, although they are now being pursued in a capitalist context. And in the political arena, one-party democracy is being successfully replaced by multi-party democracy, despite the fact that the former was never really a failure. The time when the one-party state was needed to forge national unity is over. Despite its limited success, Tanzania's one-party system - unlike others elsewhere - did, to a large degree, enable the people to participate in the political process. Critics, of course, dismissed it outright as undemocratic.

But that is a narrow definition of democracy based solely on the Western model which is not valid in all contexts in terms of local relevance. The essence of democracy is universal, but mechanisms for its articulation are contextual. For example, the no-party system in Uganda introduced by President Yoweri Museveni - under which political candidates run for office as individuals - enjoys popular support among Ugandans although it is essentially a one-party system of Museveni's own ruling party: the National Resistance Movement (NRM). And in Tanzania, the one-party system also enjoyed popular support which was empirically verified even when union parliamentarians voted to introduce the multi-party system. There was strong opposition across the country to the introduction of multiparty politics, obviously because of its divisive effects especially along ethnic lines. As Professor Harvey Glickman states in "Tanzania: From Disillusionment to Guarded Optimism":

> "Following the trend toward more open politics that was sweeping Africa, President Ali Hassan Mwinyi (who succeeded Nyerere in 1985) appointed a commission in February 1991 to examine the feasibility of multiparty politics. The commission sent representatives abroad and consulted public opinion through party auspices.

> Although the commission reported opposition to change, it concluded by recommending the adoption of a multiparty system."[55]

What is undemocratic is to deny the people the right to decide whether they want a one-party system or a multiparty democracy. Although Tanzanians now have a multiparty system, they can decide to re-institute the one-party state - if they want to by putting the matter to a referendum - which served them well since independence and helped keep the country together which could have fractured and fallen apart along ethnic lines had the multiparty system been introduced soon after the end of colonial rule. That it was not introduced, does not necessarily mean that democracy was denied; although in most cases the one-party system in almost all of the countries where it has been adopted has muzzled the opposition. As Professor K.R. Minogue states in his analytical work "Nationalism":

> "There is certainly no reason why non-European nations should follow the details of what is done in Westminster or Washington; there is equally no reason to pretend that many of the alternatives they have found must be called 'democratic," a word which sinks ever lower towards the horizon of meaninglessness. Most Afro-Asian countries are ruled in a more or less authoritarian way, as indeed they must be where the mass of the population is largely unaccustomed to political participation and lacks the habits of democratic moderation. There are, of course, exceptions to this. India has succeeded in running a large-scale democracy along broadly traditional lines; and in Tanzania the magnetic personality of Mr. Nyerere for the present sustains a form of popular consultation which it would be no violation of language to call 'democratic.' Maintaining democracy where the nation is bent on modernization has considerable political advantages,

[55] Harvey Glickman, "Tanzania: From Disillusionment to Guarded Optimism," in *Current History: A Journal of Contemporary World Affairs*, May 1997, p. 220, with the assistance of Raymond Hopkins; and Richard Mshomba, Elaine Mshomba, and Victor Kimesera, all the last three from Tanzania. See also J. Oloka-Onyango, *Uganda's 'Benevolent' Dictatorship*, ibid., pp. 212-216; and Onyango, *The Dynamics of Constitutional Politics in Uganda* (Dakar, Senegal: CODESRIA, 1997).

> but we would be unwise to make a fetish out of either the word or the institution. Perhaps it is salutary to remember that many of the achievements of civilization have been produced under authoritarian political systems."[56]

Most African leaders articulated their political views from that perspective, and even justified dictatorship in that context; which is what prompted Dr. Kwame Nkrumah to state in his autobiographical work, published in 1957 the same year Ghana won independence, the following:

> "What other countries have taken three hundred years to achieve, a once dependent territory must try to accomplish in a generation if it is to survive. Unless it is, as it were, 'jet-propelled,' it will lag behind and thus risk everything for which it has fought. Capitalism is too complicated a system for a newly independent nation. Hence the need for a socialistic society. But even a system based on social justice and a democratic constitution may need backing up, during the period following independence, by emergency measures of a totalitarian kind. Without discipline, true freedom cannot survive."[57]

It is axiomatic that the system Nkrumah talks about - even with all the professions of social justice and a democratic institution - entails instituting a one-party state which brooks no dissent. And he has in those few words outlined the underpinnings which sustained the modern African state from independence until the early mid-nineties when it started to undergo fundamental change, although many of those changes are superficial. Those underpinnings on which almost every African state rested were socialism and the one-party system.

---

[56] K.R. Minogue, "Nationalism" (Baltimore, Maryland, USA: Penguin Books, 1968), pp. 128-129.

[57] Kwame Nkrumah, *Ghana: The Autobiography of Kwame Nkrumah* (New York: Nelson and Sons, 1957); reproduced in Paul E. Sigmund, Jr., editor, *The Ideologies of the Developing Nations* (New York: Frederick A. Praeger, 1963), p. 186. See also Julius Nyerere, "One-Party Rule," in P.E. Sigmund, ibid., pp. 197-202, reprinted from *Spearhead*, Dar es Salaam, Tanganyika, November 1961.

But that foundation has now collapsed because the international situation changed following the disintegration of the communist edifice and the end of the Cold War which ushered in a new era of democratic change around the world, and acceptance of free-market ideas in former socialist countries as the best way to achieve economic development. Throughout the African continent, socialism has failed, self-reliance pursued in a socialist context has also failed, and the one-party state has been discredited. Even in Tanzania, where there was mass participation in the political process under the one-party system, multi-party politics has been enthusiastically embraced across the country, leading to the formation of several political parties, at least 13 during the last election in October 1995.

Yet in spite of all that failure across the continent, there have also been some notable achievements in different African countries, including Tanzania, as we showed earlier in the book. But through the decades, Tanzania also differed from other countries on the continent in many respects in terms of policy implementation, including fulfillment of goals other African countries pursued as well. As Glickman pointed out:

> "Tanzania's profile, in the life and career of President Julius Nyerere, was poor, earnest, caring, and honest - at least until 1985, when Nyerere formally stepped aside in a peaceful constitutional transition (which is extremely rare in Africa). Tanzania's government was stable while other African governments succumbed to coups and civil wars. The country conducted consecutive national elections at regular five-year intervals. Other one-party states ignored mass participation; Nyerere's Tanzania devised a system of constituency primaries under the party umbrella, controlled at the center, but offering a voice for localism. Other African governments extolled the virtues of Pan-Africanism; Nyerere engineered the union of his own country and an offshore neighbor. Other African governments denounced white racist governments on the continent; Tanzania took action, cutting off relations with Britain over the issue of African rule in Rhodesia in 1965, and offering shelter to the liberation parties and guerrilla forces of southern Africa.
>
> While most African governments rejected the secession of Biafra from Nigeria in 1967, Tanzania recognized Biafra's short-lived

government on moral grounds, arguing it was an act of self-defense against ethnic pogroms. While other African countries merely denounced Idi Amin in Uganda in the 1970s, Tanzania's army defeated him in battle in 1979 and drove him from the country."[58]

In addition to all that, several features also distinguished Tanzania from other African countries since the sixties soon after she won independence. Some of those factors are economic and political, others geographic as well as demographic. But collectively, they were all critical factors in the formulation and implementation of the country's policies through the decades. Many of them continue to play a role even today as Tanzania undergoes transformation from a failed socialist state to a free-market economy; and from a one-party to a multiparty democracy. As *Africa Contemporary Record* profiled Tanzania back in 1968 one year after promulgation of her socialist policies, outlining some of the country's most prominent features:

> "A number of features mark Tanzania out as significantly different from any other African State. First, its growth into a single-party State did not come about as a result of coercion: in the pre-independence struggle TANU (Tanganyika African National Union) emerged with the popular support of the overwhelming majority of its people. Second, although it has 120 ethnic groups including a number of dominant tribes, tribalism has not been a disturbing feature of its politics, although regional ethnocentricities are marked. Third, its leader, President Julius Nyerere – Mwalimu, the teacher – is the unchallenged father of the nation. He is a leader with a surer instinct about the nature of institutions than perhaps any of his contemporaries in the continent. He is both tolerant and tough; and he has a rare degree of modesty which enables him to recognize that not all his institutional reforms have been successful. Fourth, it is a huge country (bigger than Nigeria) with very poor communications which isolate its regions from each other, and from the capital. Fifth, its

[58] H. Glickman, "Tanzania: From Disillusionment to Guarded Optimism," in *Current History*, ibid., p. 217. See also Glickman, "Ethnic Conflict and Democratization in Africa" (Atlanta, Georgia: African Studies Association Press, 1995).

> leadership has been able to commit the country to sacrificing its national interests, at times, for the sake of moral principles. Sixth it is an exceedingly poor country, with a per capita income of less than £24 per year, dependent for the bulk of its exports on the rural sector of the economy, where over 80 percent of the people are to be found, and with only a tiny modern elite. Seventh, it is one of the few countries in the Third World with a well-planned strategy of socialist development.
>
> These seven features go a long way towards explaining the formulation of the Arusha Declaration with its twin themes of reliance on self-help and an idealistic commitment to egalitarianism. The tests are whether it is indeed possible to make a revolution without using violent methods, and whether it is possible to create a lively democracy, within a single-party system."[59]

Tanzania believed all that was possible and did, in fact, succeed in creating a fair amount of democracy through mass participation in the political process under her one-party system; a process some of the elite shunned. She was also able to pursue her economic policies through the decades without resorting to violence, but failed to radically transform the society into a socialist haven. And a lot more has also changed.

Mwalimu Julius Nyerere is no longer president of Tanzania; he retired in November 1985. Socialism has not only failed, it has been abandoned. The one-party system has also been abandoned. The country remains poor, but there is some hope for improvement as we will learn later on in this chapter. And tribalism, a perennial problem which bedevils every African country but which was latent and never a major one in Tanzanian politics through the decades under the one-party system, now threatens to surface and become a national concern under the newly adopted multiparty system.

However, Tanzania has one unique advantage. Unlike most African countries, Tanzania has an indigenous national language, Swahili, which has played a critical role in integrating the country's 120 different tribes into a single political entity with a shared national ethos; a task also made somewhat

[59] "Tanzania," in *Africa Contemporary Record*, op. cit., p. 213.

easier due to the fact that most of Tanzania's tribes are small and there is no single tribe or two dominating the others. And Swahili also has the additional advantage of being transtribal; it is not identified with a single tribe - it belongs to all the 120 tribes and different racial minorities, they all contributed to its evolution as its rich vocabulary clearly shows. Such linguistic homogeneity has helped to contain and discourage tribalism; so has government policy of assigning employees to different regions and districts away from their tribal homelands, and mixing in school students of different tribes where communication in one's tribal language with members of one's tribes is strongly discouraged and even looked down upon. But now that multiparty politics has been introduced, support for political candidates and membership in political parties could assume regional and tribal character at the expense of national unity. The last national elections brought this problem to the attention of a number of people:

> "Until the 1990s, Tanzania has escaped significant ethnic, racial, regional, and religious conflict. In October 1995, however, the country's first competitive elections for president and parliament raised doubts about the commitment of the triumphant – formerly monopoly – party to pluralist democracy. The fallout from the election caused serious concern about the fate of 30 years of striving toward national political integration, progress made despite 120 tribal groupings, a vast territory, and poor communications."[60]

Commitment to genuine democracy was yet another concern inextricably linked with the threat from ethnic antagonism in a pluralistic context. Like in other African countries, pluralist democracy in Tanzania today is more of an ideal than a reality in multiparty politics that spans the ideological spectrum and which must transcend ethnic and regional loyalties to acquire legitimacy. It is a problem which was dealt with, rather successfully, before the introduction of multiparty democracy because the one-party system was all-inclusive; it did not have the electorate compartmentalized into parties which compete for partisan interests. In order for multiparty politics to be fruitful, it

---

[60] H. Glickman, ibid.

must be transcendent, a goal few African countries - if any - have been able to achieve.

There is yet another problem which poses a serious threat to national unity in Tanzania. And that is secessionist tendencies in Zanzibar. Although the secessionist sentiment has not gained full acceptance on the isles, it is still strong enough to be taken seriously; it has its exponents in spite of the fact that the former island nation has always enjoyed great autonomy since the union was consummated in 1964: Zanzibar has its own government, with its own president, who also automatically serves as one of the two vice presidents of the united republic; it also has its own legislature, and judiciary, and is significantly represented in the union government as well as in other institutions of the united republic.

According to the union constitution, when the president of the united republic comes from Tanzania mainland, the first vice-president shall come from the isles and vice versa. And under an amendment passed in 1984, a citizen of Tanzania can be president for no more than two five-year terms. According to the Zanzibar constitution, also amended in 1984, the president of the isles can also hold office for a maximum of two five-year terms. The president of the united republic appoints a prime minister to run the day-to-day affairs of government. So does the president of Zanzibar; he appoints a prime minister to run the Zanzibar government.[61] The two islands also have their own seal, different from the emblem of the united republic, but a judicial system which is somewhat similar to that on the mainland:

> "The Zanzibar House of Representatives has passed three bills, establishing a Government Seal, a new Isles judicial system, and Kadhi courts. Under the Government Seal Bill, the Zanzibar Revolutionary Government will have its own seal which symbolizes the Zanzibar Government and its wealth...The seal has an emblem of the two islands of Zanzibar and Pemba which are flanked by a coconut tree and a clove tree on the left and right, respectively, and sea below the islands. The outer side of the seal is supported by a

[61] "Tanzania Embassy Newsletter," Washington, D.C., January 1985, p. 12.

> hatchet on the left and an axe on the right signifying the 1964 revolution which toppled the Sultanate oligarchy.
>
> Another bill abolishing the People's Courts and set (up) a new judicial system under the 1984 Zanzibar Constitution was unanimously passed by the House. The Bill repeals that of 1964 and will have a judicial system similar to that on the Mainland - that is primary courts, resident magistrate's courts, high and appeal courts. The Kadhi's Bill was also unanimously passed by the House. The courts will deal with matters of Islamic law provided that both parties concerned profess Moslem religion. The Bill provides for appeals from Kadhi's courts to the High Court (of Zanzibar), the case referred shall be heard by a judge and four sheikhs and the decision shall be based on the majority decision of all the five members on the bench. Such a decision shall not be appealable to the court of appeal."[62]

Yet in spite of all the freedom Zanzibar enjoys in running its own affairs, such autonomy has not satisfied many Zanzibaris on both islands. They still want to secede. Therefore devolution of power does not work in all cases to contain secessionist sentiments. And that applies to both unitary and federal states. Tanzania was a unitary state until 1995. But even if Tanzania had a federal constitution, secessionist tendencies in Zanzibar would still have continued to threaten the union because the people who want to secede see Zanzibar as a de facto separate nation with its own history and culture different from that of the mainland.

There is also a racial and religious component involved in their opposition to the union. Secessionist Zanzibaris of Arab descent want a return to a Arab rule or, at the very least, re-institution of Arab hegemony on both islands even if the president of the isles, and the majority of the island cabinet members are black, provided they can manipulate them at will. And in terms of religion, Zanzibar is almost entirely Moslem, unlike Tanzania mainland where the percentage of Christians roughly equals that of Moslems. Therefore many islanders, probably most of them, see Zanzibar as an Islamic nation

[62] Ibid.

which should be allied - and if possible even unite - with other Islamic countries.

But there are also political differences between blacks and Arabs on the isles. Arabs dominated the two islands for centuries until they were dislodged in 1964 in a revolution which was not racial but against oppression; among the most prominent leaders of the Zanzibar revolution were Zanzibaris of Arab descent such as Abdulrahman Babu who also became some of the leaders in the union government holding senior cabinet posts and other high government positions within the united republic and in the diplomatic field. Yet even their participation in the union government was not, and still is not, enough to mute secessionist sentiments being articulated on the two islands.

Therefore three features distinguish Zanzibar in its relation to the union: great autonomy the former island nation enjoys; secessionist sentiment; strong political opposition to Tanzania's ruling party (CCM) which rules both parts of the union. That alone, CCM's hegemony, has fueled secessionist demands. Strong national leadership, which commands allegiance across the spectrum on democratic basis on both islands and the mainland, will play a critical role in holding the union together. Nyerere who led Tanzania for 24 years until his retirement in 1985 - from 1961 to April 1964 (when the union was formed) as leader of Tanganyika - was able to provide that kind of leadership. So did his successor Ali Hassan Mwinyi. And the third president, Benjamin Mkapa, elected in 1995, has also been able to do that; although he may have many more years to go to contend with the problem if he wins a second term during which the tension between the islands and the mainland could get worse and even break up the union. But in spite of the success achieved by the three leaders in maintaining the union, serious problems continue to threaten the united republic:

> "Secessionist sentiment is now strong in Zanzibar... Zanzibar is also now home to the strongest regional opposition to the erstwhile ruling party. These policy differences translate into religious conflict between Muslims and Christians on mainland Tanzania, and political antagonism between indigenous Africans and residents of Zanzibar of Arab descent.
>
> A stronger asset is the country's new leader, Benjamin Mkapa, who started his presidential term in November 1995 by making public

> his family's financial assets - two houses, a farm, and four cars. His appointed prime minister is Frederick Sumaye, a former agriculture minister who, like Mkapa, maintains a modest lifestyle. Mkapa's cabinet is distinguished by youth, competence, and the absence of old faces. All but two of the mainland regions are represented, and it has more Muslims than at any time before.
>
> The quality of Tanzania's future will greatly depend on the management of five issues: dealing with refugees from Burundi and Rwanda, making progress in economic reform, battling a culture of corruption, expanding multiparty politics to more meaningful democratic government, and overcoming the threat of communal conflict."[63]

Another serious threat to Tanzania's stability comes from refugees fleeing from the fighting in Rwanda and Burundi. Tanzania has for years provided asylum to refugees from other countries including those in southern Africa when they were fighting for independence. Her policy of welcoming refugees goes back to the sixties when Nyerere promised them sanctuary as soon as Tanganyika won independence in 1961. In 1983 he was awarded the Nansen Medal of the UN High Commissioner for Refugees for his efforts to resettle refugees and exiles in Tanzania, a large number of whom were granted citizenship through the years. They were also given farm land. Even those who did not become citizens were given some land, and helped to return to their home countries whenever they were ready to. Such generosity also helped to reduce tensions without the country which could have threatened Tanzania's security if the refugees were left homeless and landless.

Although there were a lot of refugees from southern Africa living in Tanzania, it is the refugees from Rwanda and Burundi who constitute the largest exile population in the country; almost all those who came from southern Africa returned to their home countries after they won independence. By May 1997, Tanzania had the largest number of refugees on the entire continent, second only to Congo, former Zaire. There were more than 500,000

[63] H. Glickman, ibid., pp. 217-218. See also, "Tanzania: Corruption Hot Potato," in *Africa Business*, London, February 1997.

from Rwanda, and more than 200,000 from Burundi. All of them were mostly Hutus living in camps in western and northwestern Tanzania. Thousands of them have lived in Tanzania - in what was then Tanganyika - since 1963, having fled from massacres and persecution in Burundi by the Tutsis. There were also refugees from Rwanda which was ruled by Hutus until July 1994; these were mostly Tutsis.

In 1980 tens of thousands of refugees from Rwanda and Burundi were granted Tanzanian citizenship. Thousands more Rwandan refugees settled in Tanzania in 1983 after they were expelled from Uganda; these were mostly Tutsis, and a large number of them also became citizens. As the fighting continued in both Rwanda and Burundi into the late 1990s, thousands of refugees continued to flee into Tanzania, most of them seeking permanent shelter; only to be repatriated. Yet many of them kept on coming back, along with new refugees, almost all of them Hutus fleeing from Tutsi domination and persecution in the two countries.

Unless the ethnic conflict in Rwanda and Burundi is settled, the refugee problem will continue to be a great challenge to Tanzania, constantly threatening her security, draining her meager resources, and testing her hospitality she has always extended through the years to those fleeing from persecution. Rwanda's and Burundi's problems have now become Tanzania's problems, as they always have been. Strangely enough, all three were once one country known as German East Africa. But their separation did not separate their problems. Now they are united by those problems stemming from the Hutu-Tutsi ethnic warfare which has spilled into Tanzania, drawing her into the orbit of conflict.

The ethnic warfare has also been responsible for tense relations between Tanzania and Burundi, which deteriorated even further in 1997 because of border incidents involving troops on both sides when Burundian soldiers crossed the border into Tanzania in pursuit of Hutu guerrillas. Although such incidents and the refugee crisis cause security problems for Tanzania, they are not a threat to national unity because they tend to trigger exactly the opposite reaction: mobilize nationalist sentiment against an external threat.

The challenge to unity in Tanzania comes from within; and unlike the conflict in Rwanda and Burundi, it is more political than ethnic. Tribalism is something to be concerned about, but ethnic relations among Tanzania's 120 different tribes are not tense; and where antagonism exists, it has not erupted into violence - at least not on the scale it has in other African countries. But the potential for such an eruption exists if it is exploited by unscrupulous elements for their own ends, especially in the new political climate.

However, the biggest threat to Tanzania's territorial integrity comes from Zanzibar, which some national legislators from the mainland felt could be dealt with peacefully, and to the satisfaction of both sides, by demanding the same thing for the mainland the Zanzibar opponents of the union were demanding for the isles: separation. That is where the biggest challenge to unity comes from. Not only are many Zanzibaris opposed to the leadership by the CCM on the island, the party which won the national election; they want to pull out of the union entirely:

> "Civic liberty, economic liberalization, and the opening of the political system to multiparty competition have begun to expose Tanzania to the ethnic and communal conflict that bedevils other states in Africa. So far, 'tribal' conflict has been muted and open differences have been confined to the Zanzibar issue. Opposition sentiment in Zanzibar predates competitive politics... (and) led to secessionist sentiments expressed more openly as opposition parties became increasingly active. By 1993, antimainland sentiment had ensnared militant Islamism; anti-Muslim looting was kindled by a self-styled Christian fundamentalist clergyman-cum-politician in Dar es Salaam. It was clear that opposition to CCM rule in the Union would find widespread support in Zanzibar as multiparty politics heated up. In retaliation, the Union's National Assembly approved a motion urging a separate mainland government and legislature by constitutional amendment... It hardly helped matters that the Zanzibar government secretly joined the Organization of Islamic Conference, only to withdraw a few months later under heavy criticism."[64]

The Civic United Front (CUF), which is strongest on Pemba island where there is a substantial Arab population proportionally more than on Zanzibar Island, was the main opposition party to CCM in the 1995 elections - not only

[64] H. Glickman, ibid., pp. 219, and 220.

on Pemba island but also on Zanzibar. And its clarion call for strengthening commercial ties and other links with the Arab states in the Persian Gulf - where the former rulers of Zanzibar originally came from, especially from Oman - aroused fear among blacks on the two isles as well as those on the mainland that the CUF was trying to restore Arab control over the islands; a fear which, even if unfounded, was not disproved. As if to confirm that fear, the CUF won all the seats on Pemba Island for the Zanzibar legislature, a victory attributed to the large Arab population on that island.

Yet in spite of its strong ties to the Arab world, the CUF also has strong support on Zanzibar island as well, not just on Pemba, the CUF's stronghold. But the CCM candidate, Dr. Salmin Amour, won the presidency of Zanzibar precisely because of CUF's advocacy of stronger ties to the Persian Gulf states. Yet because of its secessionist sentiments which are shared by many Zanzibaris, the party enjoyed considerable support among the islanders on both isles. It has become a paradox its opponents have to contend with in contradictory ways: the CUF is feared by many blacks, yet it is also supported by the very people who fear it, on both islands, because it supports secession many Zanzibaris, black and Arab, also support. So what can be done?:

> "The Zanzibar issue rankles. The CCM is divided as to how far to extend an olive branch to the CUF, which has overwhelming support in Pemba and is supported by half or more of the archipelago's total population. Zanzibar President Amour's victory reflects class fears in Unguja (the other name for the larger island also known as Zanzibar), where peasants worry about a return of nationalized plantations to Arab ownership or a reversal of their breakup. Opposition figures have wondered why Nyerere, if he can attempt to mediate in Burund, cannot do the same in Zanzibar. Mwinyi (who is from Zanzibar island), Nyerere, and Mkapa quietly explored a government of national unity there at the end of 1995. Unrest and protests, especially on Pemba, continued through last year (1996)."[65]

[65] Ibid., p. 221.

The challenge to unity also continues. So does the challenge to the old ruling party, CCM, under the new political system of multiparty politics as was clearly shown in the 1995 national elections. There were four presidential candidates. The leading contender was Benjamin Mkapa, leader of CCM. He won 62 percent of the vote; the three opposition candidates collectively won 38 percent. Mkapa's opponent was former Deputy Prime Minister Augustine Mrema, leader of the NCCR-Mageuzi (National Convention for Construction and Reform: Chama Cha Mageuzi - a Swahili name meaning Reform Party, as opposed to the ruling Chama Cha Mapinduzi which means Revolutionary Party).

In parliamentary elections, there were four main parties. They won 98 percent of the seats and slightly over 95 percent of the vote. CCM won 186 of the elected seats - the rest are assigned by nomination; the CUF won 24 seats, and the NCCR-Mageuzi won 16. But the combined total of opposition seats in the National Assembly came to 60; while CCM had a total of 124 including seats for nominated members.

Therefore the ruling CCM has a commanding majority in the union parliament. However, the combined opposition also has a respectable presence in the legislature - 60 seats is a significant number, although not enough to reverse or reform the CCM agenda - as well as on the national political landscape which is gradually being transformed since the one-party system was abolished in 1991. The challenge that lies ahead in the political realm is whether this fledgling multiparty democracy will become a transcendent phenomenon or simply an exercise in cheap politics dictated by narrow partisan interests in the name of national unity.

The last general election in 1995, the first in multiparty democracy, showed that there are cracks in the Tanzanian body-politic which, instead of being closed as they were under the one-party system, are now being widened by multiparty politics. The voting was conducted along well-defined lines which showed a number of overlapping divisions: between Pemba Island and the main Zanzibar Island. Pemba islanders voted overwhelmingly for their own candidate, while Zanzibar islanders did the same for their own, to be the president of the two islands - collectively known as Zanzibar - as it is allowed under the Constitution of the United Republic of Tanzania. There was also a split in the vote between black Africans and Arabs on both islands, each racial group voting overwhelmingly for its own candidates. Blacks on both islands supported Dr. Salmin Amour, from the main Zanzibar island who went on to win the presidency of the two isles, while Arabs on both islands voted for Shariff Hamad from Pemba, for the office.

There was also a split in the vote between the former island nation of Zanzibar - which is composed of both Pemba and Zanzibar - and the mainland formerly known as Tanganyika, over the issue of union of the two former independent countries. Voters from both islands strongly supported the CUF which wants to end the union. Another division in the voting pattern was between Christians and Muslims on the mainland - there are hardly any Christians in Zanzibar; between Africans and Asians on both Zanzibar and the mainland; and, to a lesser degree, between allied African ethnic groups as well as regions on the mainland, threatening to fuel tribal and regional competition which through the decades was not a major problem in Tanzanian politics under the one-party system.

Such are the unintended consequences of multiparty politics - in spite of all its advantages over the one-party system in many areas - in African pluralistic societies. Their very composition demands a high degree of political dexterity to accommodate and harmonize conflicting interests - ethnic and regional, racial and religious, political and economic, social and cultural - for the sake of democracy whose articulation in the African context remains largely experimental. Success of democracy in Africa will require innovations in the political system which have never been tried anywhere else, but without compromising the essence of the democratic tradition. Uganda under Museveni is trying to do just that through no-party electoral contest in which political candidates run, not as members of political parties presenting party manifestos to the electorate, but simply as individuals offering their own agenda for the nation. But there is also reason for concern that if its underlying principles of free and fair competition in the electoral process on an individual basis are not properly implemented, the no-party system political blueprint could be no more than a manifesto for a new form dictatorship clumsily disguised in the same old rhetoric Africans across the continent are so much used to.

Tanzania may also have to introduce its own innovations, including limiting the number of political parties to three so that a third party could constitute a third force between the two major parties which will inevitably emerge in the new dispensation. The third party would be able to throw its weight behind one or the other of the two dominant parties to effect major policy changes, and act as a moderating influence on both. Even a return to the status quo ante should not be entirely ruled out, if that is what the people want because they fear multiparty contests may break up the country. But the one-party system intended to keep the country united should be re-instituted only after it has been determined in a national referendum that - that is what the people really want.

Under the reformed one-party system, there should be no one particular ideology which the party follows. The party should be open to all ideologies. People should be free to formulate whatever policies they want to campaign on and promote; and opponents of government policies in parliament should be allowed to form an opposition group - as well as cross the floor - within the same party which will, for all intents and purposes, be a national political movement that has dispensed with divisive party politics but which allows and encourages robust political debate. In African contests, almost all of which are composed of several different tribes, multiparty politics degenerates into tribal politics; therefore, more often than not, the multiparty system in those countries is no more than multi-tribal parties.

Tanzanians have only to look north, at their next-door neighbor Kenya, where the 1997 general election was contested along tribal lines; Kikuyus voting for their fellow Kikuyu for president, Luos for their own, as did the rest, each of the major tribes as well as the others with its own political - frankly speaking, tribal - party. It was a division which proved to be a windfall for the long-serving brutal autocrat, President Daniel arap Moi, who comfortably - and gleefully - coasted to victory. Had his opponents united behind a single candidate, Moi would be history today. But tribal politics made that impossible. That is what multipartyism means in Africa: multi-tribalism. And many Tanzanians are aware of that. However, giving multiparty democracy a chance is the right thing to do, although extremely difficult to achieve in Africa. But Tanzania has one great advantage against multi-tribal politics because her tribes are small, making it impossible for any particular tribe or tribes to dominate the rest and win elections on their own strength - let alone rule the country.

But Tanzania's well-being will also be determined by the state of her economy which, like her political system, is also undergoing transformation. It is an ideological challenge which has been compounded by the fact that although socialism has been abandoned, it has not been entirely jettisoned. Still change is inevitable, however slowly. There is no other choice. Even the old guard in the country's ruling political party, CCM, who want to maintain the status quo and continue to pursue some of the old socialist policies - refusing to dismantle the state monopoly of a number of enterprises - while only grudgingly implementing free-market ideas, are being inexorably propelled in the new direction the country has taken. We live in a new era of fundamental change round the globe of which Tanzania is an integral part, however marginal her economy. Like all the other African countries, Tanzania plays only a peripheral role in the global economy because she is underdeveloped. But she has also undergone an ideological conversion and adopted a new strategy for economic development. We focus on that next in order to assess her potential for growth and try to see how far she has gone in this new direction.

FREE-MARKET APPROACH TOWARDS TANZANIA'S ECONOMIC GROWTH

Ten years after he retired from the presidency in 1985, Julius Nyerere looked back at his leadership during which he led Tanzania for almost three decades since independence. They were years of successes and failures, also of hope and despair. Probably the biggest failure was in the economic arena where the government, as opposed to the private sector, played the most decisive role as the owner of the country's major assets and imposed severe restrictions on income and private ownership of property, thus robbing the people of the incentive to work. The restrictions were made even more stringent by high taxes, some of the highest in the world. All that and a combination of other factors, including international ones beyond Tanzania's control, led to tragic failure: the economy virtually collapsed. As Nyerere himself, one of the extremely few African leaders who publicly admit mistakes, conceded in his farewell speech in November 1985:

"I failed. Let's admit it."[66]

---

[66] Julius Nyerere, in his farewell speech upon stepping down as president of Tanzania, delivered in Dares es Salaam, November 1985, issued as a press release by the Tanzania Ministry of Information and Broadcasting; Nyerere, quoted by James C. McKinley, Jr.,

The transportation system was dilapidated, agricultural production declined, and industries were producing at half their capacity, due to failed economic policies. But Nyerere also left behind a record of great achievements. He was able to maintain peace and stability in Tanzania throughout his leadership, while many other African countries descended into chaos, torn by civil wars, ethnic conflicts, military coups, and state violence unleashed by security forces against countless innocent civilians. Very few African leaders can claim to have maintained peace and stability for almost 30 years straight as Nyerere did in Tanzania. The only other exceptions during that period were Zambia, Botswana, Swaziland, Ivory Coast, and Gambia. And while other African countries imposed one-party dictatorships, Tanzania's one-party system allowed mass participation in the political process on democratic basis and held elections at regular intervals in which even some cabinet members who were also members of parliament lost their seats, humbled at the polls by their opponents who were just ordinary citizens.

Under Nyerere's leadership, Tanzania also made great progress in education and health, unlike many other African countries endowed with even greater resources. In fact it was during Nyerere's tenure that Tanzania became one of the countries which made the greatest advances in combating illiteracy. Because of that, Tanzania today has a higher literacy rate than India; yet India is a major country, fairly developed, with some of the most educated people in the world including the third largest pool of scientists after the United States and the former Soviet Union.

Nyerere will also always be remembered for other great achievements. His support for the African liberation movements - all of them based in Tanzania - in their struggle against colonial rule and white racist regimes is unequalled by that of any other leader on the continent. And his commitment to African unity also produced tangible results unmatched anywhere else in Africa. It was on his initiative that the union of Tanganyika and Zanzibar was formed, the only union of independent countries which was ever formed and that still exists on the continent today as the United Republic of Tanzania.

"Tanzania's Nyerere Looks Back: Many Failures, and One Big Success - Bringing a Nation to Life," in the *International Herald Tribune*, September 2, 1996, p. 2. See also McKinley on Nyerere and Tanzania in *The New York Times*, September 2, 1996. On Nyerere's retirement speech, see also *Daily News*, Dar es Salaam, November 1985.

Even with his failed economic policies, all those achievements, and much more, shall endure as a monument to his great leadership. And in the economic field, he said ten years after his retirement that he would do many things differently if he could turn back the clock. But he remains unshaken in his belief in socialism. As he stated in an interview in his home village of Butiama in northern Tanzania in 1996 where he returned after he retired from the presidency:

> "I would still write the Arusha Declaration. I believe in it. It is right."[67]

But Nyerere acknowledged that socialism never mixed well with the traditional ways of African villages. It is possible, he said, to have farmers own a tractor in common, or to cooperate in buying fertilizer or selling grain. But he said that in hindsight it was a big mistake to collectivize the individual farms, or *shambas* in Swahili, which families had owned for generations:

> "You can socialize what is not traditional. The shamba can't be socialized."[68]

Nyerere also said it was a mistake to nationalize sisal - one of the country's major export crops which is grown on large plantations owned by private companies before being nationalized - and other industries, especially in the manufacturing sector, as well as banks.

But he still defends mobilizing the people into ujamaa (collectivized) villages. It was the right thing to do, he said, if only to make the most of the schools, roads and health clinics the government had built and others it could afford to build. Yet that is also what caused some of the country's major problems. Many people resented being put together in ujamaa villages, a move which led to low morale and low productivity. Tanzania, with her meager resources, also spread herself too thin providing free services in all those areas: education was free, medical service was free - people didn't have to pay a cent for all those services; and that included people who could afford

---

[67] Nyerere, quoted by J. McKinley, ibid.
[68] Ibid.

to. Free services were provided across the country in all those areas and others. Such policy was justified on the grounds that the vast majority of the people were desperately poor and could not afford those services on their own - which is one reason why Tanzania's taxes were among the highest in the world in order to help pay for those services in a country which was also, and still is, one of the poorest in the world. And that was indeed the case; most Tanzanians could not afford those services on their own. Therefore, providing them free was the right thing to do; it was social equity, and no on quarreled with that. But it also proved to be costly, and contributed to the country's economic ruin. Even the poor should have been asked to pay a token fee, and the rest should have been assessed a fee based on their income for whatever service they got. School fees should never have been abolished entirely, nor should have all fees for medical service, but ujamaa villages should have been.

Abolishing ujamaa villages would have boosted production on family- or individually-owned farms because private ownership is an incentive to higher productivity. People tend to work harder for themselves than they do for groups, and care more about their own property than they do about communal property. With farmers earning more income on family and individual farms, and paying lower taxes, they would have been able to pay at least some fee for the social services being provided by the government. There would have been no need for the government to impose high taxes on the people to pay for the services they themselves would have been able to afford or pay at least something for them.

Putting people into ujamaa villages, and making them pay high taxes when they were not producing much due to low morale as a result of being forced to live in those collectives, were some of the biggest disincentives to productivity Tanzania suffered during the last 30 years. And she has not recovered yet. According to a 1995 Word Bank report, Tanzania ranked 172d out of 174 countries in world income tables; her per capita income was a mere $100; her international debt burden is overwhelming - more than 200 percent of GDP (Gross Domestic Product) in 1996; and half the government's budget depends on foreign aid,[69] which is fast dwindling in this new world order now

[69] World Bank Report, 1995.

that the Cold War is over and big powers are no longer interested in buying the friendship of small poor countries with financial aid and other inducements to keep their adversaries out of those countries.

Therefore Tanzania's failed economic policies cost the country enormously. Ujamaa villages might have been successful if the people moved into those settlements willingly, attracted by their benefits, and were allowed to move out of them if they were not satisfied with the life there; and if they did not have to pay high taxes. But even such voluntary collective settlements would probably not have provided catalytic change in the economic transformation of Tanzania because their main attraction would have been social services - schools and clinics - provided by the government, not profit. This incentive, profit, comes from family and individual farms where farmers work hard for themselves, and even harder if they pay lower taxes, because they are able to keep for themselves most of what they earn. Ujamaa villages did not generate that kind of income and profit for individuals and families living in those collectives where they were also burdened with high taxes on meager earnings. The result was economic failure which may take Tanzania decades to overcome.

Yet with great achievements in health and education, and provision of social equity, Tanzania's economy was therefore not a total failure. There was, however, one failure Nyerere probably regretted the most. He said his greatest failure was that although he managed to form a union with Zanzibar in 1964 to create Tanzania, he never succeeded in persuading neighboring countries to form a larger one, a move he said would have made the region a powerhouse:

> "I felt that these little countries in Africa were really too small, they would not be viable - the Tanganyikas, the Rwandas, the Burundis, the Kenyas. My ambition in East Africa was really never to build a Tanganyika. I wanted an East African federation. So what did I succeed in doing? My success is building a nation out of this collection of tribes."[70]

[70] Nyerere, quoted by J. McKinley, ibid.

Nyerere also reflected on the changes taking place in the political arena in Africa, especially since the early nineties when the wave of democracy swept across the continent, although most of that was sheer optimism which produced few real changes. Nonetheless, Nyerere said:

> "A new leadership is developing in Africa, especially in this part of Africa. The military phase is out. I think the single-party phase is out."[71]

Also out are the old economic policies which have ruined Africa, losing an entire generation of development. International donors and lenders, tired of seeing their money go down the drain, played a critical role in changing the economic policies of African countries. They demanded imposition of austerity measures to rejuvenate the economies through financial discipline, adoption of free-market policies, and maximum sacrifice from the people of those countries. The leading international financial institution, besides the World Bank, in this new revival has been the IMF (International Monetary Fund), although its stringent conditions for aid have not always been valid in all contexts, one of them being Tanzania which differed with the IMF over the country's economic policies.

In 1984 when Nyerere was still president, he explained in detail Tanzania's stand on IMF proposals as they related to the country's development and financial woes. He said the major difference between Tanzania and the IMF was not based on the conditions demanded by the latter but the extent to which such conditions could be applied in Tanzania. In an interview with local and foreign journalists at the State House in Dar es Salaam on November 22, Nyerere said that none of the IMF packages ranging from massive devaluation, reduction of government deficits to liberalization of imports had helped improve any Third World economy. As he explained:

> "They (international financial institutions) advised us to liberalize imports in 1977 when we had surplus in foreign reserves and we did. But we have been in trouble ever since."[72]

[71] Ibid.

Nyerere said IMF imposition of the ready-made prescriptions on poor countries as a condition for aid was unacceptable:

> "Any serious Third World government will ask serious questions. I cannot sign an agreement (with the IMF) and then have riots on the streets. You may be the economic experts but I am the political expert - allow me at least to say how much the people can take."[73]

He went on to explain that blind acceptance of the IMF packages would force the government to turn the police force against the people. The President said the government was flexible in its economic policies and had taken a number of measures similar to those recommended by the IMF; and went on to stress:

> "We don't say we don't change but we say how much should we change. Every government will have to ask that. Every government asks that."[74]

He said Tanzania needed the financial resources offered by the IMF to pay for her raw materials and spare parts but insisted that the negotiations must be balanced. Commenting on government involvement in running the economy, Nyerere said all governments, including that of the United States, had to make decisions dealing with the economy. He cited as an example the deliberate decision by the American Government to maintain "huge deficits" in its annual budget:

> "Those deficits are a government decision and it pervades the total economy."[75]

---

[72] Nyerere, quoted in "Mwalimu Explains Stand on IMF," in *Tanzania Embassy Newsletter*, op. cit., p. 8.
[73] Ibid.
[74] Ibid.
[75] Ibid.

Nyerere said the higher degree of government control of the economy in Tanzania was basically historical because most of the economic infrastructure, including industry, was created by the government, pointing out that little was inherited from the colonial powers (first Germany, and then Britain). As he put it:

> "In Tanzania we do a little bit more than they (other countries) do. It is partly historical, party ideological... but mostly historical."[76]

But he insisted that Tanzania would continue to pursue socialism and self-reliance as the only means to development. However, he told the press conference, collectivization in the rural areas would continue to be voluntary:

> "It has never been the intention to force collectivization in Tanzania."[77]

It is true that forcing the people to live in ujamaa villages had never been the government policy. But some overzealous officials who implemented that policy resorted to intimidation and other tactics to mobilize people into those collective settlements. Peasant farming was collectivized between 1973 and 1976, triggering riots and retaliatory violence against government agents enforcing the policy.[78] President Nyerere reported that by mid-1975 over 9 million Tanzanians - close to about half the entire population - had been moved into more than 6,900 ujamaa villages. And in 1976 the government launched a massive sweep of Dar es Salaam, the capital and the country's largest city, and rounded up thousands of the unemployed and sent them to rural areas to work in their home villages or in new settlements.[79]

But Nyerere never entirely ruled out capitalist involvement in the socialist transformation of Tanzania. In fact, the Arusha Declaration he authored almost single-handedly welcomes such participation. As he explained in the

---

[76] Ibid.

[77] Ibid.

[78] "Tanzania," in *Readers Digest 1986 Almanac and Yearbook* (Pleasantville, New York: Reader's Digest Association, 1985), p. 665.

[79] Ibid.

interview in 1984 almost exactly one year before he retired, Tanzania would continue to invite foreign private firms to invest in the country under mutual agreements which did not compromise the principles of either party. He told a questioner that this was not a capitalistic tendency. He said Tanzania has been willing to cooperate with private companies all along, citing the General Tyre (East Africa) Company formed jointly with an American firm shortly after the Arusha Declaration was issued in February 1967. As he told the journalists:

> "I have been advised that it is correct to use capitalists to develop socialism."[80]

But socialism failed to develop the country's economy, despite some success in import-substitution industrialization, an achievement which is sometimes overlooked when people talk about the country's failed economic policies. But the failure was disastrous, and no amount of clever sheet-balancing can mitigate its effects.

Besides some achievement in import-substitution industrialization, there was also an emphasis on food production in order for the country to be self-sufficient in that area. But such self-sufficiency was also emphasized at the expense of export-crop growth on which the country depends to earn foreign exchange. And it was a noble objective; people can't eat cotton or coffee or tea or tobacco. Food comes first before export crops. However, even food production declined due to lack of incentives, as did export-crop growth for the same reason including high taxes on export crops which, besides the ones we just named, include cashew nuts, pyrethrum, and cloves among Tanzania's major exports.

As production declined, budget deficits grew. The end of the coffee boom of the 1970s and soaring oil prices also had a devastating impact on Tanzania's fragile economy, especially in 1979, the same year the country fought a full-scale war against Idi Amin's forces (from November 1978 - April 1979) which cost Tanzania $500 million;[81]an astronomical amount for such a poor country. The country's poor economic performance continued to

---

[80] Nyerere, quoted in *Tanzania Embassy Newsletter*, ibid.
[81] "Reader's Digest 1986 Almanac," ibid.

take its toll. The infrastructure crumbled, especially roads, electricity supply, communications and transportation - with only a few vehicles on the road compared with the country's needs, and most of them in dilapidated condition. The Tanzania-Zambia railway service virtually collapsed. Buses did not run regularly. Fuel became scarce or too expensive. The currency was overvalued, farmers suffered because of policies biased against them, and corruption became rampant as the economy decayed. As Glickman, who did his study in Tanzania, states:

> "Policy bias against farmers, an overvalued currency that cheapened imports, and a bloated and politicized bureaucracy made gaining the ability to grant licenses, tariff protections, and franchises the chief goal of the ambitious and powerful. A political class acquired a vested interest in controls, which strangled enterprise. From 1980 to 1985, per capita income fell by 12 percent."[82]

It was during this period, between 1981 and 1985, that President Nyerere engaged in negotiations with the IMF and other international financial institutions to help revive the economy. That marked the beginning of the end of Tanzania's socialist policies. It was a fundamental change Nyerere was not enthusiastic about; which explains why he was opposed to some of the IMF proposals - the extent to which liberalization of the economy should be carried out - and entered into those negotiations only reluctantly. However, Tanzania had no choice but to comply with the IMF conditions if she was to reverse the decline of her economy. As Adebayo Adedeji, the Executive Secretary of the UN Economic Commission for Africa, stated in 1983 when negotiations between Tanzania and the IMF were still going on:

> "The donor countries and institutions have the last word, rather than the governments themselves, such as in the recent controversy between the IMF and Tanzania. I think, in the final analysis, that the IMF won. This is the grueling reality of poverty. When you are poor,

[82] H. Glickman, *Tanzania: From Disillusionment to Guarded Optimism*, ibid., p. 219.

> you can never be right. It is the rich country that is right, because it is the only one that can help you out."[83]

Like all the other African countries, Tanzania had to adopt stringent austerity measures as a condition for financial aid from the IMF. Those measures included structural adjustment programs which demanded reducing controls on marketing and currency exchange rates as well as cutting overall public expenditure. Implementation of the programs led to recession and caused a lot of hardship on the people, not only in Tanzania but also in other African countries. The suffering seemed to last forever. As Joe Mensah, a lawyer and senior civil servant in Accra, Ghana, stated in 1989:

> "How many years does one have to live on earth, and how many of those must be spent in hardship?"[84]

When Ali Hassan Mwinyi succeeded Nyerere as president in November 1985, he continued to implement the IMF structural adjustment programs, and agreed to further austerity measures. One of those was the Economic Recovery Program of 1986 - it was implemented well into 1992 with IMF backing as the Economic and Social Action Program - which produced some positive results, especially in freeing foreign exchange, reducing tariffs, and breaking down crop-marketing cooperatives which exercised almost absolute control over the farmers in terms of price control: they literally owned what the farmers produced, "in the name of the people."

Implementation of those measures has led to some improvement in the economy, especially in agriculture. Farmers growing export crops, traders, and small manufacturers have benefited from this economic growth, but most of the people in Tanzania have experienced exactly the opposite because there has not been enough improvement: public sector salaries have dropped, social services have declined, and the incentive to produce remains low. The country still has a long way to go before it achieves significant economic growth.

---

[83] Adebayo Adedeji, interviewed by Margaret A. Novicki, in *Africa Report,* September-October 1983, p. 14.

[84] Joe Mensah, quoted by Colleen Lowe Morna, "Surviving Structural Adjustment," in *Africa Report,* September-October 1989, p. 48.

One indicator of the country's poor economic performance is its dependence on foreign aid. As late as 1996, about $1 billion annually was still considered almost the minimum amount needed to rejuvenate the economy through structural adjustment programs and other measures. But these reforms have not been implemented fast enough. And corruption is rampant; it is one of the major reasons why economic reforms have proceeded so slowly:

> "The slow pace of economic reform, and complaints about corruption, led the IMF to delay granting credits from 1992 until 1996. Balance of payments problems have not been fully conquered."[85]

In fact corruption was one of the biggest campaign issues during the 1995 presidential election. The leader of Tanzania's opposition party (NCCR-Mageuzi), Augustine Mrema, focused on the issue during the election, waging a relentless campaign against misappropriation of public funds and the government's failure or unwillingness to fight corruption; a subject which has received extensive coverage in the media as much as corruption in other African countries have. As one publication, "African Business," February 1997, headlined one of its major stories: "Tanzania: Corruption Hot Potato".[86]

But in spite of all the economic problems Tanzania faces, there have also been some encouraging signs for improvement. Beginning in early 1995, the IMF and the World Bank have become optimistic about Tanzania's performance, partly because of an increase in the rate of growth in gross domestic product (GDP). By 1997, Tanzania was one of 12 countries chosen for favorable treatment in allocation of funds from the two financial institutions.

But corruption also has had long-term effects on the country, not only in terms of misuse of public funds and office but also in the area of ethnic and race relations; and in terms of economic performance and provision of services:

---

[85] H. Glickman, ibid.

[86] "Tanzania: Corruption Hot Potato," in *Africa Business*, No. 218, London, February 1997.

> "The economy's decline in the 1980s and the misuse of public office permitted corruption to expand and seep downward from the higher ranks. Since economic reform benefits those who have entrepreneurial skills and some private capital, the small Asian merchant community has been the target of bribery charges, which increases communal tensions, especially in coastal towns. The difficulty in uprooting corruption is tied to the slow pace of dismantling government controls and to the sluggishness in improving the standard of living of ordinary people. They miss social services and education assistance, but they have not yet seen much rise in incomes. On the plus side, cabinet resignations over corruption charges have begun to establish stronger political accountability. On the minus side, since the tiny Asian - and in Zanzibar, Arab - communities are strongly represented in trade and finance, and seem to live better than the vast majority of ordinary Africans, communal relations are also strained."[87]

The situation is similar to what is going on in neighboring Kenya where during the 1997 presidential campaign when violent demonstrations took place in the streets of Nairobi against President Daniel arap Moi's autocratic and corrupt regime, some of the demonstrators openly complained about economic exploitation by the Asians. Many people in Tanzania feel the same way but the criticism is more muted and may get less as the economy improves, as it is bound to, as a result of the new economic reforms which have already produced some good results in a relatively short period of time. Economic forecasts have been improving since the mid-1990s. In 1997, Tanzania's economy grew about 5 percent, and was projected to grow 6 percent by 1999. Inflation was down from 25 percent to 19 percent, according to 1997 statistics,[88] and incomes are expected to rise gradually, increasing the purchasing power of many Tanzanians as inflation drops even further. And it is expected to, following implementation of the new economic reforms; and abandonment of the old economic policies which robbed people of the

[87] H. Glickman, ibid.
[88] Ibid.

incentive to work, discouraged foreign investment, and stunted economic growth.

In fact the 5 percent economic growth Tanzania achieved in 1997 was a commendable performance. Many countries in sub-Saharan Africa achieved that growth rate by the mid-1990s. It was the highest in decades in the region, as the economies were liberalized. The private sector is now going to be the locomotive of change, not only in Tanzania but throughout Africa. As President Benjamin Mkapa defined the new course:

> "The Rubicon of reform has been crossed. Government has no business doing business."[89]

One of the first areas which the Tanzania government opened up to the private sector was the beer industry. In 1993, the Tanzania government sold parts of its share in the business to a South African company as part of its privatization program. The brewery was modernized, and output by Tanzania Breweries Ltd. in 1995 recovered the 1985 levels, and the company paid its first dividends in 20 years; a remarkable performance within only three years after part of the industry was privatized.

Other African countries which have introduced significant political and economic reforms include Ghana, Zambia, Zimbabwe, and Botswana which we focused on in the previous chapter; and Mali, Benin, Ethiopia, and Uganda - which in 1997 had the highest economic growth rate in Africa after emerging from a decade of ruin during which Idi Amin ravaged the country's economy and left it in tatters. Tanzania still faces enormous economic problems; but she also has great potential for growth, including mineral wealth, some of it recently discovered; for example the immense coal and iron ore deposits in the southwestern part of the country in Rungwe District, Mbeya Region. And many foreign investors are being attracted to the country. As Robert Greenberger of *The Wall Street Journal* reported from Dar es Salaam, Tanzania's capital, in December 1996:

---

[89] Benjamin Mkapa, quoted by Robert S. Greenberger, "Africa Ascendant: New Leaders Replace Yesteryear's 'Big Men,' and Tanzania Benefits," in *The Wall Street Journal*, December 10, 1996, p. A-1.

> "Tanzania isn't Taiwan, one of Asia's economic successes, and it won't be any time soon. But the record in this Indian Ocean nation (on the East African coast), with its rich mineral resources and still-widespread poverty, suggests that successful reforms are possible in Africa. The gains in Tanzania are coming despite enormous and still potentially devastating obstacles: a ponderous bureaucracy, a crumbling infrastructure and embedded corruption that still finds government officials demanding handouts from businesses. After shrugging off a close encounter with bankruptcy in the early 1980s, Tanzania's economy is now growing... Government spending has been slashed and one-third of some 400 state-run industries dismantled. The handful of high-rises sprouting amid the capital's faded colonial-era buildings is a sign of growing confidence. So is the IMF's recent decision to grant Tanzania a $234 million loan. Last month, the government was host to an investment conference attended by more than 500 executives from 38 countries. They signed deals that could bring $786 million of new investments, compared with $1.2 billion for all of last year."[90]

One of Tanzania's biggest problems during its socialist years was shortages. The country was plagued with shortages of all kinds of items including soap and cooking oil - and sometimes even water in the capital, Dar es Salaam, and other towns due to breakdowns and lack of spare parts; not all the time but quite often. The water was also often dirty, left untreated. Brown water coming out the taps was not uncommon even in some hotels in Dar es Salaam. Light bulbs were a luxury for many people, they weren't available all the time, and when they were, many people couldn't afford them. Drinking glasses were another luxury for many people, either unavailable or totally out of reach due to exorbitant prices.

There was a also a shortage of food. Sometimes even salt wasn't available, let alone "luxury" items such as bread. And commodities like soft drinks, another luxury, were, of course, also totally out of reach even for people with regular income from government and other public-sector jobs. To

---

[90] R.S. Greenberger, ibid.

get any of these items, and this is only a partial list, you had to bribe someone. And bribery still goes on today. That is why corruption is still rampant and was one of the hottest issues during the 1995 general election. But with the liberalization of the economy through privatization of assets and other reform measures, there is now change on the horizon. The word "shortages" may no longer be in the lexicon of many Tanzanians:

> "The result is a promising, if mixed, picture. The capital's downtown stores are well-stocked with food and cartons of televisions and stereos. But its well-paved streets are a bit deceptive; when the autumn 'short rains' arrive each afternoon, small lakes appear quickly, because drainage is poor. (But) the mood is upbeat in the air-conditioned Sheraton hotel, where foreign executives eat lunch with prospective Tanzanian partners and the staff tries with limited success to persuade guests to turn off their noisy cellular phones while dining. Those phones represent something of a leap into the modern age; Tanzania's old ones are so unreliable that affluent citizens bypass them for something new. For a joint venture launched by Mobitel, a unit of Luxembourg-based Milicon International Cellular SA, Tanzanian sales have more than doubled in the past year."[91]

Mobitel began the joint venture in Tanzania with the state-owned telephone company in 1994. By December 1996, it had about 6,000 customers in Dar es Salaam alone, most of them businessmen. And sales were expected to double annually for several years to come. During its socialist years, the Tanzania government would not have allowed such a joint venture to be launched. That is why the Tanzania Telephone Company remained a state monopoly for years since socialism was adopted as a national ideology in 1967 following the Arusha Declaration.

Although Mobitel is one of the success stories in Tanzania's privatization program, the company is still hampered in its operations by too much bureaucracy. As Ron Ross, Mobitel's manager in Tanzania, explained, it takes

[91] R.S. Greenberger, "Tanzania is an African Success Story," in *The Wall Street Journal*, ibid., A-15.

three months for Mobitel to get customs clearance from the Tanzania government for the $1 million-equipment it imports every month. By glaring contrast, it takes only a week to get such clearance in Europe. But Ross was not exasperated despite all the trouble going through the bureaucratic maze:

> "I'm an optimist. It's just that I think (reform) will be a gradual process. A few years ago, I thought it would be explosive."[92]

The privatization process may be slow in Tanzania, but it is still a step forward, and may be even a great leap into the future. When we look at the past, that does indeed seem to be the case: a giant leap. When Tanzania adopted socialism, she was virtually locked in place in terms of economic development, going nowhere. Just within ten years after most industries were nationalized and almost half the entire country's population moved into ujamaa villages, half of the 330 state-owned enterprises had gone bankrupt, agricultural production had declined dramatically, the economy was stagnant, and many people hardly had enough to eat:

> "James Adams, the World Bank's country director for Tanzania, recalls driving here from Kenya in the early 1980s. Stores were empty, medicine unavailable and supplies so scarce that he carried extra cans of gasoline in his car. At one time, the World Bank made more loans per capita to Tanzania than to any other nation. But by the mid-1980s, it was threatening to close the spigot unless reform began."[93]

It was when those reforms began in earnest that Nyerere retired from the presidency, although he himself played a critical role in introducing the measures when he engaged in negotiations with the IMF to revive the economy. But he stepped aside to let his successor, Ali Hassan Mwinyi, proceed with the rest to open up the economy to private-sector participation for the development of the country. Besides the brewery, other major assets

---

[92] Ron Ross, quoted ibid.

[93] R.S. Greenberger, ibid.

whose shares - a substantial portion - have been sold to private investors include the Tanzania Tobacco Company, a state monopoly for years since nationalization, and a cement factory. However, privatization of smaller assets is much harder because they are not economically viable and their bookkeeping is poor, making it almost impossible to make a realistic assessment of their potential.

The man who is in charge of much of Tanzania's privatization program is George Mbowe who heads the commission assigned the task of dismantling state enterprises and selling them to private investors. Despite the failure of socialism, Mbowe offers a balanced perspective probably most critics of Tanzania's failed policies don't. Besides other valid reasons why socialism failed, although Mbowe may or may not agree with us on those reasons, there is no question that Tanzania tried to do too much with too little:

> "Nearly three decades ago George Mbowe was a bright young man with a graduate degree from Williams College in Williamstown, Massachusetts, and a key role in Mr. Nyerere's nationalization drive... Even as he takes apart what he helped create, Mr. Mbowe refuses to condemn the past. 'I would not say (ujamaa) was a failure. It's just that the government spread itself too thin, building schools and roads.'"[94]

The legacy of socialism is an enduring phenomenon, but the government now is gradually pulling out of a number of areas of economic activity to allow private-sector initiatives fuel the economy. However well intentioned, this laissez-faire approach has had unintended consequences which are acknowledged even by some of the greatest beneficiaries of the new economic policies: Tanzanians of Indian origin. They constitute less than one percent of the country's population of 30 million but are a formidable force in the economy. They dominate local trade as well as the import-export business; and they are also one of the most highly educated ethnic groups in Tanzania. As Jeetu Patel, who owns several businesses in Dar es Salaam, stated:

[94] George Mbowe, cited ibid.

> "It's true that we are resented. The indigenous people are mostly poor. When they see that a nonindigenous person has a better life, they say, 'why him and not me?'"[95]

Such resentment will inevitably subside when Tanzania prospers and when there is more wealth to share, an egalitarian ideal deeply rooted in traditional African society but whose elevation to a national ethos during Tanzania's socialist years proved disastrous precisely because socialism failed to produce wealth. In pursuit of that goal, Tanzania even decided to establish a stock market. In 1996 Fratern Mboya, head of the official Capital Markets and Security Authority established in 1994 to develop a stock market, drew up plans to license six brokerage firms and expected an initial 10 listings once the exchange went into operation.

Big foreign companies have also become major participants in Tanzania's privatization process. In 1993, the government invited Ocelot & TransCanada Pipelines to participate in a $300-million development and pipeline project to transport natural gas 125 miles to the capital Dar es Salaam from the Tanzanian island of Songo Songo in the Indian Ocean. In 1998, gas-generated electricity replaced power from a creaky hydroelectric system which is often plagued by outages. Such replacement would not have been possible had it not been for the gas from Songo Songo island and the involvement of major foreign investors to help Tanzania exploit the natural resource. As James McCardle, the project's general manager, stated:

> "This program wouldn't have been possible 10 years ago. The thinking (then) would not have allowed a foreign corporation to control the project."[96]

Tanzania's potential for economic growth is expected to increase in all areas of the economy as a result of privatization. When the country abandoned her collectivization policy, ending ujamaa villages whose farms reverted to private ownership, the agricultural sector - which is the country's

[95] Jeetu Patel, ibid.

[96] James McCardle, ibid.

backbone of the economy - began expanding 5 percent annually. But besides agricultural products, Tanzania also has other resources which can contribute substantially to her economic growth once the private sector starts playing a big role in the exploitation of those resources.

Tanzania is, of course, world-famous for her wildlife. She has the largest game parks and reserves in the world. Serengeti is virtually synonymous with African safari. In terms of agriculture, Tanzania may not be a major food producer, but she has the potential to become one. In addition to the cash crops we named earlier, Tanzania's agricultural products include the following principle food crops: maize, bananas, rice, pulses, sorghum, millet, yams, cassava, coconuts, sugar cane, wheat, white and sweet potatoes. Fish is another important food resource from the Indian Ocean, Africa's three Great Lakes - Victoria, Tanganyika and Nyasa - all of which are part of Tanzania, as well as from other freshwater lakes and rivers.

In addition to that, large numbers of cattle, sheep, goats and poultry, are also raised. Tanzania's other products include refined petroleum, aluminum goods, wood products, and construction materials. The country also has a major textile industry. It is also one of the few African countries where motor vehicles are assembled.[97]

Tanzania once ranked among the world's leading producers of diamonds, especially industrial diamonds. Although production declined through the years, it is expected to go up again. Other minerals extracted in significant quantities include gold, tin, gemstones, one of which is the world-famous tanzanite discovered in 1967; salt, gypsum, phosphates and kaolin. Also immense deposits of coal and iron ore have been found near Lake Nyasa, and there are plans to start their production on a large scale, an effort which requires large foreign investment. The discovery of coal and iron ore - critical to the manufacture of steel - could play a big role in the industrialization of Tanzania which is impossible without steel. But that is not all:

> "Other treasures lie beneath the ground. Bill Bali, resident manager of Sutton Resources Ltd., a private Canadian concern, says Tanzania has

---

[97] *Columbia Encyclopedia* (New York: Columbia University Press, 1993), p. 2692; and *1997 Almanac* (New York: Houghton Mifflin, 1996), p. 273.

rich deposits of nickel, cobalt, diamonds and perhaps offshore oil. 'We estimate the overall mineral wealth could be $5 billion to $8 billion,' he says. Ian Mitchell, managing director of South African-based Stanbic Bank, Africa's largest, adds that major South African mining companies, including DeBeers Consolidated Mines Ltd., already are exploring here. 'In the next two years, they should move from exploration to mining,' he predicts. Indeed, experts say Tanzania's overall prospects are bright if reformers persevere."[98]

In addition to her natural resources, Tanzania has another very important asset without which all the minerals and agricultural resources would mean very little. It is impossible to develop without it. The leadership provided by Nyerere for almost 30 years was critical to the survival of Tanzania as a nation, making it possible for many investors from around the world to invest in Tanzania today. As Robert Greenberger reported from Dar es Salaam in *The Wall Street Journal*:

"Nyerere... was a skilled nation builder. He fused Tanzania's 120 tribes into a cohesive state, preventing tribal conflicts like those plaguing so much of Africa. That reassures investors. The tobacco arm of RJR Nabisco Holdings Corporation, for example, which this year (1996) acquired 51 percent of the state-owned cigarette maker, plans to use the venture as a base for selling across the continent. Natwar Gotecha, chairman and chief executive of the cigarette company here, says, 'This is a politically stable country. There's a built-in bias toward sorting out problems through dialogue'."[99]

Conflict resolution through dialogue, and leadership transcending ethnic loyalties: that is why Tanzania has not been torn by tribal conflicts; and that is why she has never had a single military coup in almost 40 years since independence despite several attempts to subvert the government. It is one of the very few countries to escape these scourges Africa has been afflicted with

[98] R.S. Greenberger, *Tanzania Is An African Success Story*, ibid.
[99] Ibid.

since independence. And they continue to threaten the existence of African nations today.

Probably one of the best indicators of Tanzania's success in implementing her privatization program is the improvement in the income and standard of living of some of the employees working for companies the government has sold to private investors, although it retains a controlling interest in all of them. The rise in income is also better appreciated by providing a contrast. For example, there are Americans who live on about $400 a month in the richest country in the world with a per capita income of $28,000, according to 1998 statistics;[100] there are, of course, a few countries with a higher income but in the aggregate not as rich as the United States. Yet in Tanzania, one of the 10 poorest countries in the world, with a per capita income of only about $200 which is one of the lowest in Africa, there are people who live on almost the same amount per month ($400) as many Americans do; thanks to privatization which increased their income six times, although even this - is not enough for comfortable living in Tanzania itself. Such a phenomenal increase took place within three years at Tanzania Breweries after the government sold a larger number of shares to a South African beer company which streamlined and rebuilt the entire operation for maximum efficiency:

> "This pleases Joseph Mbuya, a technician in crisp blue overalls who has worked here for 17 years. His salary and benefits were boosted to about $310 from $53 (almost a six-fold increase), as productivity gains let the company cut the payroll to 2,000 from 3,200. Now he has cash to spruce up his house and for an occasional night out with his wife at a neighborhood pub serving goat on a spit. 'Privatization is very good,' he says. 'People get more money. There's more things to buy. That's what we want.'"[101]

Of course people who have lost their jobs as a result of privatization may not be as enthusiastic about private-sector incursions into the economy as

---

[100] Cited by Donald G. McNeil, in contrast to Mozambique's per capita income in *International Herald Tribune,* September 14, 1998; p. 2. See also *1998 World Almanac* (New York: World Almanac Books, 1997), p. 832.

[101] Joseph Mbuya, cited by R.S. Greenberger, *Tanzania is an African Success Story*, ibid.

those who have kept theirs and seen their incomes go up like Mbuya's, for example, at Tanzania Breweries. But even they, the losers, have not been entirely left out in the cold. The 2,000 employees who lost their jobs at Tanzania Breweries received a termination package. So did the 15,000 who lost their government jobs when the austerity measures mandated by the IMF and other international donors and lenders were implemented:

> "President Mkapa deals with austerity's backlash partly by using aid from other nations, mainly Scandinavian countries, to silence some of the grousing. Some of the 15,000 government workers who have been laid off receive lavish severance packages that can equal five year's pay."[102]

And all Tanzanians will, in the long-run, benefit from privatization and other new economic reforms when their standard of living and incomes go up. So will they when corruption goes down if the authorities decide to fight it more aggressively, although it will never be entirely eliminated; that's simply a fact of life in every country, that's the kind of world we live in. But it is also a fact of life that the less there is to go around as a result of poor economic performance, the more widespread is corruption all the way to the grassroots level.

Under those conditions you can't even buy a loaf of bread, if it's available, or buy a bus ticket or even apply for a job let alone get one, without bribing someone. You can't get medical treatment without slipping a few extra shillings under the table because, as the nurse or doctor might put it, "I've got to eat too! We all have." It goes on and on. Of course the well-connected even carry on illegal business transactions across the border, smuggling goods. All that still goes on today, but even more blatantly so during Tanzania's socialist years when "everybody" was hungry. In fact in terms of smuggling, some of the biggest traffickers were government officials, and the leaders of cooperative unions which had a virtual monopoly on what the peasants produced – setting prices, intimidating farmers, taking bribes, and dictating marketing policies in general to the detriment of the farmers. As

---

[102] R.S. Greenberger, ibid.

Professor Horace Campbell, a Jamaican and socialist himself who taught at Makerere University in Uganda, stated in 1975 in his essay "Socialism in Tanzania: A Case Study":

> "The obvious failure of collectivization... manifests itself in the present shortages in Tanzania. The food shortage in Tanzania is also a problem of the ideological bankruptcy of the petty bourgeoisie. While Tanzania is begging Canada for aid to avoid famine, the kulaks smuggle maize to Kenya to sell in order to earn foreign exchange. This outrageous sabotage by powerful bureaucrats in the TANU party, reinforces the correct view that the petty bourgeoisie act in their own interest, in spite of the plight of the peasantry. The border between Kenya and Tanzania was closed for sometime during December 1974, partly to end the smuggling of food and partly to check excessive demands of a trucking company, Kenatco, owned by the Kenyatta family... Leading members of the Tanznaian petty bourgeoisie have shares in Kenatco... (Also) the Americans said that Tanzanian bureaucrats clandestinely begged the U.S. to help them overcome food shortages. Meanwhile, the mabepari - local capitalists - smuggle grain to Kenya for reexport to Europe."[103]

Also in the forefront of the economic strangulation of the peasants were the agricultural cooperatives, ostensibly working in the interest of the masses. It was an empty claim which was exposed by the peasants themselves in a display of candor typical of Tanzania's mass participation in the democratic process at the grassroots level. That the cooperative unions were corrupt is beyond dispute:

> "The cooperative sector was riddled with corruption, mismanagement, and petty thievery. The Union Committee men and

[103] Horace Campbell, "Socialism in Tanzania: A Case Study," in *The Black Scholar*, Vol. 6, No. 8, Sausalito, California, May 1975, pp. 48, and 51. See also *Daily News*, Dar es Salaam, Tanzania, January 11, 1975; Henry Mapolu, "The Organization and Participation of Workers in Tanzania," in *Africa Review*, Vol. 2, No. 3, 1972; and Issa Shivji, "Silent Class Struggle," (Dar es Salaam: Tanzania Publishing House, 1973), pp. 24-36.

> corruptive employees - usually the more literate elements in rural Tanganyika - openly exploited the poor peasants. This was the case throughout East Africa... The rural poor (in Tanzania) testified to the special committee of cooperatives in 1966 (and thereafter in other forums) that 'our incomes have been dwindling and what is worse, we are continually being overtaxed.'"[104]

Such hegemonic control by the cooperatives over the farmers is going to be an anachronism in a free-market economy which is now being gradually introduced into Tanzania. The success of this economic transformation will be determined not by speed, that's how fast - however haphazardly - Tanzania pursues her new policies, but by fundamental structural changes in what is still in a number of areas a state-dominated economy. However, the pace of change is encouraging; so are the results. Practically every sector of the economy is being transformed, and the new government policies are attracting investors from all over the world.

Australian, Canadian, and African mining companies such as Ashanti Goldfields of Ghana and DeBeers of South Africa, are now involved in developing the gold resources in northern Tanzania just south of Lake Victoria. Several other international firms and consortiums have committed substantial amounts of money to infrastructural development, farming, manufacturing, and tourism. To facilitate the economic transformation, the IMF has also demanded that, as a condition for aid, the government must step up revenue collection, fight corruption - which is endemic - and improve the country's overall macroeconomic management before it slides back into its dismal past. As Daniel Yona, Tanzania's finance minister, stated:

> "We have accepted the regimen of fiscal and monetary discipline, and we have passed with flying colors."[105]

---

[104] Horace Campbell, "Socialism in Tanzania," ibid., p. 44. See also "Report of the Special Committee of Inquiry into Cooperative Movement and Marketing Boards" (Dar es Salaam, Tanzania: Government Printers, 1966), p. 4.

[105] Daniel A.N. Yona, quoted by Richard Synge, "Tanzania: Industries Revive as Privatization Takes Center Steps," in the *International Herald Tribune,* June 11, 1997, p. 8.

He was referring to the release in 1997 of a $40-million installment of a three-year enhanced structural adjustment loan approved in 1996. The IMF's approval of the loan package was seen by investors, creditors and donors as an expression of confidence in Tanzania's economic performance. Yona pointed out that the macroeconomic benchmarks were being met: in 1997, inflation stood at about 15 percent and was expected to fall below 10 percent in the next several months; the exchange rate had been stable at about 600 Tanzanian shillings to the dollar for 1996; economic growth was around 5 percent; and the foreign exchange reserves had been helped by a favorable rescheduling of foreign debts. All those factors pointed out by Yona are grounds for optimism among foreign investors who want to invest in Tanzania. As Harvey Glickman also points out;

> "This optimistic portrait of Tanzania's economic future is based in part on a renewed influx of foreign aid. The end of 1996 marked the renewal of IMF credits flowing from a new expanded structural adjustment fund: $234 million in special drawing rights, available semiannually, to coincide with progress in economic reforms to 1999. These credits were augmented when the World Bank approved an additional $100 million, largely for a new road program. If replenished regularly, this program will stretch to 10 years. The Paris Club of lending countries is expected to restructure Tanzania's debts. A November 1996 investors' forum (in Dar es Salaam) produced plans for $786 million of projects. Direct investment inflows are rising."[106]

Concurrent with the inflow of new investments was Tanzania's disposition of a number of other public-sector operations which were being put up for sale. Analysts said that the first results of foreign direct investments made in the past five years (since 1992) would show over the next 12 months (in 1998 and beyond) in the form of a dramatic increase in gold exports and a sharp revival in the production of goods and services for domestic consumption. Newly established investors in Tanzania include Coca-Cola,

[106] H. Glickman, *Tanzania: From Disillusionment to Guarded Optimism*, op. cit., p. 221.

R.J. Reynolds, South African Breweries which bought substantial shares in Tanzania Breweries, Sheraton International and a number of companies owned by the Aga Khan.[107]

More investment was expected to come in as a result of the privatization and commercialization of the telecommunications, power and banking sectors in 1997 and 1998. The process was to be facilitated by the opening up of Tanzania's first stock exchange at the end of 1997 and a listing of public-sector company shares. Tanzania's privatization program is intended to enable ordinary people buy shares in the state-owned enterprises which are being disposed of as well as in the new companies that are being established in the country. Tanzania's first president, Julius Nyerere, who still wields enormous influence in the country and across the continent, has played a major role in this transformation because of his approval of the new policies. Although he was out of office when Tanzania changed course, his approval of the changes was considered critical to the adoption of the new policies. As Richard Synge points out:

> "Now that the long-running shift from socialism to capitalism has been approved even by the former president, Julius Nyerere, who remains influential in the affairs of the country, it seems likely to run its course."[108]

The disposition of the state assets also required some ideological reorientation among the people who had been schooled in the virtues of socialism, hence in the vices of its very antithesis, capitalism, they were now being asked to embrace after being taught for so long how evil it was; remember, many Tanzanians had also been opposed to the introduction of the multiparty system after living under a one-party state whose superiority over its antithesis they had come to accept even if just for one reason that the one-party system would continue to keep the country united while the multiparty system could break it up along tribal lines. They were, of course, overruled:

---

[107] R. Synge, *Tanzania: Industries Revive as Privatization Takes Center Stage*, ibid.
[108] Ibid.

> "(President) Mwinyi appointed a commission in February 1991 to examine the feasibility of multiparty politics. The commission... consulted public opinion... Although the commission reported opposition to the change, it concluded by recommending the adoption of a multiparty system."[109]

The introduction of capitalism, in place of socialism, was also met with some skepticism, although not everybody was opposed to it just as not everybody was opposed to the adoption of the multiparty system. As Finance Minister Yona stated with regard to the new economic policies:

> "It has taken time to get people on the side of divestiture, but we are winning the argument. Most areas are up for sale. We have already disposed of the beer, cigarette and cement industries, and now we are concentrating on parastatals like the airline, harbors, National Milling Corporation and sisal industries."[110]

In 1997, there were 200 enterprises which were still state-owned. The task of disposing of those companies was assigned to the Parastatal Sector Reform Commission headed by George Mbowe whom we encountered earlier. Mbowe planned to sell them all by 1998, but admitted that he was facing continuing resistance from company managers and politicians. Obviously, many of them are nostalgic about the good old days of socialism or are still convinced of its triumph over capitalism as a historical inevitability; while others, even if capitalist-oriented, may be opposed to selling the assets to foreigners purely for nationalistic reasons. Despite such opposition, there is no question that the new economic policies which have been pursued for more than 10 years, especially since 1986, have produced results.

Evidence of the benefits of economic reform can be seen clearly in Dar es Salaam where the construction industry is booming. South African and South Korean firms have taken the lead in putting up tall office buildings and modern housing projects, something unheard of in the past when Tanzania

---

[109] H. Glickman, ibid., p. 220.

[110] D. Yona, quoted by R. Synge, ibid.

trod the socialist path. The country's second largest commercial city, Mwanza on Lake Victoria, is also developing fast, with banks and other services moving in. For example, Citibank Tanzania opened a second branch in Mwanza in July 1997. Other major international banks were expected to follow suit. As Tanzania's Citibank managing director, Emeka Emuwa, stated:

> "As investors come in and as the free market reforms get under way, they are improving the prospects for services."[111]

And as Tom Bowen, manager of Standard Chartered Bank Tanzania, put it:

> "More projects will come up as privatization of the parastatals progresses. There is a strong commitment on the part of the government, which is willing to talk to any investors."[112]

Bowen anticipated that the enormous growth in Tanzania's mining industry over the next few years will be followed by further investments in farming and manufacturing, especially by South African companies which are now some of the biggest investors in Tanzania; not too long ago, before the end of apartheid, South African investors would not even have been able to set foot on Tanzanian soil.

Among the minerals targeted for further exploitation is gold. New gold production from the ore-rich Geita region south of Mwanza started in 1998 at the Golden Pride mine opened up by Samax and Resolute Samantha, a Canadian/Australian joint venture. Its initial output was projected to be 160,000 ounces of gold per year. Other companies which prepared feasibility studies on similar mining operations in the region include Sutton Resources, Pangea, and Ashanti Goldfields.

In 1997 mining companies operating in Tanzania also won attractive terms in a deal made with Energy and Mines Minister Abdallah Kigoda, who

---

[111] Emeka Emuwa, quoted ibid.

[112] Tom Bowen, ibid.

approved exemptions for them from import taxes during construction and reduced sales taxes and import duties after the grace period expires. As Jeremy Pearce, the financial director of Samax, said:

> "Ever since our project was established, we have had support from the highest level."[113]

It will take many years for Tanzania to develop, but some significant achievements as a result of the new economic policies are expected within a relatively short period of time, an optimistic view shared by Frank Vogl, an investment consultant who formerly worked for the World Bank. As he put it:

> "Over the next three to five years, Tanzania will begin to score some successes that will be noticed internationally."[114]

Vogl concedes that there is some bureaucratic paralysis investors sometimes encounter when they try to launch or pursue their projects in Tanzania. But he is also quick to remind them of the procedural delays that are common in the United States before the authorities approve projects. By contrast, the delays in Tanzania are comparatively short; in a country which is also expected to set an example in a number of areas other African countries may emulate. For example, James Adams, the World Bank's country director for Tanzania, says Tanzania's approach to private-sector participation in utilities such as telecommunications and power supply will set it apart in Africa and also show that high levels of performance are achievable and sustainable. A pioneer project to generate electricity from gas - pumped from Songo Songo island - was already under construction in 1997 by Independent Power Tanzania Ltd., a company owned by Tanzanian and Malaysian investors.

As a member of both the expanding markets of the Southern African Development Community and the East African Cooperation initiative, Tanzania is in an ideal position to increase its supply of such services. And

[113] Jeremy Pearce, ibid.

[114] Frank Vogl, ibid.

although the Tanzania Electricity Supply Company (TANESCO) is still state-operated,, it was preparing in 1997 to work with private-sector companies and with neighboring countries in selling power in the region. Also a power-link with Zambia, already under construction in 1997, would make Tanzania a full member of the Southern African Power Pool.

Agriculture and tourism are also some of the areas which have great potential for rapid development. South African farmers and ranchers, and others elsewhere, are among those who had expressed great interest in acquiring long-term leases on state-owned land. In fact tourism is already one of the fastest-growing industries after years of poor performance, made even worse by Kenya's skillful but deceptive marketing strategy of using Tanzania's tourist attractions to draw tourists to Kenya. New hotels and game lodges are springing up in Tanzania to meet the phenomenal increase in the number of tourists expected to reach half a million visitors in the year 2000 alone. Not only does Tanzania have the largest game parks and reserves in the world – Serengeti, Ngorongoro, and Selous - and the world-famous Mount Kilimanjaro; it is also the only country in East Africa whose territory includes all the three Great Lakes: half of Lake Victoria is in Tanzania; so is half of Lake Tanganyika and half of Lake Nyasa. And its beaches along the coast on the Indian Ocean and on the islands of Pemba and Zanzibar have always been a great tourist attraction, drawing visitors from all over the world.

However, Tanzania's great potential for development is not restricted to one sector of the economy. The economic changes taking place across the country have many people believing that within the next ten years, Tanzania could become one of the most successful economies on the continent. Whether or not that will indeed be the case remains to be seen. But the potential for such phenomenal growth exists, both in terms of manpower and resources. Besides agriculture, the mainstay of the economy, Tanzania's mineral wealth is also significant and exceeds that of many other African countries. In fact, it is one of the few mineral-rich countries on the continent where some countries have virtually none, at least not yet.

Gold production at the country's modern gold mine in Geita, northern Tanzania, began in 1998 as we have already noted. But it is also significant to remember that Tanzania has been producing gold in that area for years, just as she did around Lake Rukwa in the southern highlands of the southwestern part of the country. She has also been producing gold and other minerals for decades but is going to boost production during the coming years. Other minerals in line for increased production include nickel and gemstones. However, this is not to downplay the country's agricultural potential. As Richard Synge reported from Tanzania in 1997:

> "The country also has massive potential in agriculture, with an expanding output of crops such as tea, coffee, cotton, sisal, flowers and vegetables."[115]

Private-sector participation by foreign investors in the agricultural sector is critical if the country is to harness its full potential. Because of low national savings, it is obvious that Tanzanian investors alone cannot raise sufficient capital to develop the agricultural and mining - as well as the tourist - sectors of the economy without foreign involvement in the privatization process; a point underscored by President Mkapa:

> "The process cannot be frozen to wait until such a time when Tanzanians will have sufficient capital to be more active participants in the privatization process..., (although) we do not have the means to turn Tanzania into an investors' paradise overnight."[116]

The good news for Tanzania, short of her own capital, is that foreign investors have invested in mining, farming, manufacturing, tourism and other sectors of the economy including financial. More investment is expected from both local and foreign investors when the government reduces the heavy tax burden which has suffocated Tanzanians and scared away foreign investors for years as much as the country's socialist policies did. The private sector has also urged the government to improve the work performance of employees whose appetite for corruption frustrates investors and impedes progress:

---

[115] R. Synge, "Tanzania: Building Boom in Dar es Salaam Is Sign of Progress," in the *International Herald Tribune,* December 8, 1997, p. 12.

[116] Benjamin Mkapa, quoted by R. Synge, ibid. See also Synge, "Tanzania: Listening Hard to Investors," in the *International Herald Tribune,* December 8, 1997, p. 12.

> "It was in this context that Mr. Mkapa recently announced the dismissal of more than 1,500 civil servants for corruption and dishonesty."[117]

All the sectors of the economy are now open to private investors, although not everything has been privatized. But the financial sector is one area which is fully open to investors. That is a big change, for, until recently, it was the exclusive domain of the state-owned National Bank of Commerce (NBC). Another very encouraging sign is that to match the arrival of foreign banks such as Citibank and Standard Chartered, many small institutions owned by Tanzanians have also opened up for business in the financial market. And the NBC has been reorganized as a conventional commercial bank focusing its banking services on corporate, large business and larger personal clients. It is the largest commercial bank in the country but is also expected to be opened up to private capital.

In the mining sector, at least four new gold mines were expected to go into production between 1998 and the year 2000. All four are located in the Geita area south of Mwanza, and all four will use the latest technology to maximize the rate of extraction used by companies from Australia, Canada, Ghana and South Africa. The capital-intensive projects launched by the mining companies will also contribute to development in a region that largely lacks modern infrastructure just like the rest of the country does. And more minerals are expected to be found, including gold itself:

> "The north-central regions of Tanzania are situated on one of the world's most ancient continental crusts... which is likely to contain some of the richest base and precious metals in the world. Gold has been mined here since time immemorial and was exploited by Arab traders, who have been present in the region since the 16th century. Even now, at least 500,000 Tanzanians are thought to earn a living from gold mining and trading, although the government receives no revenue from this source."[118]

---

[117] R. Synge, *Tanzania: Building Broom in Dar es Salaam Is Sign of Progress*, ibid.

[118] R. Synge, "Tanzania: in Gold Mines: Modernization," in the *International Herald Tribune*, December 8, 1997, p. 13.

Besides the four gold mines, another rich mining project which is being developed involves a nickel and cobalt deposit at Kabanga, west of Lake Victoria. It is being developed by South Africa's Anglo-American Corporation and Canada's Sutton Resources, and will be in production by the year 2001. It has been projected that the Kabanga mine will produce at least 35 million pounds of nickel per year. And more mines are expected to be opened.

Investors' confidence in Tanzania's great mineral potential is easily gauged by the degree to which foreign companies are willing to commit their financial resources to the mining projects. All those involved have invested heavily in the operations, further encouraged by mineral discoveries in other parts of the country which had never even been known to have minerals; for example, the gold mine near the town of Nzega which is in western Tanzania, as opposed to the gold mines in Geita in northern Tanzania south of Lake Victoria. And the amount of money committed to the projects is substantial, running into the hundreds of millions of dollars, an astronomical amount no investors would sink in any mining project unless they expected something in return - a far higher amount than what they put in. As Richard Synge says about those projects, involving only gold, without even including other minerals such as diamonds, nickel and cobalt:

> "The Samax/Resolute project, known as Golden Pride, evolved from a discovery by Canadian-registered Samax in 1990 near the town of Nzega in an area that had not been known to contain gold... Resolute recently reported that Golden Pride's resource base has increased from 2.4 million ounces to 2.7 million ounces of gold... Starting from September 1998, Samax/Resolute's $50 million investment is scheduled to go into production at a rate of not less than 150,000 ounces of refined gold per year, at an operating cost of $235 per ounce. Even more substantial is Sutton Resource's project at Bulyanhulu, where the presence of 5.6 million ounces is indicated. The company's $20 million exploration development program includes deep drilling to establish underground mining operations. The company anticipates investing at least $200 million before going into production in two years' time, with an operating cost currently

> estimated at only $150 per ounce. Other gold projects will not be far behind. The leading projects are those at Buckreef, Golden Ridge and Geita."[119]

And then there are, of course, the immense coal and iron ore deposits near Lake Nyasa in southwestern Tanzania which have yet to be exploited, already attracting even more investors to Tanzania. Also more nickel and cobalt mines are expected to be opened following the discovery of large deposits of the two minerals at Kabanga, west of Lake Victoria. As Michael Kenyon, president of Sutton Resources, put it:

> "Success will spur more exploration, and with the development of new mines will come infrastructure."[120]

There is no question that the involvement of foreign companies in Tanzania's mining industry will encourage technological innovation and the development of modern infrastructure in the country. That is something which would not have been possible during the country's socialist years when such large-scale foreign investment was unheard of in a nationalized economy. Foreign investment and private-sector participation was not against the law, but it was severely restricted, and discouraged by socialist policies and very high taxes.

Tanzania's socialist policies and high taxes also discouraged the development of another area of the economy, tourism, due to lack of private-sector involvement. But since the new economic policies were introduced during the late 1980s, the number of tourists started going up. For example, it went up from 200,000 tourists in 1992 to 326,000 in 1996, and is expected to reach 500,000 by the year 2000, and will probably keep on going higher thereafter.

But there is also a limit to how far Tanzania will go in expanding tourism, although it is impossible to measure that in terms of absolute numbers. However, it is a fact that the country does not want to get into mass tourism

---

[119] Ibid.

[120] Michael Kenyon, quoted ibid.

because of the environmental impact on wildlife from too many visitors. That is why there are so few charter airlines with direct flights to Tanzania, unlike those going to Nairobi and Mombasa in Kenya, the two main regional destinations in East Africa for tourists. It is from those two cities that tourists travel to Tanzania, mainly overland in tour buses and vans, instead of flying.

Yet, even with its regulated tourism to minimize environmental impact, Tanzania still has great potential for growth in this industry which can be greatly exploited with private-sector participation. It was private-sector involvement, for example, which led to the sale of the inefficient Tanzanian airline, Air Tanzania, to an international company in 1998; the airline is a major carrier of tourists within the country, and many people see that there are excellent commercial possibilities in the country's tourist sector. As one tour operator who specializes in East Africa said:

> "Considering Tanzania's potential, we are still just scratching the surface."[121]

The same can be said of farming and mining - "We are still just scratching the surface" - the other two most important sectors of Tanzania's economy which is undergoing radical transformation from socialist to capitalist; just as the country underwent fundamental change in the political arena from the one-party state to a multiparty democracy.

But while Tanzania may have successfully met the ideological challenge by undergoing an ideological conversion from socialism to capitalism, and from one-partyism to multipartyism, the challenge to unity remains a perennial problem. It has always existed in the form of secessionist tendencies in Zanzibar, and also in the form f real potential for ethnic and regional rivalries on the mainland even if those rivalries don't erupt into violence; which they probably won't, given the history of the country.

All those secessionist sentiments and potentially explosive ethnic and regional conflicts were effectively contained under the one-party system whose capacity for integrating different ethnic and racial groups into a single

---

[121] Quoted by R. Synge, Tanzania: From Kilimanjaro and Serengeti to Lake Victoria and Zanzibar," in the *International Herald Tribune,* December 8, 1997, p. 13.

national entity cannot be denied; it is a system that is probably unequaled in that area by its antithesis, the multiparty system, because of the latter's tolerance for partisanship in the name of democracy even at the expense of national unity. It is also worth remembering that Tanzania's unity under the one-party system was achieved without mass regimentation, despite the system's shortcomings.

Had Tanzanians been regimented into unity, the country would have fractured and fallen apart along ethnic and regional lines when multiparty politics was introduced, for example, as the former Yugoslavia did, following the collapse of communism. That Tanzania, a multiethnic nation itself, did not fall apart had less to do with its genius - all countries claim to have - for maintaining unity than with the national ethos that was inculcated into its citizens by the one-party state. Although the country did not break up when multiparty democracy was introduced, that does not mean it won't some time in the future, if Zanzibar secedes – although that is a remote possibility - while the mainland remains intact.

Therefore the challenge for the future is whether or not the unity which still exists in Tanzania today, can still be maintained under the multiparty system without accentuating the cleavages that exist and which may lead to ethnic and regional conflicts - even to national disintegration - in the name of democracy. It is as much a challenge to unity as it is to the ideology of tolerance we call democracy, whose name has been invoked throughout history to fight oppression, glorify partisanship, and even justify some of the worst forms of tyranny. It is an even bigger challenge for the United Republic of Tanzania which is a merger of two independent states, although the two surrendered their sovereignty upon consummation of the union. But the union may now be threatened by the petty nationalism of the Zanzibar secessionists who see their part of the united republic as a different country, and by the cheap politics of partisanship pursued under the guise of multiparty democracy.

Multiparty democracy may be able to transcend partisan politics. But it may not be able to maintain national unity on the basis of partisanship which, unfortunately, is its very essence in the multiparty politics of the multiethnic societies of Africa we call countries today. Whether we like it or not, we Africans should simply face the fact that, more often than not, multiparty politics in African countries is no more than multi-tribal or multi-regional politics, each political party drawing its greatest strength from a particular tribe or tribes in the name of "national" unity.

The task for Africans, in all the countries on the continent, is to navigate the treacherous waters between dictatorship for the sake of national unity and tribalism in the name of multiparty democracy. We focus next on how those fragmented countries may continue to survive and thrive as viable entities despite the disunity within.

CHAPTER THREE

AFRICA'S POTENTIAL FOR ECONOMIC GROWTH: BASIS FOR REGIONAL INTEGRATION AND VIABLE STATES

ALMOST ALL AFRICAN countries are underdeveloped. And the majority of them don't practice democracy. But that is not the main reason why they are not developed.

If democracy is the key to economic prosperity, then that is news to the people of Indonesia, Malaysia, Singapore, South Korea, and Thailand, who for decades have endured authoritarian rule and sometimes outright dictatorship while making spectacular economic progress. By contrast, African countries, which also won independence during the post-World War II era like their Southeast Asian counterparts did, have been marking time. They are almost the exact opposite in every conceivable way except dictatorial rule.

Democracy has also eluded the People's Republic of China. Yet China, under communist dictatorship, has the fastest-growing economy in the world and is destined to become a super power, the only one capable of challenging the United States, probably within the next generation. It is already a formidable force in the global arena. It will take African countries, combined, several years to produce what China produces in one year; and several months to produce what she produces in a single day. Yet China is still a developing country, part of the Third World just like all the African countries, except South Africa which is both part of the First and the Third World.

On country basis, for example China vis-a-vis Tanzania, the comparison may be unfair; but not when all of Africa's economies are combined versus China's. Africa has about half the population of China, is more than three times her area, and has far more potential wealth. But unlike China, Africa is not united, and is therefore poor and powerless. As Dr. Kwame Nkrumah stated in his book "Dark Days in Ghana" which he wrote soon after he was overthrown in a CIA-masterminded coup in February 1966:

> "While we remain divided, no single progressive independent African state is safe. The continent is disunited and powerless in world affairs."[122]

Many Africans argue that Africa is not united because she has so many different tribes and races. True enough. But so does India, in fact even more so. The racial composition of modern India is exceedingly complex due to centuries of immigration into the continent. Demographers generally refer, however, to four main groups: Caucasoid, Mongoloid, Australoid, and Negroid - which, of course, does not mean they are black African; the term also applies to other dark-skinned people, for example, those in Papua New Guinea and other islands in the Pacific and elsewhere.

India's cultural complexity is also enormous. It is true that more than 1,000 different languages and dialects are spoken in Africa. But that does not match India's linguistic allogeneity: more than 1,500 languages and dialects are spoken in India; Papua New Guinea is another linguistically diverse country where more than 700 different languages are spoken yet is united. Africa has more than 730 million people; India has more than 950 million. Yet India is united, under one federal government, and is democratic. It is, in fact, the largest democracy in the world. Why not Africa, even if under five regional governments instead of one? East, Central, West, North, and Southern African federations. Unfortunately, African unity on a continental or subcontinental scale remains as elusive as ever.

---

[122] Kwame Nkrumah, *Dark Days in Ghana* (New York: Monthly Review Press, 1966). See also Nkrumah, *Africa Must Unite* (New York: Frederick A. Praeger, 1963).

Yet Africa's potential for economic growth is enormous, although it has been squandered through the years. As we pointed out in chapter one, it is true that in 1965 Nigeria was richer than Indonesia, Ghana richer than Thailand, and Zambia richer than South Korea. Add to the list, Uganda. That all those African countries were then richer than their Southeast Asian counterparts, is an empirical fact. It was a point also underscored by President Yoweri Museveni of Uganda in his speech at the United nations in February 1997 when he reminded his audience that in 1965 Uganda was "more prosperous than South Korea and Nigeria more prosperous than Indonesia."[123]

So what happened? It is also worth remembering that 1965 was only three years after Uganda won independence (in October 1962), four years after Nigeria won hers (in October 1960), eight years after Ghana did (in March 1957), and just one year after Zambia won hers (in October 1964), all from Britain; hardly enough time for the new African governments to have achieved so much progress - within so few years - and outstrip their Southeast Asian counterparts. The claim is further - in fact even more strongly - refuted by the economic ruin and political chaos during the next 30 years after independence, not only in the African countries we just named here but in most across the continent. They all ended up being the poorest in the world.

One of the strange paradoxes about Africa is that some of her richest countries are also among the poorest. Therefore most of the poverty in those countries is not due to lack of natural resources but due to wrong economic policies, mismanagement including well-meaning incompetence, sheer waste, and rampant corruption.

No case better illustrates the utter waste of such potential than that of Zaire - now the Democratic Republic of Congo - under Mobutu Sese Seko, one of the most brutal dictators on the entire continent. He ruled a vast country endowed with an abundance of minerals and other natural resources including enormous agricultural potential, making it potentially one of the richest countries in the world. In fact in terms of mineral wealth, it is the richest country in Africa - richer than South Africa.

[123] Yoweri Museveni, in his speech to the UN General Assembly, February 1997; cited by Tom Stacey, "African Realities," in *National Review*, May 19, 1997, p. 30.

The newly-renamed Congo is estimated to have more than 60 percent of the world's cobalt and the greatest supply of high-grade copper.[124] The country produces 90 percent of the world's small industrial diamonds[125], and still has an enormous reserve of those. The extent of Congo's gold reserves has never been properly assessed, but it is believed to be immense. And Congo's minerals are special. What makes them so special is not just the huge reserves, seemingly endless, but the quality of the ore. The country has some of the world's highest-grade copper, cobalt and zinc.

In addition to the enormous reserves of gold, diamonds, cobalt, copper, and zinc, Congo also has huge quantities of uranium, iron ore, silver, tin, manganese, bauxite, coal, radium, germanium, cadmium, petroleum, and an immense hydroelectric potential from the Congo River, one of the world's largest, and from other numerous rivers across the country. And it is believed to have even larger quantities of all those minerals. Exploration continues, and more discoveries are expected soon. And as Thierry Naudin, economics editor of "The European" stated in November 1996, Congo (then Zaire) has more than a dozen of vital minerals in huge quantities, but did nothing with all that enormous wealth through the decades to help its own people when it was under Mobutu; an indictment equally applicable to most of the other African countries:

> "In much of Africa, if a country is poor it seems bound to remain so indefinitely, and if it is rich, as Zaire is, it seems destined to be systematically plundered by a ruling minority... Zaire, which is about as large in area as the European Union, sits on some of the world's richest reserves of gold, diamonds, copper, cobalt and another dozen metals. The state's water resources are adequate to generate the energy required to exploit those minerals, and could also support an agricultural sector big enough to feed Zaire's population of 44 million. Nearly four decades after independence , the country might

---

[124] Howard W. French, "Sure, Africa's Troubled. But There Is Good News: (However), In Even the Successful Countries, Greed and Autocracy Threaten Stability," in *The New York Times*, June 15, 1997, p. E-16; *Columbia Encyclopedia* (New York: Columbia University Press, 1993), p. 3031.

[125] Ibid.

have been expected to have developed some manufacturing sector of its own.

But something is very wrong, and none of this potential has been realized. In terms of overall production and income, Zaire is back to its 1958 pre-independence levels - and now has a population three times as great. Its per capita output - under $120 per year today, against $377 in 1960 - is one of the lowest in the world. Like many countries in the region, since the 1960s it has swung from being an exporter to an importer of foodstuffs."[126]

Besides minerals, Congo also has a lot of agricultural potential to become a major food exporter. The principal food crops are maize, yams, rice, cassava, plantains, groundnuts, pulses, bananas, vegetables, mangoes and oranges and other fruits. Other main agricultural products and export crops are coffee, palm kernels and oil, rubber, quinine, tea, sugar cane, cocoa and cotton. Rubber, coffee, cotton, tea and palm products are produced commercially in limited quantities on small farms. The main plantation commodities are palm products, coffee, sugar cane and rubber. Substantial numbers of goats, sheep, cattle and poultry are also raised. Fishing in the Congo River and the country's many other large rivers and lakes is also an important industry. But it is very underdeveloped in spite of its potential for commercial success on a large scale.

Approximately 55 percent of Congo is covered with forest, itself a great source of wealth. Considerable amounts of ebony and teak are produced annually as well as other valuable woods. Congo's numerous rivers form the backbone of the country's transportation network. Unnavigable parts of the Congo River - the main artery - are bridged by rail lines; the river also handles oceangoing vessels straight from and into the Atlantic Ocean.

Yet in spite of all that wealth, the country ended up being an international beggar, unable even to feed itself, because of corrupt leadership. During 32 years of kleptocratic rule, Mobutu bled the country to death, and Zaire ended up being one of the poorest countries in the world, almost all of which are in

[126] Thierry Naudin, "Europe Can Help Africa, But Only If Africa Helps Itself," in *The European*, November 21, 1996, p. 22.

Africa. His personal wealth was equal to the national debt, at the very least. He amassed a fortune in the billions of dollars (estimates range from $5 to $10 billion), making him one of the five richest men in the world. The list goes on.

Neighboring Congo-Brazzaville, also known as the Republic of the Congo, is another country endowed with an abundance of natural resources, agricultural and mineral, including oil which accounts for 70 percent of the government's income.[127] The country's major crops are rice, yams, cassava, corn, peanuts, maize, bananas, beans, fruits such as mangoes and oranges, and vegetables. In fact fruits are so abundant and such an important part of the diet that the streets of Brazzaville, the country's capital, are lined with mango trees. Cash crops include palm kernels and oil, sugar cane, cocoa, coffee and tobacco. Sugar cane and tobacco, raised primarily on plantations, are the leading export crops, followed by coffee, cocoa, palm products, and groundnuts. Timber is another major export. Livestock and poultry, as well as fishing, are also important economic activities.

In terms of minerals, oil is the most important export. Others are potash, lead, zinc, gold, copper and diamonds. Natural gas is another major natural resource being exploited.

Congo-Brazzaville is one of the richest countries in Africa and in the entire Third World. Her people enjoy a higher standard of living than those in many other black African countries. Yet much of the country's wealth goes to only a relatively few people, distributed on tribal basis, depending on whose tribe is in power. If the president is a member of the Bakongo tribe, from the south and the largest in the country, his people are going to get a larger share of the pie. If he is a northerner, northerners are going to be the greatest beneficiaries. Even the struggle for power is fought along tribal and regional lines.

President Pascal Lissouba, who was overthrown in October 1997 after a four-month civil war by his long-time rival and former military dictator Denis Sassou-Nguesso, had been trying to perpetuate himself in office since the last bout of fighting in 1993 between northerners and southerners for control of

[127] "Congo," in *1986 Reader's Digest Almanac and Yearbook* (Pleasantville, New York: Reader's Digest Association, 1985), p. 534.

the country. Lissouba is a member of the Bakongo tribe from the south where Brazzaville is located and mainly inhabited by the Bakongo. Sassou-Nguesso is a northerner belonging to the Mbochi tribe.

For his part, Nguesso, one of the extremely rare African heads of state to step down (after he lost the election to Lissouba in 1992), had been working just as hard to win back the presidency by fair means or foul. Towards this end, he used his personal fortune to mobilize a heavily armed private militia known as the Cobras - composed mostly of northerners - to maintain control over much of his native northern Congo and serve as a counterweight to President Lissouba's government troops who constituted the national army. Nguesso also moved his militias to his neighborhood in the capital Brazzaville. When the fighting erupted in June 1997, the two sides became locked in fierce combat for control of the capital. But finally, Nguesso's Cobra militia with the help of Angolan troops routed the national army and took over Brazzaville; a clear-cut case of ethnic and regional rivalry so typical of African politics. As one senior West African diplomat in Abidjan, Ivory Coast, stated:

> "What you have in Congo is a very rich state in deep decay. Unfortunately, there are no saints in this picture. The name of the game in Congo is being in charge so that you and a few people from your ethnic group can profit from the country's huge oil earnings."[128]

Neighboring Gabon is another fabulously rich country. It has a lot of oil and other natural resources more than enough for its small population of just over a million people to enjoy one of the highest standards of living in the world; and some of them do, but they are only a handful of the elite.

Besides petroleum, Gabon also has large deposits of iron ore, manganese, gold, uranium, natural gas, lead, zinc, copper, and diamonds. In fact, it is one of the world's leading producers of uranium. Its agricultural products include cocoa, coffee, vegetables, fruits, rice, pulses, palm products, cassava, bananas, and taro. Fishing is also an important part of the economy.

---

[128] An unidentified West African diplomat in Abidjan, Ivory Coast, quoted by Howard W. French, "Shells Rain on Center of Brazzaville: France and U.S. Strive to Evacuate Citizens," in the *International Herald Tribune*, June 10, 1997, p. 4.

Unfortunately, the raising of livestock is inhibited by the scourge of the tsetse fly.

Gabon also has an abundance of forest products, a thriving lumber industry especially the production of okoume (a softwood used in making plywood), mahogany, and ebony; and rivers with substantial hydroelectric potential. The country's annual revenues from exports is usually higher than the cost of imports. The main exports are crude petroleum, forest products especially timber, uranium, manganese, and cacao. The other minerals are also important exports.

Because of the country's wealth, large numbers of immigrants from other French-speaking African countries, as well as from English-speaking Nigeria especially from the east, work in Gabon, mostly harvesting cash crops. The people of Gabon have the highest per capita income in black Africa, and second only to Libya's on the entire continental mainland. They also have one of the highest literacy rates in Africa.[129]

Yet after more than 30 years of autocratic rule and rampant corruption under President Omar Bongo who has ruled the country since November 1967, the people of Gabon are still mired in poverty in spite of all that wealth. And disease and malnutrition give Gabonese one of the lowest life expectancies in the world, with the average man dying by the age of 25.[130] Like all the other tyrannies in several countries across the continent, President Bongo's dictatorship is notorious for ignoring the basic needs of the people, uses terror to intimidate them into submission, and thrives on tribal rivalry, dividing the opposition. Gabon's squandered wealth would have made it one of the most highly developed countries in the world in telescoped time. It still has the potential to become one, but under a totally different kind of leadership.

Other rich African countries notorious for squandering wealth include Cameroon where President Paul Biya has muzzled the opposition while enormously enriching himself; Nigeria where General Sani Abacha ruled with an iron first and is reported to have squirreled away an estimated $4 billion making him and his cronies some of the richest men in the world just within

---

[129] "Gabon," in ibid., p. 558; *1997 Almanac*, (New York: Houghton Mifflin, 1996), p. 191.

[130] *1986 Reader's Digest Almanac*, op. cit., p. 558.

five years since he seized power. In fact he was already rich even before then, when he served as defense minister under General Ibrahim Babangida whom he eased out of power in 1993. But he got even richer, and faster, when he became the helmsman himself. Nigeria is the richest black nation in the world, second only to predominantly black but multiracial South Africa; yet its people are among the poorest because of waste and corruption. As Ken Saro-Wiwa, the Nigerian writer who was executed by Sani Abacha on November 10, 1995, lamented: while other oil-rich countries used their money for development, Nigeria squandered hers, with the rulers enriching themselves.[131]

Although Saro-Wiwa was from Eastern Nigeria, he supported the federal military government during the Nigerian civil war against the secession of Biafra, fearing that the Ibos would dominate his tribe, the Ogoni, and seize for themselves all the oil wealth coming from Ogoniland. Yet he was not very optimistic either, about the future after the federal forces won the war; and wrote bitterly that "the resources of the Ogoni and other ethnic minorities in the Niger River Delta could be more easily purloined while paying lip service to Nigeran federalism and unity."[132]

That is exactly what happened. Nigeria's military rulers have been looting the national treasury for decades. There has been some development, granted, but it has not meant much for the vast majority of the people. The petrodollars are either stolen or wasted on grandiose projects. The military rulers, almost all of them northerners since 1966, constitute the core of the problem. They are accountable to nobody, as they continue to squirrel away billions of petrodollars into their personal accounts at home and abroad. As Wole Soyinka bluntly states in his book, which is a searing indictment of Nigeria's military rulers, "The Open Sore of a Continent: A Personal Narrative of the Nigerian Crisis":

> "(Nigerians have one important task to fulfill and that is), the immediate, overall mission of rooting out the military from Nigerian

---

[131] Ken Saro-Wiwa, *A Month and a Day: A Detention Diary* (New York: Penguin Books, 1993).

[132] Ken Saro-Wiwa, quoted by David Rieff, "The Threat of Death: The Ruin of Nigeria, the Ruin of Africa," in *The New Republic: Africa is Dying*, June 16, 1997, p. 38.

politics, rescuing the nation's wealth from its incontinent hands, and terminating once and for all, its routine murders of innocent citizens on the streets of Lagos and other visible centers of opposition."[133]

One of the people killed was the wife of Moshood Abiola, winner of the 1993 presidential election who was imprisoned by Sani Abacha when he tried to claim his office. She was a tireless campaigner for the release of her husband and for democracy; and for that, she paid a heavy price, with her life, when Abacha's henchmen unleashed a fusillade of bullets on her car, killing her in broad daylight in the streets of Lagos in 1995; the killers paid with petrodollars for a job well done. Denying the people democracy and silencing the opposition has been one of the most effective ways to guarantee theft of the nation's wealth by the soldiers which could be used for development, not only in Nigeria, but in other African countries as well.

But those are not the only rich countries in Africa. Others endowed with an abundance of natural resources include the Ivory Coast, Ghana, Zimbabwe, Botswana, Angola, Namibia and, of course, South Africa. Even some of the poorest have stumbled upon unexpected wealth. Chad was once the poorest country in Africa, with the lowest income. Now it has the potential to become one of the richest because of the recent discovery of large quantities of oil in that barren land. There has been some petroleum exploration since 1977, but it was interrupted through the years by the civil war which wracked the country from the sixties until the eighties.

Mali is another one. It is still one of the most poverty-stricken nations in the world. Yet the country has extensive mineral resources: uranium, gold, diamonds, iron ore, manganese, copper, phosphate, bauxite and lithium, all of which remain largely unexploited because the poor transportation system of the landlocked nation cannot handle large ore shipments. That will change when foreign investors willing to exploit the minerals and develop the necessary transportation and communications facilities invest in the country on a large scale. In fact Mali's future already looks bright with increased

[133] Wole Soyinka, *The Open Sore of a Continent: A Personal Narrative of the Nigeran Crisis* (New York: Oxford University Press, 1996). See also D. Rieff, *The Ruin of Nigeria, The Ruin of Africa*, op. cit., p. 34; and Crawford Young, "The Impossible Necessity of Nigeria: A Struggle for Nationhood," in *Foreign Affairs*, November/December 1996, pp. 139-143.

exploitation of only two of its resources, cotton and gold, without even mentioning the rest also scheduled for further development. Both the adoption of new economic policies and change of leadership have played a critical role in improving the country's prospects. As *The Economist* points out:

> "Mali's President Alpha Oumar Konaré... enjoys a reputation in the United States and elsewhere as one of the few truly democratic leaders to have emerged in the past decade... First elected in 1992, Mr. Konaré, an archaeologist and veteran pro-democracy campaigner, had to cope with the legacy of the 23-year reign of Moussa Traore, one of Africa's less savory army-backed autocrats. The treasury was empty. Five years later, Mali is praised by the IMF and the World Bank as a case of successful structural adjustment in extremely difficult circumstances. Cotton production is booming: Mali is now second only to Egypt among African producers. And it will soon be Africa's third-biggest gold producer."[134]

And if the rest of its abundant minerals are fully exploited, and its wealth well-spent, Mali could end up being one of the richest countries not only in Africa but in the entire developing world. Its potential for such growth is beyond dispute, as shown by its quantum leap from being a small producer of cotton to being second only to Egypt today on the entire continent; and soon to be the third largest producer of gold in Africa.

Therefore, we see that even some of Africa's poorest countries are not as poor as they seem to be, as their potential wealth clearly shows. Chad and Mali are just two examples; they are poor yet potentially rich.

The Central African Republic is yet another one. Not only is it extremely poor; it is also landlocked, has no railroads, and not enough all-weather roads. Hardly any are paved. Rivers are the chief means of transportation.

But in spite of all the poverty, the Central African Republic has more resources than several other countries in the world. Cotton, tobacco, and coffee are its main cash crops. Others include cocoa, rubber, and palm products. Timber is also an important export product. The country's large

---

[134] "Mali: Take A Horse to Water...," in *The Economist*, July 26, 1997, p. 39.

tropical forests provide the potential for a substantial lumber industry, but lack of good transportation facilities makes the export of large amounts of lumber and other forest products difficult.

However, the country's best hope for improving its economic situation lies in the development of its mining industry. Mining was formerly limited to diamonds, another leading export, but has become increasingly important with the extraction of uranium, begun in 1972. Gem and industrial diamonds account for over half the value of the country's exports. In the 1970s the French Atomic Energy Commission cooperated with the Central African Republic in developing mining and refining facilities to exploit a large deposit of uranium found in the eastern part of the country. The country's mining industry, as well as its agricultural and forest products such as timber, can contribute substantially to economic growth, but inadequate transportation remains a major obstacle to such development.

Corruption has been another retarding factor to economic development. So has waste of the country's wealth. For example when Jean-Bédel Bokassa was president, he renamed the country the Central African Empire on December 4, 1976, and crowned himself Emperor Bokassa I, the first socialist emperor of Africa as he described his title, in a ceremony which cost $25 million in such a poverty-stricken country. The coronation was held at the Bangui sports stadium in the country's capital, Bangui, but was not attended by most of the other African leaders.

Such waste of the nation's wealth has been devastating to most African countries. But if properly managed, even the poorest can conquer poverty and stop begging, with African leaders trotting round the globe pleading for help.

Another country which seems to be permanently locked in poverty is Burkina Faso, formerly Upper Volta. It is one of the 10 poorest countries in the world. Traditionally, large numbers of the male labor force migrate to the Ivory Coast and (to a lesser extent) to Ghana to work in factories and on farms. However, their earnings contribute virtually nothing to Burkina Faso's economic development. Also the annual cost of the country's imports is usually much higher than its earnings from exports, and the nation relies heavily on debt servicing from other countries.

Burkina Faso is an agricultural country. But less than 10 percent of the land is suitable for cultivation, and droughts through the years have severely limited agricultural production. However, the country has great potential for growth in the agricultural sector if, with international help, it can successfully mount a campaign to exterminate what is probably one of its biggest enemies: black flies.

Actually, Burkina Faso has more fertile land than the 10 percent that is now being cultivated. But much of that land is in the valleys where it remains fallow because people fear the river-blindless disease carried by black flies along the rivers. The country has several unnavigable rivers. The major ones include the Komoé River in the southwest which flows through the Ivory Coast to the Gulf of Guinea; in the center are the Black, Red, and White Volta rivers, which join in Ghana to form the Volta River; and in the northeast are several small tributaries of the Niger River.

All the valleys around those rivers have fertile land, and would be under cultivation had it not been for the black flies scaring the people away. Therefore Burkina Faso's agricultural potential is more than enough to meet the country's needs for food and other necessities, and is also enough to boost the production of its cash crops which include cotton, the major export crop. Besides cotton, the other principal agricultural commodities include sorghum, millet, maize, groundnuts, sugar, rice, yams, cassava, fruits and vegetables.

Large numbers of cattle, sheep, goats and poultry, are also raised. Fishing from the country's several rivers, forestry and lumbering, are also major economic activities. Mining is another important industry. Burkina Faso's mining industry is small, mainly producing manganese, phosphates, and gold-bearing quartz. But there are also untapped deposits of zinc, nickel, lead, bauxite, and uranium. The country also has a good road network; and a railroad that runs from the capital Ougadougou to the seaport of Abidjan in the Ivory Coast. Such good transportation will undoubtedly facilitate the exploitation of the country's resources.

All that agricultural and mineral potential - as well as forestry products and fishing - is a lot of wealth for what is today still one of the world's poorest countries. It can lead to Burkina Faso's economic growth, especially once the black flies are exterminated, and foreign investors participate in the exploitation of the country's minerals and other resources.

Guinea is another country which is one of Africa's poorest. Yet it also has the potential to become one of the richest. Some of the world's largest bauxite deposits are in Guinea. They are mined jointly by Guinea and international companies. The country also has large deposits of iron ore, gold, and diamonds, that are mined under joint ventures with foreign investors but which have not yet been fully exploited.

The significance of the country's minerals was dramatically noticed during the 1970s when just one of them, bauxite, boosted Guinea's income at a phenomenal rate. From 1972 to 1976, Guinea's export revenues rose nearly 800 percent when two large bauxite mines went into production.[135] And increased production of all the minerals - iron ore, gold, diamonds, and bauxite itself - all of them found in abundance, will greatly fuel the country's economic growth.

The mining sector now generates over 90 percent of the nation's export revenues.[136] Mineral exports increased throughout the 1980s, creating a favorable trade balance. But there is still room for more improvement. Guinea has some light industry but a lot of potential for growth in that area. However, inadequate transportation facilities have hampered industrialization, although expansion of the mineral industry has led to improvement of the road network.

Guinea also has a lot of agricultural potential which, when fully exploited, will contribute significantly to the country's economic growth. Predominantly agricultural like the rest of the African countries, Guinea produces rice, millet, cassava, coffee, tea, bananas, palm kernels, citrus fruits, yams, pineapples, peanuts, maize, and vegetables. Fishing and livestock are also an important part of Guinea's economy.

Few countries endowed with so much can, realistically, be considered poor. But African countries are, because their economic potential has not been fully exploited. In terms of natural resources, some countries around the world have virtually none. Yet they are developed. Singapore has none, not even many people; it is no more than a city-state, yet an economic powerhouse that dwarfs African countries several times its size and which are endowed with an abundance of natural resources it does not have. Japan also hardly has any natural resources; yet it is now a world economic giant.

But they all have one important resource every country in the world has: people. It is just that some countries use theirs better than others do. Those

---

[135] *1986 Reader's Digest Almanac*, op. cit., p. 568.
[136] *Columbia Encyclopedia*, op. cit., p. 1161.

endowed with even more resources besides people should be able to do even better. That is why even some of the poorest African countries - for example the ones we have looked at here - all of which are endowed with other natural resources besides people, are not really that poor. They just have not done enough for themselves with what they have as much as they should have.

Sierra Leone is one of those perennial contenders, all of them in Africa, for the poorest country in the world. And all the poorest countries in the world are, of course, in Africa. Yet Sierra Leone has some of the largest deposits of diamonds, bauxite, titanium dioxide, and iron ore on the entire continent. Other minerals found in the country include gold and rutile. Altogether, they account for about half of the country's foreign-exchange earnings.

But the country's mining industry is dominated and controlled by companies based in Britain, Switzerland, and the United States which, through the years since independence, have worked with the country's rulers - civilian and military- to siphon off the country's mineral wealth into their own coffers. Smuggling has always been a thriving industry in Sierra Leone since the Margai brothers - Dr. Milton Margai, the country's first prime minister, who was succeeded by his younger brother Sir Albert Margai - were in office during the sixties and virtually gave official sanction to the illegal traffic by participating in it themselves. Smuggling, especially of diamonds, has now become an integral part of the country's economy virtually indistinguishable from legal economic activities. The problem was compounded by the civil war which wracked Sierra Leone during the 1990s when both government soldiers and the rebels of the Revolutionary United Front (RUF) engaged in looting the country's wealth, especially targeting diamonds.

In addition to its great mineral wealth, Sierra Leone also has a lot of potential for economic growth in other areas, especially agricultural. The main food crops are rice, cassava, maize, millet and groundnuts. The leading cash crops, most of which are exported, are palm kernels, cacao, ginger and coffee. Poultry, cattle, sheep and goats are also raised. Fishing is also an important industry, and the capital Freetown has excellent port facilities, some of the best on the continent. But Sierra Leone has limited rail and road networks, a handicap that hampers economic growth. And the cost of its imports is usually slightly higher than its earnings from exports, a problem which further stunts economic growth. However, it is an imbalance that can be rectified with increased production in both the mining and agricultural sectors, and when diamond smuggling is brought under control.

Neighboring Liberia, founded by freed African-American slaves when they returned to their native continent, is another poor African country with an underdeveloped economy and a poor infrastructure. Yet it is one of the world's 10 leading producers of iron ore and natural rubber.

Beginning in 1926, Liberia encouraged American companies to develop rubber plantations that became a mainstay of the economy. Until the 1950s, Liberia's economy was almost totally dependent upon subsistence farming and the production of rubber. The American-owned Firestone plantation was the country's largest employer. Then in 1955, huge iron-ore deposits were discovered at Mount Nimba on the border with Guinea. More were found at Bomi Hills and at Bong. With the discovery of the high-grade iron ore at all those sites, the production and export of minerals became the country's major cash-earning economic activity. Shipments from the mines began in 1963. Iron ore now accounts for over half of the nation's exports. Other important minerals found in Liberia include gold, diamonds, barite and kyanite.

Rubber and timber, produced mainly on foreign concessions, are the main nonagricultural exports. Iron ore, rubber, and diamonds constitute the largest share of the export earnings. Much of Liberia's industry is concentrated around Monrovia and is directed toward the production of iron ore. But the lack of skilled manpower and technology has impeded growth of the manufacturing sector of the economy just as it has in all the other African countries, except South Africa. Liberia's economic development is also hampered by lack of adequate transportation. Internal communications are poor, with few paved roads and only a few short, freight-carrying rail lines.

Liberia also derives substantial revenues from maritime activity. A large merchant fleet sails under the Liberian flag - over 2,000 ships.[137] Most are owned by Americans and other foreigners who register the ships in Liberia to avoid strict control. Low fees and minimal control over shipping operations under the Liberian flag have made the Liberian merchant maritime fleet one of the world's largest.

---

[137] *1986 Reader's Digest Almanac*, op. cit., p. 600.

In addition to minerals and rubber, other major exports include lumber and coffee. Liberia also produces rice, cassava, sugar cane, tobacco, cocoa, palm kernels, citrus fruits, vegetables, yams, and okra. However, a lot of rice, which is the country's staple food, is imported. But efforts have been made to develop intensive rice production and to establish fish farms. Fishing has also always been an important part of Liberia's economy. Tourism is also a leading industry, boosted by Liberia's history and fame as one of the most well-known African countries because of its founding by African-American freed slaves.

Yet with all that economic potential, Liberia remains one of the poorest and least developed countries in the world. But it has the potential wealth to become one of the richest and one of the most developed on the African continent. Unfortunately, a lot of Liberia's potential was wasted during the seven-year civil war, started by Charles Taylor, which devastated the country through much of the 1990s. As Taylor said during the 1997 presidential campaign:

> "They say I brought the war, so let them give me the chance to rebuild the country. I sincerely want to rebuild what they claim I have destroyed."[138]

He went on to win the election. And in spite of the devastation inflicted by the war on the country, Liberia still remains potentially rich enough to achieve spectacular economic growth once all of its resources are fully mobilized to achieve that goal.

Togo is another African country which is one of the poorest on the continent. Freed slaves also played an important part in its founding, although not as much as they did in Liberia and Sierra Leone. Freed slaves from Brazil were the first traders to settle in Togo, but it was the Germans who founded the German colony of Togoland in 1884. After the Germans were defeated in World War I, the colony was divided between the French and the British. The British portion voted in a plebiscite in 1956 for incorporation with Ghana,

---

[138] Charles Taylor, quoted in "Liberia on the Home Stretch," in the *New African*, No. 352, London, United Kingdom, May 1997, p. 17.

which took place in 1957 when Ghana won independence; while French Togo became independent three years later on April 27, 1960.

Togo today also has the distinction of being one of the smallest countries in Africa, a factor which accounts for its poverty. It resisted President Kwame Nkrumah's efforts to unite it with Ghana, a merger which could have made the new and bigger nation more economically productive than Togo is today by itself with only a few resources and a tiny domestic market.

But in spite of Togo's poverty, the small West African country located between Ghana and Benin (formerly Dahomey) is not an entirely hopeless case and may, in fact, make great progress once the resources it has are fully exploited. Other than its farmland, Togo's most important natural resources is a huge deposit of phosphates. Exploitation of major deposits of phosphates at Akoumapé in the southern part of the country began on a large scale in 1963, just three years after the country won independence. In 1988 Togo was the world's ninth leading producer of phosphate ores. Today phosphates constitute about half of the country's exports. Other minerals found in the country include small quantities of chromite, bauxite, limestone, and iron ore, all of which are mined. Marble is also quarried. But the country has the resources which can help it improve its economic situation, even though those minerals, except phosphates, do not exist in large quantities.

In the agricultural sector, Togo produces cocoa, coffee, palm kernels, groundnuts, fruits, vegetables, cassava, millet, maize, rice, sorghum, pulses, and yams, most of it for local consumption. Livestock and fishing are also an important part of the economy. Togo's major exports are phosphates, cocoa, coffee, palm nuts, cotton, groundnuts, fish, cassava flour and starch. The leading cash crops - coffee, cacao, and palm crops - are raised mainly on plantations in the southern part of the country. Cotton and groundnuts are grown in the north. Togo's livestock industry involves the raising of large numbers of sheep, goats, hogs and cattle.

Many non-African countries with far less than that - with virtually nothing - have ended up richer, much richer, than Togo and all the other African countries endowed with even more resources. There is no reason why Togo should not be able to, with all the resources it has, in spite of the fact that it is one of the poorest countries in the world.

Formerly known as Dahomey, Benin is another small poor African country. It is bordered by Togo on the west and by Nigeria on the east.

Although Benin is small, 43,483 square miles, it is about twice the size of Togo which has an area of 21,925 square miles.

But Benin is not a hopeless case either, in spite of its poverty. Like all the other African countries, its economy is overwhelmingly agricultural. The chief crops are maize, cassava, yams, millet, sorghum, groundnuts, pulses, cacao, cotton, coffee, tobacco, rice, kapok, cashew nuts, palm nuts and kernels. Large numbers of sheep, goats and pigs constitute a significant part of Benin's economy. There is also a sizeable freshwater and ocean fishing industry.

Benin also has several minerals. They include chromite, low-quality iron ore, ilmenite, and titanium. But they have not yet been exploited on a large scale. Petroleum was discovered offshore back in 1968 and has been increasingly exploited since then. And in the 1980s, Benin began to develop its vast hydroelectric potential through the Mono River Dam project. There is also a developing tourist industry. Long beaches, a tradition of hospitality to visitors, and unspoiled wildlife reserves provide the potential for a boom in tourism.

Now, to call a country endowed with so many agricultural, mineral and maritime resources, desperately poor is something which may surprise many people who are really poor. Yet Benin itself is indeed poor, as shown by the extremely low standard of living of the vast majority of its people; and for the same reason that the rest of the Africans are poor. African countries are poor, in fact most of them are desperately poor, because they are underdeveloped. Almost all of them have a lot of potential wealth - agricultural and forestry products, minerals, and fishing in Africa's numerous rivers and lakes, and from the ocean. But most of that potential wealth has not been exploited. That is what makes them so poor.

Look at Benin and Israel for example. Compare and contrast the two in terms of natural resources. Israel has virtually nothing by comparison - it is dwarfed by Benin, one of the poorest countries in Africa. Yet Israel, founded in the desert and much smaller than Benin, is one of the most successful economies in the world.

The maritime plain of Israel is, of course, remarkably fertile. And the country has some natural resources: sulfur, copper, phosphates, potash, and bromine. But Israel has also transformed a significant portion of the desert into fertile land through an extensive irrigation scheme. But because of its climate, Israel cannot produce a wide range of agricultural products which Benin and other African countries are able to produce. Therefore there is no reason why Benin cannot produce more than what it produces now, and why it should be permanently trapped in poverty, with all the resources and the good climate it has.

Also on the list of the poorest countries in the world is Niger, a huge country north of Nigeria which is tens of thousands of square miles - 132,506 altogether - bigger than Nigeria; this difference is, in fact, the area of some of the biggest countries in Africa.

The northern four-fifths of Niger is covered by the wasteland of the Sahara Desert. The climate is hot, dry and dusty. Because of lack of employment and arable land due to arid conditions, there is a significant migration of seasonal workers from Niger to Ghana, Nigeria, and Chad. The only fertile cropland in Niger is in the 300-mile-long valley of the Niger River in the southwestern part of the country and near the border with Nigeria in the south.

But Niger also has large quantities of minerals. In the early 1970s a Franco-Niger company began to excavate large high-grade uranium deposits and also opened a uranium-ore concentrating plant. Another uranium mine was opened in the late 1970s, and a third in 1986. Increasing uranium-ore exports boosted the gross national product at an annual rate of 10 percent during the late 1970s. But falling uranium prices caused the nation's economy to stagnate in the 1980s.

Niger also has large deposits of iron ore and phosphates, but exploitation of these important minerals is handicapped by the nation's poor transportation system. There is no railroad to the nearest port, which is 1,000 miles away on the Atlantic coast of Nigeria. And there are few hard -surfaced roads for use by trucks. Consequently, much freight has to be flown in and out of the country. Most of Niger's all-weather roads are confined to the fertile south and southwest. Other minerals found in the country include tin ore, coal, gypsum, natron and salt.

There is also a small but growing fishing industry, centered mainly on the Niger River in the southwest and on Lake Chad in the southeast. Large numbers of poultry, goats, cattle, sheep and camels are also raised. But their numbers have dwindled through the years because of persistent droughts. In spite of the harsh climate, Niger is still able to grow a number of crops. The main ones are millet, sorghum, cassava, groundnuts, rice, cotton, sugar cane and dates - which are grown in the desert. The chief exports are uranium, groundnuts and their products, cotton, meat, hides, and live cattle. Niger's exports are expected to increase when all the other minerals, besides uranium, are fully exploited. Among those targeted for increased production include iron ore and phosphates. Niger's potential for economic growth is further shown by the country's increasing value of its exports which, if sustained, will exceed the value of its imports and enable the country to earn more foreign exchange.

If a nation like Singapore had the resources poverty-stricken Niger has, it would probably consider itself the richest on earth. Niger is poverty-stricken because it has not harnessed its potential.

Next we look at the Gambia and Guinea-Bissau, also in West Africa, the two countries being some of the smallest on the continent. The Gambia is the smallest. It is also one of those countries which, even by African standards of poverty, some people may say has nothing.

It is true that the Gambia has no known minerals. And despite attempts at diversification, Gambia's economy remains overwhelmingly dependent on a single commodity: groundnuts and their by-products. It is the most important cash and export crop. But the country also has other products. They include swamp rice, millet, sorghum, maize, cassava and beans. Livestock raising, especially cattle, is also an important economic activity. Fishing is one of the country's two main occupations, next to agriculture, and generates a significant amount of income through the export of dried and smoked fish. In fact, the commercial fishing industry has great potential for expansion, but such growth is contingent upon the construction of adequate port facilities to handle the increased volume of trade. Gambia also exports palm kernels, hides and skins.

Gambia's transportation system is one of the main obstacles to the country's development. There has been a lot of improvement in Gambia's road system, but it has not been extensive enough. However, the Gambia River, which extends the length of the country, provides excellent transportation and remains the country's main artery in its transportation system. Gambia's other exports include cotton, lint and beeswax.

Gambia's economic growth is also partly facilitated by the tourist industry. Improvements in the infrastructure and a heightened popular interest in the country largely because of Alex Haley's epic "Roots" - which partially took place in the Gambia - helped spur a threefold increase in tourist arrivals between 1978 and 1988. The village of Juffure attracted an unusual number of foreign visitors to the ancestral home of Kunta Kinte, the main character in "Roots," which is a historical-fiction book. Gambia's President, Sir Dawda K. Jawara who was overthrown in July 1994, declared Juffure a national monument when he was still in power. The village has changed little since Kunta Kinte, a composite character, was captured by slave traders in 1767. However, even without Kunta Kinte, the Gambia has always attracted visitors. The country's beaches on its 50-mile Atlantic shoreline have always been a major tourist attraction. Except for its Atlantic coast, Gambia is surrounded by Senegal. The country is only about 20 miles wide but about 200 miles long from east to west.

But probably the best way for Gambia, and for other African countries as well, to achieve economic development is through regional integration. And if that cannot be achieved soon, a bilateral approach is the next best step to take; for example, Gambia integrating with Senegal as the two countries tried to do in their confederation of Senegambia which lasted from 1982-89. Unfortunately, it collapsed. But there seems to be no other way to economic prosperity for the two countries, besides stronger economic ties between them, unless all the countries in the region achieve full economic integration as the Economic Community of West African States (ECOWAS) and the Southern African Development Community (SADC) are attempting to do. Otherwise African countries will be permanently stuck in poverty, all their potential wealth doing them no good.

From the Gambia we go to Guinea-Bissau, the smallest but also the first of the three Portuguese African colonies to win independence. Guinea-Bissau is bounded by Senegal on the north and by Guinea on the south. It has an Atlantic coastline indented by many rivers which are also an important source of fish as much as the Atlantic Ocean is. Besides the mainland, many people also live on the offshore islands of the Bijagos archipelago as well as on the other smaller islands in the Atlantic, carrying on a thriving fishing industry.

Guinea-Bissau's economy depends on farming, livestock, raising, lumbering, and fishing. But it is still one of the poorest countries in Africa. The country spends four times more for imports than it receives from exports.

Yet this small very poor country of only about one million people has the potential to become rich once all of its resources are exploited. It has deposits of bauxite, petroleum, and phosphates, none of which are being fully exploited. Only bauxite is mined, but only in limited quantities. Exploitation of the minerals is also being hampered by lack of transportation facilities. Guinea-Bissau has no railways, and hardly any roads, let alone paved ones. Internal communications depend mainly on deep estuaries and meandering rivers. The country has many rivers, some with wide swampy estuaries.

Agriculture forms the backbone of the country's economy. Rice, palm oil, cassava, sugar cane, cotton, and coconuts are some of the main products. Cashew nuts, groundnuts, fish, shrimp, palm kernels and wood are the major exports. Guinea-Bissau also has some of the most fertile agricultural land in West Africa.

With improved transportation and communications facilities, foreign investment, and integration of Guinea-Bissau's economy with those of neighboring countries especially Guinea, Senegal and Gambia, Guinea-Bissau's potential for economic growth would be easier to exploit for the benefit of all the countries involved. The country is too small, and faces too many obstacles, to pursue economic development on its own without integrating its economy with those of its neighbors.

In fact, most African countries are too poor and too weak to survive on their own as viable economic entities, although the majority of them are rich in terms of natural resources. It will take bold initiatives by Africans themselves to correct the situation. And that includes surrendering at least some of their sovereignty to achieve the common goal of regional cooperation. Much of that effort has, in the past, come from outside Africa, even leading to the establishment of some regional organizations on the continent for the benefit of Africans because African countries were seen as being too weak to pursue economic development on their own. As Adebayo Adedeji stated when he was still the Executive Secretary of the UN Economic Commission for Africa (ECA):

> "In West Africa, the Economic Community of West African States (ECOWAS), the West African Economic Community (CEAO) and the West African Rice Development Institute (WARDA) were in fact established by the ECA... In a continent full of many small states, the

> majority of which have less than 10 million people, ECA believes that economic cooperation must be part and parcel of national policy because, with the exception of Nigeria and maybe Egypt, none of the countries has a population base that can constitute the basis for rapid socioeconomic transformation."[139]

One of those countries is Senegal, which we are now going to look at, as we continue with our survey of West African countries. Although Senegal is not as underdeveloped as the other West African countries we have looked at, it is not rich either. Nor is it one of the poorest of the poor in West Africa or on the continent as a whole.

Because its capital Dakar, which is located on the westernmost part of the continent, was the capital of the French colonies in West Africa, Senegal is more industrially developed than most other West African countries except Nigeria, Ivory Coast, and Ghana which, together with less developed Cameroon, are the economic powerhouses of West Africa. Dakar is the busiest port in West Africa, and its modern international airport is the main stopping point for flights from Europe to South America.

Senegal's per capita income is also one of the highest on the continent. Senegal is primarily an agricultural country, but industry in the cities, especially Dakar, is growing. About 27 percent of the country's land area is arable, which is a fairly high percentage. Arable land in most countries is usually under 20 percent. 30 percent of Senegal's arable land is used for pasture.[140]

The country's main food crops are rice, maize, millet, sorghum, cassava, pulses, groundnuts, sugar cane, vegetables and fruits. Groundnuts are the main export crop. Some of Senegal's largest industrial establishments process groundnuts into oil and oilcake; and groundnuts, their oil and oilcake account for a bigger percentage of Senegal's exports than any other commodities.

Large numbers of cattle, sheep and goats are also raised, but drought conditions now and then significantly reduce the population of the livestock. Senegal also has a large fishing industry, but it has been severely affected by

[139] Adebayo Adedeji, interviewed by Margaret A. Novicki, in *Africa Report,* September-October 1983, pp. 12, and 16.

[140] *Columbia Encyclopedia,* op. cit., p. 2475.

illegal fishing which is being carried on by commercial fishermen from European countries. Unfortunately, Senegal does not have the requisite naval power to keep foreign trawlers and other fishing vessels out of its territorial waters.

Like most African countries, Senegal is also endowed with a number of minerals. They include high-grade iron ore, gold, phosphate rock, and limestone. Offshore deposits of petroleum have also been discovered, and prospects are excellent that more oil, and probably other minerals as well, may be found as exploration continues.

Therefore in addition to groundnuts and their byproducts, Senegal's major exports include calcium phosphate, canned fish, hides and skins, high-grade iron ore and gold. Tourism and forestry are also among Senegal's leading industries.

Unlike many countries in the region, Senegal also has a relatively good transportation system that facilitates economic growth. The west-central part of the country which includes most of the largest cities such as the capital Dakar, which is also the country's largest is well served by railroads and major highways. A railway also runs from Dakar to Mali. And the discovery of petroleum deposits offshore has placed Senegal in line as one of Africa's oil-producing, may be even oil-exporting, countries once full production begins.

Next we look at the economic powerhouses of West Africa, which are also some of the richest countries on the continent: Nigeria, Ivory Coast, Ghana, and Cameroon. We start with the Ivory Coast, and then move on eastward.

The Ivory Coast, also known as Côte D'Ivoire is the wealthiest member of what was formerly French West Africa. The country has enjoyed a high economic growth rate since independence in 1960, a record unequaled anywhere else on the continent except by Botswana. However, the Ivory Coast still is a predominantly agricultural country despite steady industrialization since the sixties. French personnel have, since independence, played and continue to play a major role in the country's economic development. And thousands of other French men and women still live in the country today, especially in Abidjan, one of the most cosmopolitan cities in Africa.

Ivory Coast is endowed with many natural resources and has, since independence in 1960, used foreign aid and loans to diversify its agriculture. The country is one of the world's largest coffee producers, and cocoa is also one of the most important exports. Ivory Coast also has a lot of mineral resources. They include crude oil, iron ore, diamonds, manganese, cobalt, bauxite, and copper. The production of timber, which is another major export, includes mahogany and other hardwoods.

Other major economic activities include livestock raising, fishing and the canning of tuna. The production of rubber has also increased substantially in recent years, and rubber is now one of the country's major exports. Together with coffee and cocoa and other agricultural and forest products, petroleum is also one of Ivory Coast's most important exports.

The country's economic development has proceeded rapidly since independence mainly because of the unusually liberal terms offered to foreign investors. In 1972 Ivory Coast was also among seven Francophone countries which set up the West African Economic Community (CEAO) - inspired by the UN Economic Commission for Africa (ECA) - to promote trade and economic cooperation among the member states.

When French President Giscard d'Estaing visited the Ivory Coast in 1978, he praised the country for having "proved it is possible to escape from the curse of underdevelopment in the framework of a free economy."[141]

---

[141] Giscard d'Estaing, quoted in *1986 Reader's Digest Almanac*, op. cit., p. 588. See also Kaye Whiteman, *France's Year in Africa*, in Colin Legum and John Drysdale, *Africa Contemporary Record: Annual Survey and Documents 1968 - 1969* (London: Africa Research Ltd., 1969), pp. 29-30:

"In recognizing Biafra, President Charles De Gaulle (of France) based his argument on self-determination, and on hostility to federations in general. All those he mentioned were British creations, including Canada - where he equally applies the self-determination principle in Quebec - but the real analogy he is making is the two federations the French had created in West and Central Africa, which were systematically dismantled in the late 1950's as independence approached. France at the time was accused of balkanization - of creating a host of unviable mini-states in order to maintain a neo-colonial influence over them, but of late the French have been emphasizing that their decolonization did at least avoid a Nigerian war. It is significant that wealthy Ivory Coast and Gabon were the 'Biafras' of these failed federations, and it has been claimed that De Gaulle may have been influenced by President Houphouet-Boigny (of Ivory Coast) towards Biafra rather than the other way round."

Production of petroleum began in 1980 from fields discovered in 1978-80. By 1983 Ivory Coast became an oil-exporting nation. But drought and failing cocoa and coffee prices hurt the nation's economy from 1982-85, making the Ivory Coast the largest per capita debtor in Africa. And in an act of total waste of the nation's resources, President Felix Houphouet-Boigny announced in March 1983 that the nation's capital would be moved from Abidjan to Yamoussoukro, his birthplace. It was. A Catholic himself, he also ordered the building of the largest Christian church in the world, Notre Dame de la Pax, in the capital city Abidjan before he ordered the capital moved to his birthplace. The church was built as he ordered.

Houphouet-Boigny also, like Malawi's Life President Dr. Hastings Kamuzu Banda, alienated his country when he advocated and conducted dialogue with white-ruled South Africa in defiance of the collective wish of the Organization of African Unity (OAU) which was opposed to that. Yet he presided over a thriving economy, probably the most prosperous in Africa, although he also squandered wealth while many of his people continued to live in squalor. In fact the majority did not benefit much from the country's spectacular economic growth.

But because of its rapid economic growth, the Ivory Coast became one of the most industrialized countries on the African continent; an achievement which became a symbol of national pride. The country's industries include the production of petroleum and assembly of cars.

Therefore, De Gaulle also contends that the dissolution of the French African colonial federations contributed to economic growth, especially in Ivory Coast and Gabon, although that is a controversial thesis. In this book, we contend otherwise. A large population base and an equally large domestic market, fuels economic growth as the case of Nigeria clearly demonstrates. Otherwise there would be no such rich and powerful black nation had the Nigerian Federation collapsed. Natural resources are not enough to develop a country to the maximum. For example, Canada has 30 million people and a lot of natural resources, and is a developed country. But if it had as many people as the United States has, in such a vast expanse of territory and with so much resources, it would be a super power today. Its 30 million people are not enough to make it one, in spite of the country's vast resources and territorial size. Had the French African federations emerged from colonial rule as collective entities without breaking up, they would be as rich and as powerful as Nigeria is, which remained intact as a federation; they would perhaps be even richer than Nigeria, but definitely richer than the Ivory Coast and Gabon are individually.

In addition to coffee and cocoa, other agricultural crops grown for export include cotton, bananas, pineapples, sugar cane, coconuts and palm kernels. And economic productivity and exports have also increased because of the introduction of IMF-sponsored reforms in what was already a free-market economy. The country's economic prosperity has also had an impact on neighboring countries. Many people from Burkina Faso, Mali, Liberia, Ghana, Sierra Leone, Guinea, Senegal, Togo, Benin, Niger, and even from Nigeria, live and work in the Ivory Coast. Its rapid economic growth has also attracted tens of thousands of people from different parts of the world outside Africa. As James Rupert reported from Abidjan in December 1996:

> "More than any other city in West Africa, Abidjan works. The evidence is that foreigners keep coming- enough to make Abidjan West Africa's most cosmopolitan city. Tens of thousands of Europeans, Asians and Americans are in Abidjan to do business. The demand for luxury villas in the suburbs where these foreigners live has risen by as much as 50 percent in the past two years, real estate agents say. And hundreds of thousands of Africans - mostly from Burkina Faso, Mali, Guinea and Niger - have come to seek work as manual laborers, servants or petty traders. Their demand for housing, in poor neighborhoods or outlying shantytowns, has risen as well. There is a foreign middle class, too. As in many West African cities, most small shops seem to be owned and managed by Lebanese, and there are Indian and Vietnamese businesses, as well."[142]

More than 2 million immigrant Africans live in Ivory Coast, attracted by the country's economic prosperity unequaled anywhere else in West Africa. There are even many from Nigeria, an economic powerhouse itself but with fewer opportunities for them than in the Ivory Coast. As Mohammed Traore, a single Guinean in his 20s who drives a taxi through the jammed streets of the country's bustling former capital city and commercial center of Abidjan,

---

[142] James Rupert, "Life Is Better in Abidjan, Despite All the Hardships," in the *International Herald Tribune,* December 6, 1996, p. 2. See also J. Rupert on Abidjan, Ivory Coast, in *The Washington Post,* December 6, 1996.

said about groups of young men peddling watches and calculators and clothes as well as other merchandise:

> "A lot of them come from Nigeria, for the same reason I came from Guinea. We just want to make money, to have a life and get married."[143]

The Ivory Coast, with a robust economy provides them with the opportunity to do just that, by enabling them to make enough money and return to their home countries to realize their dreams. These are the people who take jobs Ivorians won't. And these are also the people who help to keep the economy going, and growing. They have been doing that for decades. As Rupert stated in his report from the former Ivorian capital:

> "For decades, unemployed people from Burkina Faso and other neighboring countries have provided the labor for Ivory Coast's huge cocoa and coffee harvests and for whatever menial tasks Ivorians have chosen to avoid."[144]

Undoubtedly, the Ivory Coast is going to play a major role in the economic development of the region, especially when the countries involved establish stronger economic ties. But also the challenge for neighboring countries is to learn what the Ivory Coast has done and what they haven't or failed to do so that they can duplicate its success, but without mortgaging their independence as Ivory Coast has done by becoming a French satellite.

Neighboring Ghana, east of Ivory Coast, is also another regional powerhouse and one of the most prosperous countries on the entire continent. It was once the world's leading producer of cocoa. Before then, another African country, the island nation of Sao Tome and Principe in the Atlantic Ocean which was a Portuguese colony, was the world's largest producer of cacao until 1909, and the crop is still the country's most important export commodity. Then it was surpassed by Ghana. But Ghana's production of the

[143] Mohammed Traore, quoted ibid.
[144] J. Rupert, ibid.

crop has declined since the 1970s, and the country is no longer the world's largest producer of cacao beans, from which cocoa and chocolate are made. However, it still remains one of the largest.

Ghana also has one of the world's largest man-made lakes, Lake Volta in the southeastern part of the country, which was formed when the Akosombo Dam (125 yards high) was built across the Volta River in 1964-65. The dam, which is the principal unit of the Volta Development Project, regulates the flow of the Volta River, stores water for irrigation, and generates hydroelectricity that supported a large aluminum industry until 1983, when the huge smelter at Tema was shut down.

All that was accomplished during the presidency of Dr. Kwame Nkrumah, Ghana's first president and hero of the African independence movement who led the Gold Coast to become the first black country on the entire continent to emerge from colonial rule. Nkrumah promoted development projects like the Volta River hydroelectric and aluminum plants; and built many schools, hospitals, and factories. He also introduced many reforms in education, transportation and other social services, as well as in the economic sector; and launched Ghana on the road toward industrialization. Because of what he started, and the momentum he provided, Ghana today is one of Africa's most industrialized countries.

However, Ghana's economy is still predominantly agricultural. Besides cacao, the country's most important export crop, Ghana also produces coffee, oil palms, coconuts, maize, rice, groundnuts, cotton, yams, tomatoes, plantains, cassava, and a variety of vegetables and fruits for export as well as for local consumption. For example, Ghana is one of the biggest exporters of pineapples in Africa, most of which are shipped to Europe and North America.

Ghana is also rich in minerals, The main ones are gold, diamonds, manganese and bauxite. They constitute the second-largest export, followed by forest products, mainly timber. Fish, especially tuna, and aluminum, are also major exports. Rubber is another main cash crop.

In 1978, Ghana added oil to its list of major products when offshore petroleum was discovered in commercial quantities. Exploration for more oil and other minerals continues. Livestock raising, especially cattle and sheep, is also an important part of Ghana's economy. The country's well-developed manufacturing sector includes major activities such as aluminum smelting and the processing of cacao. And there has been recent expansion in the construction, mining, and manufacturing sectors.

In terms of transportation, Ghana has a large road system; and its railways connect all the major cities and commercial centers in the southern part of the country to facilitate access to the sea. Ghana has another important asset. Compared with other African countries, Ghana has a high level of education in general, and one of the largest numbers of university graduates on the entire continent. Such a relatively high level of education and skilled manpower is critical to economic growth, and partly explains why the country is ahead of so many others in terms of economic development. And mainly because of economic reforms, Ghana today has one of the fastest-growing economies in Africa.

But it is Nigeria, more than any other country, which stands out as the economic powerhouse of the continent - with the exception of South Africa. It is the world's second -richest black nation (after South Africa), but the most heavily populated. Nigeria also is one of the world's 10 leading producers of petroleum, forestry products, natural rubber, and tin.

Petroleum is Nigeria's biggest export. It derives 90 percent of its revenues from oil. Nigeria is the second-largest supplier of oil to the United States, surpassed only by Saudi Arabia, and the biggest producer of petroleum in sub-Saharan Africa. But Nigeria also has one advantage over several other oil-producing countries in the world. It produces high-grade oil, with a low-sulfur content, an advantage which puts its oil in high demand round the globe because of its low levels of pollution.

Nigeria also has the largest number of university graduates in black Africa who have studied abroad and at its national universities. Since independence in 1960, the country has built several universities and colleges through the decades, a record unmatched anywhere else on the continent. Nigeria is also one of the most urbanized countries in Africa, with several large cities in all parts of the country, but especially in Western Nigeria. In fact, Ibadan is the largest indigenous city in black Africa which has existed for hundreds of years, long before the coming of Europeans. Its history is typical of Yorubaland in the west whose kingdoms were based on city-states, an achievement unparalleled anywhere else on the continent.

In addition to the large number of educated Nigerians, especially in the cities among the Yorubas and the Ibos in Western and Eastern Nigeria, respectively, there is also a large community of expatriates working in different fields. Most of those expatriates are employed by foreign firms, including oil companies in the country's major industry: oil production.

Petroleum production on a significant scale began in the late 1950s, and by the early 1970s, it was by far the leading earner of foreign exchange. The growing industry attracted many people to the cities, a migration pattern which adversely affected agricultural production. But even with the decline in agriculture through the years, Nigeria's revenues remained high, thanks to oil; and the country's large and robust economy encouraged the Nigerian leadership as far bask as the 1970s to play a more active role in world affairs and try to promote the interests of all Africans including those in diaspora. As David Rieff states:

> "The aftermath of the Biafran war coincided with the oil boom of the 1970s, with the era of OPEC. The Nigerian authorities were obsessed with exploiting the resource. Within a few years of the end of the civil war, there had occurred a huge increase in exploration and extraction activities... (Nigeria was) a state besotted by fantasies of wealth and global importance. This was a time when there was much talk within the Nigerian elite of the country acquitting an 'African' nuclear bomb and a seat on the Security Council, when the government believed that Nigeria was destined not only to lead Africa, but also to be a beacon for the African diaspora in Europe and North America."[145]

But not all of that was fantasy, especially the possibility of acquiring a seat on the UN Security Council. It is a prospect which is discussed even today, regarding South Africa which, together with Nigeria, is a leading contender for a permanent seat on the Security Council to represent Africa. And because of Nigeria's stature in the Third World, and as the largest black nation in the world, the suggestion that it should - like India, another major Third World country - be given a seat on the UN Security Council is something that has been discussed through the years since the sixties, shortly

[145] David Rieff, "The Ruin of Nigeria, the Ruin of Africa," in *The New Republic*, op. cit., p. 37.

after Nigeria won independence. Professor Benjamin Cohen of Harvard University, a specialist in international relations especially the United Nations, is one of those who seriously discussed the subject in his book 'The United Nations," published in 1961, contending that Nigeria and India, as well as Brazil and Iran, are major Third World countries which should be given permanent seats on the UN Security Council.[146] We can add others, such as Egypt and Indonesia, with Egypt representing the Arab world more than the African world; for, although Egypt is an African country geographically, spiritually it is part of the Middle East, and is the leader of the Arab world which overflows continental boundaries from Africa to Asia Minor. By contrast, Nigeria identifies itself with only one continent.

And the role Nigeria has played in Liberia and Sierra Leone as the leader of the West African peacekeeping force (known as ECOMOG) during the 1990s has only confirmed its status as a regional power in that part of Africa. It is only one of the three regional powers on the continent, the other two being South Africa and Egypt. And its oil wealth continues to provide Nigeria with the means to play a major role in African and international affairs. In fact, it is one of the few African countries which earn more from exports than they spend on imports. But Nigeria also stands out among those few countries because its earnings are huge, second only to South Africa's on the entire continent. Nigeria's earnings from oil alone exceed $10 billion annually, and its domestic product (GDP) is an impressive $122.6 billion, contrasted with South Africa's GDP of $133 billion.[147] However, in the 1980s, revenues from Nigeria's petroleum exports fell as a result of a decline in world oil prices and the government took measures to bolster the agricultural sector. But revenues from oil rose again, and with earnings from other exports, Nigeria remains a formidable economic and military power on the continent.

In addition to oil, Nigeria also has natural gas. Other minerals Nigeria produces include coal, tin, columbite, iron ore, limestone, lead, tantalite, and gold. Nigeria also exports large quantities of cacao, groundnuts and their by-

---

[146] Benjamin V. Cohen, *The United Nations: Constitutional Developments, Growth and Possibilities* (Cambridge, Massachusetts: Harvard University Press, 1961), p. 98. See also Adonis Hoffman, "Nigeria: The Policy Conundrum," in *Foreign Policy*, No. 101, Washington, D.C., Winter 1995-96, pp. 146-158.

[147] *1997 Almanac*, op. cit., pp. 242, and 264.

products including oil, palm nuts and oil, rubber, cotton, skins and hides, and textiles. Sorghum, millet, soybeans, maize, yams, rice, bananas, fruits, and vegetables are also among the chief crops. The raising of livestock, especially goats and sheep, as well as poultry is also an important part of the economy. Timber is another major export. Fishing is also a major industry; so is tobacco production.

All those products combined have enabled Nigeria to achieve spectacular economic growth, an achievement which has also been made possible by the enormous contribution of labor and skills from the country's large population of more than 120 million. One out of every seven Africans is a Nigerian.

Next we go to Cameroon, one of the biggest producers of oil in Africa. It is also one of the most prosperous countries on the continent, mainly because of the revenues it gets from petroleum. But Cameroon has other natural resources. By encouraging foreign investment, the country has been able to build hydroelectric power plants and railroads to develop its large deposits of bauxite, thus becoming the largest aluminum-producing nation in Africa. It is also one of the world's leading producers of cocoa.

Offshore oil wells began production in 1977, and by 1981 were producing about 100,000 barrels a day. An oil refinery built in 1975 - 81 made Cameroon self-sufficient in petroleum products. Huge natural gas reserves discovered in the country held promise for increased prosperity in the future, but a plan to begin production was rejected because of prohibitive costs. The government receives 60 percent of its revenues from oil and gas produced by foreign companies. In addition to bauxite and petroleum, Cameroon's mineral resources also include gold and tin.

In terms of agricultural products, Cameroon also produces coffee, tea, bananas, palm products, tobacco, rubber, and groundnuts, all of them grown mainly on plantations, and all of them commercially important. Cotton is another major export crop. The principal subsistence crops are bananas which are also exported; cassava, yams, plantains, millet, sorghum, rice, and groundnuts, another major export. Palm oil and sugar cane are also an important part of the economy.

Other leading economic activities include livestock raising, especially cattle and sheep; forestry, especially the production of timber which is another major export; and fishing, prawns being one of Cameroon's major exports. In fact fishing and forestry follow agriculture as leading occupations.

And despite the occurrence of periodic droughts, food production in Cameroon meets domestic demand, which is not the case in a number of other African countries.

Stability through the decades has also helped Cameroon build roads and railways critical to economic growth. The nation's road and railway network was further improved in the 1980s, facilitating more industrialization some of whose important activities include oil refining and paper milling. The Edéa Dam on the Sanaga River provides the bulk of the country's electricity and powers a large aluminum smelter. All the finished aluminum is exported.

But Cameroon's stability was rocked during the 1980s when a mutiny by President Paul Biya's guards almost overthrew his dictatorial government. The rebellion was suppressed by loyal army troops on April 8, 1984, with 500 to 1,000 persons killed in the fighting. In the following weeks, scores of persons were executed for allegedly plotting to overthrow the government.[148] And in 1986, a natural disaster struck: 3,000 persons died as a result of clouds of toxic gas of volcanic origin emanating from Lake Nyos.[149]

However, none of that interfered with the country's economic growth. The nation's fifth 5-year development plan for 1981 - 86 called for the expenditure of $7.6 billion, an impressive commitment, to improve agriculture and industry while further utilizing the country's abundant natural resources.[150] Since 1982, President Biya has consistently implemented conservative fiscal policies which have helped to promote economic development. And Cameroon today stands out as one of the success stories on a continent mired in poverty despite its vast natural resources. However, Cameroon itself could achieve greater economic growth and meet its people's needs had it not been for the country's leadership raiding the national treasury.

South of Cameroon is Equatorial Guinea, which before independence was called Spanish Guinea, the second least populated country on the continental mainland; Djibouti is the least populated. Equatorial Guinea is also the only Spanish-speaking African country. It consists of two provinces: the mainland territory of Rio Muni bordered by Cameroon on the north, Gabon on the

---

[148] *1986 Reader's Digest Almanac*, op. cit., p. 519.

[149] *The World Almanac and Book of Facts: 1992* (New York: Pharos Books, 1991), p. 745.

[150] "Cameroon," in the *1986 Reader's Digest Almanac*, ibid.

south, and the Gulf of Guinea in the Atlantic Ocean on the west; and the island province of Bioko. The tiny republic has several islands in the Gulf of Guinea, the largest of which is Bioko (formerly Fernando Po) about 100 miles northwest of Rio Muni.

The other islands, all of which are under the jurisdiction of Bioko, are Pagalu (formerly Annobón), Corisco, Elobey Grande, and Elobey Chico. Although Rio Muni is 13 times bigger in area than the largest island of Bioko, and has about 75 percent of the country's entire population, it is still poorer than the island; a disparity which has been a source of tension between the two provinces and one of the reasons why Bioko wants to secede.

Agriculture, including forestry, is the mainstay of the country's economy, engaging most of the labor force. Cocoa, grown on farms and plantations in Bioko, is the main export, followed by coffee, wood, and bananas from the mainland. Despite the richness of its soil and its potential natural resources, the country is exceedingly poor, a characteristic so typical of so many other African countries, not just Equatorial Guinea.

The island of Bioko has abundant fertile volcanic soil; the island is made up of three extinct volcanoes. And Rio Muni has three major rivers along which are forests of okoume, mahogany, and walnut which also grow along the coast. In addition to cocoa, coffee, wood and bananas, other agricultural products include rice, plantains, cassava, sweet potatoes, palm kernels and oil, sisal, vegetables, and fruits. There is also a small fishing industry that is being developed in a joint effort by Spain, Nigeria, and Morocco.

There are no railways anywhere in Equatorial Guinea. But the island of Bioko, which is more developed than the mainland, has a good road network, while Rio Muni lacks adequate transportation. Livestock raising, especially cattle, is also an important economic activity. Petroleum deposits have also been discovered offshore, and gold, manganese, and uranium are believed to exist.

Economic conditions declined during the 1970s because of labor and capital shortages caused by the brutal dictatorship of President Masie Nguema. One third of the population fled the country and sought refuge in neighboring countries, foreign investment declined, and donor countries reduced or suspended aid. The flight of capital proved specially disastrous for such a poverty-stricken country.

It partially recovered during the following years, but the country still has one of the lowest gross domestic products in Africa, and carries only a small amount of foreign trade. Although Equatorial Guinea's economy is weak, it still attracts some foreign workers who are not always satisfied with their wages, only to invite swift retribution, sometimes, when they protest. For example, when Nigerian migrant workers demanded higher wages during the 1970s when Masie Nguema was still in power, they were brutally suppressed, a move that led to strained relations between Nigeria and Equatorial Guinea. In 1976, 45,000 of them were evacuated amid charges of a reign of terror. Nguema was deposed and executed in 1979.

But relations between the two countries improved, and Nigeria today is one of Equatorial Guinea's major trading partners, and could help fuel the latter's economy through stronger economic ties. Aware of the imperative need for regional integration, Equatorial Guinea joined the Central African Customs and Economic Union (UDEAL) in 1983 and the franc zone in 1985. The country has some natural resources, as we have seen, but it is too small a nation to achieve substantial economic growth without integrating its economy with those of neighboring countries.

After looking at the economic potential of all the countries in Central and West Africa, in that order, we now turn our attention to East Africa, and start with Eritrea in the far northeastern corner of the continent.

The newly independent nation which won independence from Ethiopia in 1993 has about 4 million people in an area of 45,754 square miles, making it one of the smallest countries in Africa. But it is also one of the most dynamic, having fought for independence since 1962 without giving up the struggle. However, it is also one of the poorest in the world.

Much of Eritrea is mountainous, and its narrow Red Sea coastal plain is a torrid zone, one of the hottest and driest places in Africa. However, the cooler central plateau has many fertile valleys which support agriculture. Eritrea's economy and infrastructure were severely damaged by the long war for independence and by natural disasters. But the new nation inherited the entire coastline of Ethiopia when it won independence - because the coastline has always been part of Eritrea - and has long-term prospects for revenues from the development of offshore oil, offshore fishing, and tourism. Although the development of all those projects needs foreign investment, the government of Eritrea has adopted a much more independent policy with regard to foreign aid as a catalyst for the country's economic growth. According to *New African*:

> "The Eritrean government has gone cold about multi-party politics. The promises at the time of independence have been quietly dropped... The government is also cracking down on corruption... (and) is adopting a puritanical, self-reliant policy born of the liberation struggle. IMF loans have been rejected as their acceptance would mean 'aid dependency.' There are however negotiations for soft loans from the EU (European Union) Investment Bank, and the World Bank's IDA. Food aid has been accepted from Western donors, particularly the US. The food for work policy forces the hungry to work on government projects such as road building and construction to buy food aid at a subsidized price.
>
> The government is also cracking down on NGOs (Non-governmental organizations) saying that they all must leave by the end of the year, except those involved in health and educational projects. In future all expatriates working in Eritrea will have to pay a 38 percent rate of income tax.
>
> The government says that this will prevent an aid dependent mentality from developing, while speeding up post-war reconstruction. But the food security issue goes deeper than this. 'Unless we produce our own food we will not be independent,' says Ibrahim Said, the director of the Relief and Rehabilitation Commission."[151]

So the struggle continues, this time for economic independence, which demands as much discipline and unity as the liberation war itself did. For a country with scarce resources, the task is even more difficult, and divisive politics is a luxury it cannot afford when it is involved in national reconstruction especially after a devastating war which wrecked the economy. Although Eritrea's resources are limited, they are still enough to fuel economic growth.

---

[151] "Eritrea; End of the honeymoon," in the *New African*, op. cit., p. 23.

The country's main crops are cotton, wheat, and coffee. The central highlands also produce fruits, and hides and skins. Eritrea's major minerals are salt and copper, but its most important one is oil when full production begins. Then the country's economy is expected to grow exponentially, as the economies of other African oil-producing countries have. Therefore, although Eritrea remains one of the poorest countries on the continent, it also has the potential to become one of the most developed. It is one of the paradoxes of Africa that some of her poorest countries are also, potentially, some of the richest.

Next we look at neighboring Djibouti, south of Eritrea. Once known as French Somaliland and later as Afars and Issas, the names of its two main tribes, Djibouti owes its existence as a nation largely to its location on the Gulf of Eden at the southern entrance to the Red Sea, making it an important stopping place for vessels travelling through the Suez Canal. And Djibouti as a country is important mainly because of the capital city's port, Djibouti, which is the terminal of the Djibouti-Addis Adaba railway that carries 60 percent of Ethiopia's exports. Most Djiboutians live in and around Djibouti, the port city and capital, from which the country itself takes its name. They work mainly in the extensive shipping trade for which the port city is famous.

But the country is desperately poor. In fact Djibouti is one of the African countries which seem to be permanently stuck in poverty, without any hope of redemption. Most of the country is stony desert, with little or no vegetation other than thorn bushes. The climate is hot. Temperatures average above 90 degrees Fahrenheit from May to October, often soaring above 110 degrees. Rainfall is usually scant, but in some years torrential rainfall causes flooding. Because of the character of the terrain, agricultural activity is limited. Only about 10 percent of the land can provide pasture for livestock. Nomadic tribesmen - the Afars originally from Ethiopia, and the Issas from Somalia - lead poverty-stricken lives tending herds of goats, sheep, camels, and cattle. Hides and skins and live animals are the main exports. Industry is negligible.

Many Djiboutians are dependent on khat, a narcotic leaf that is a mild stimulant when chewed while still fresh. About 10 tons a day of khat are imported from Ethiopia. The drug is legal, so the government collects about $15 million a year in import duties.[152]

The only important industry in the capital Djibouti is the production of salt from the sea. There is also a camel market in town. Out of a total population of about 430,000 in the whole country, almost 400,000 of them - close to the entire population - live in the capital, which is a free port.

The nation is economically underdeveloped and nomadic pastoralism is the chief occupation. In addition to income derived from import duties imposed on the importation of khat from Ethiopia, and from the export of hides and skins and live animals, the government also gets revenues from transit taxes, fees, trade, and services. Not only the port of Djibouti but the nation's air and rail hubs are also important to commerce. Manufacturing is limited to shipbuilding and repair, building and construction, production of compressed or liquid gas, and the manufacture of foodstuffs such as dairy products and mineral-water bottling. The principal agricultural products are goats, sheep and camels - a livestock industry which entirely eclipses crop production. Djibouti imports most of its consumer goods.

In addition to sea salt, Djibouti's other natural resources include limestone, gypsum, perlite, diatoms, and geothermal energy. But it is as a port and railway terminus that Djibouti can play a critical role in the economic development of the country as a whole. With some ingenuity, Djibouti has the potential to become Africa's Singapore.

We then move on next door to Somalia. The collapse of Somalia is the subject of another book, to which we have devoted an entire chapter, but only briefly looked at the country's economic potential.

Somalia is one of the world's 25 poorest countries. Most Somalis live as nomadic herdsmen, raising camels, cattle, goats, and sheep. The country has some deposits of iron, but its most important mineral is uranium. Oil and other minerals have been discovered but have not yet been produced commercially. They include bauxite and gypsum, in addition to iron, uranium and oil. That is an impressive list for a desperately poor country. Therefore in terms of natural resources, Somalia is not really a poor country, just like most African countries are not, since they all have minerals and enough arable land

---

[152] *1986 Reader's Digest Almanac*, op. cit., p. 542.

to achieve economic growth, however limited because they are not united in a harmonious economic ensemble.

But arid, semidesert conditions make Somalia relatively unproductive. In fact Somalia is mainly desert. The country's most fertile area is between the Shibeli and Juba rivers in the south. And wildlife includes big game and many species of antelope.

Like all the other African countries, Somalia's development is hampered by various factors, among them undeveloped natural resources, poor infrastructure, lack of investment - foreign and domestic, periodic droughts, and shortage of skilled labor and high-level manpower. Somalia has no railways and only a few roads which are impassable during the rainy season; hardly any are paved.

Somalia's main exports are live animals - goats, sheep, cattle, and camels; hides and skins, clarified butter (ghee), and bananas. Bananas are the major cash crop. Other crops include citrus fruits, sugar cane, cotton, sorghum, rice, maize, beans and peanuts. Meat and fish (especially tuna) canning, sugar refining, oilseed processing, leather tanning, and the production of cotton textiles, iron products, soap, shoes and cement are the major industrial activities and products. Most of those industrial products are exported.

But all that was before the collapse of Somalia as a nation. Somalia is dead. It is no more than an amorphous collection of rival clans competing for power and territory within the boundaries of what used to be one of Africa's 53 independent countries. And what was once one of black Africa's most ethnically homogenous countries, composed almost entirely of members of the Somali ethnic group except for a few Bantu tribes in the south as well as some Arab and Asian and European communities, also turned out to be one of its most tragic failures. The Somalis may unite again and rebuild Somalia as one country. But prospects are bleak.

Next we look at the economic potential of Ethiopia, black Africa's oldest nation with 2,000 years of recorded history, and one of the most ancient kingdoms in the world whose monarchy was ended in 1974 when Emperor Haile Selassie was deposed.

One of the poorest countries in the world, Ethiopia has the third-largest population in Africa after Nigeria and Egypt. It is also a country known for its beautiful mountains, some of them snow-capped, and numerous deep valleys. But Ethiopia also has several large lakes in the southern part of the country.

The main agricultural products are coffee, teff and other millets, sorghum, barley, wheat, maize, plaintains, peas, potatoes, groundnuts, cotton, sugar cane, tobacco, fruits, and vegetables. Large numbers of poultry, cattle, sheep and goats are also raised. No large-scale mineral deposits have been found in Ethiopia, but limestone, potash, gold, copper, platinum, iron ore, and sulfur are extracted in small quantities. Ethiopia's main exports are coffee which accounts for more than half the nation's exports, oilseeds, hides and skins, and grain.

Ethiopia continues to have one of the least developed economies in the world. The country's future lies in its agricultural potential since it does not have any large quantities of minerals, at least not yet. But economic development has been hindered by poor transportation. There is only one railway - the only other one which was also Ethiopia's serves only Eritrea which is now a separate country, having won its independence from Ethiopia. Besides the single rail line, most of Ethiopia's roads are not usable year round.

A deposit of natural gas has been found, but a general lack of natural resources has hampered industrialization. Therefore without agricultural development, economic growth is almost impossible; and should droughts occur again, another catastrophe may hit Ethiopia with consequences too ghastly to contemplate as happened during the 1970s and 1980s when hundreds of thousands of Ethiopians died from starvation. And without regional integration involving the economies of all the East African countries, none of them can exploit their potential to the maximum to achieve development.

South of Ethiopia is Kenya, once one of the most prosperous countries in Africa. Like all the other African countries, Kenya is mostly agricultural, but industry is growing. In fact Kenya is the most industrialized county in East Africa.

The country's main crops are coffee, tea, sisal, pyrethrum, maize, and wheat. Others include coconut, cashew nuts, cotton, sugar cane, beans, rice, cassava, bananas, potatoes, fruits and vegetables. Large numbers of cattle and poultry are also raised. The chief minerals produced are limestone, soda ash, copper and salt. Other minerals include gold, diatomite, barytes, magnesite, felspar, sapphires, flouspar, and garnets, but they are found only in small quantities.

Kenya's major exports are coffee and tea. But fluctuations in their world prices have a devastating impact on the economy. Other exports include timber, sisal, sugar, pyrethrum, fruits and vegetables. Fishing is another major industry. Most of the fish comes from the Indian Ocean and from Lake Victoria, which is also known by its African name as Lake Nyanza. However, the single most important contribution to foreign exchange earnings is tourism, which attracts more than 700,000 visitors each year. The nation's leading tourist attractions are its coastal beaches and the national park sanctuaries for lions, elephants, leopards, cheetahs, giraffes, zebras, gazelles, and other wild animals. However, Kenya's tourism suffered during the late 1990s due to a number of factors:

> "Kenyan authorities began a hunt yesterday (February 16, 1998) for the killing of a British tourist who was stabbed to death and robbed while vacationing at a luxury safari camp... Kenyan tourism is already reeling under a combination of natural and man-made calamities, including ethnic violence on the coast in July (1997), floods caused by the El Nino weather phenomenon, uncertainty over last December's (1997) elections, and violence in the Rift Valley last month (where hundreds of Kikuyus were killed in 1992 by members of President Daniel arap Moi's Kalenjin tribe because the Kikuyus are not welcome in the region and also because they voted against President Moi in the 1992 and 1997 presidential elections). The number of visitors to the East African country dropped to 600,000 last year from a peak of more than 850,000 in 1994."[153]

In spite of the setback in tourism, Kenya still has a lot of potential for economic growth, although there has been deterioration of the economic situation in general through the decades. One of Kenya's advantages is that it has a well-developed transportation system, and in the 1980s the railways were further improved. But the system has not been well-maintained. The road and railway network - critical to economic development - and the

[153] "Tourist at Kenya Resort is Stabbed to Death in Robbery," in *The Boston Globe*, February 17, 1998, p. A-16.

economy as a whole have deteriorated since Moi became president following the death of Kenya's first president and founding father of the nation, Mzee Jomo Kenyatta, on August 22, 1978. He is said to have died at 89, but had no record of his birth and is believed to have been older than that. Hundreds of thousands of Kenyans lined the route of his funeral procession.

The deterioration of Kenya's economy is due to rampant corruption through the years under Moi's presidency. There was corruption under Mzee Jomo Kenyatta as well, but it got worse under Moi to the point where Kenya has now become one of the poorest and most corrupt countries in the world. Yet it used to be one of the richest in Africa.

The rejuvenation of the country's economy will greatly depend on whether or not the government fights corruption. Kenya's agricultural potential is enormous - it has some of the most fertile land on the continent - and its tourist industry is probably the largest in Africa, assets which can be used to fuel and sustain economic growth indefinitely. Kenya once had a vibrant economy precisely because it exploited those resources and attracted foreign investment, although the vast majority of the wananchi (the people) did not benefit from such prosperity. The country's wealth was almost exclusively for the elite as is still the case today. But the country still has the potential to become one of the richest, and most developed, in the entire Third World.

South of Kenya is Tanzania, which was the subject of the last chapter, as a case study. Therefore we turn west of Kenya and look at Uganda, one of the fastest-growing economics on the continent. It is a success story to which we are going to devote more time, as we look at Uganda's phenomenal growth from a continental perspective as well.

Uganda is, without question, the most fertile country in Africa. Winston Churchill called it "the pearl of Africa." And there is a saying in Uganda, given credence by foreigners as well, that if you stick a dry twig into the country's fertile soil, it will sprout food the next day. As *The Economist* put it:

> "Uganda is so fertile that people say a walking stick stuck in the ground will sprout bananas the next morning. But Ugandan peasant farmers, who produce more food than their families can eat, find it hard to deliver the food to people who want it and need it in eastern

Zaire, Rwanda and Burundi. Up to 40 percent of African crops are lost to poor transportation and poor storage."[154]

Unlike all the other African countries which are only partly fertile and some hardly at all, most of Uganda is made up of fertile land, a plateau whose elevation of 4,000 feet gives the country a mild climate. Except in the arid north, temperatures rarely exceed 85 degrees or fall below 60 degrees Fahrenheit.

Uganda's chief food crops are bananas, sweet potatoes, maize, pulses, cassava, millet, sorghum, groundnuts, fruits, and vegetables. The principal cash and export crops are coffee, cotton, tea, tobacco, sugar cane, and groundnuts. Large numbers of poultry, cattle, goats, and sheep are also raised. Fishing, especially in Lake Victoria and River Nile, as well as in the country's other lakes and rivers, is also a very important part of the economy. And a lot of hardwood, especially mahogany, is another major export. But it is coffee which is the leading export, and Uganda is one of the world's major producers.

Copper was once Uganda's main mineral for export, but it has been virtually mined out. But the country has other minerals, although they are extracted on a small scale: tin, iron, beryl, tungsten, gold, cobalt, limestone, and salt.

Uganda also has a lot of hydroelectric potential. It has a large hydroelectric plant at Owen Falls, one of the largest in Africa, located on the Nile River where it leaves Lake Victoria. Uganda's healthy economy is also clearly shown by the fact that the annual value of its exports is usually considerably higher than the value of its imports. Coffee accounts for 95 percent of the total value of exports, followed by cotton, copper, and tea. But the other cash crops and minerals as well as wood products, especially mahogany, are also important exports.

Uganda's economy was devastated during Idi Amin's reign of terror, but it made spectacular recovery under President Yoweri Museveni, a former socialist, who embraced capitalism in order to develop his country. And he set

---

[154] "A Survey of sub-Saharan Africa: Africa for the Africans - Withering Indictment," in *The Economist*, September 7, 1996, p. 12 of the survey.

aside his socialist beliefs probably unwillingly, since he admits he is still a follower of Julius Nyerere whose belief in socialism remains unshaken, as we saw in the previous chapter. As Peter Graff reported from Uganda's capital Kampala in December 1997 after interviewing Museveni:

> "(Museveni is) a former guerrilla leader who spent much of his life in exile in socialist Tanzania and received his education at the University of Dar es Salaam, then a hotbed of post-colonial leftist radicalism. At the time, Tanzania's patriarch, Julius Nyerere, was a hero to most students for implementing the policy of 'ujamaa' (African socialism)... Museveni still considers himself a disciple of Nyerere, but says common sense drove him to abandon socialist economics. His fellow leftists, he now says, simply misjudged human nature. 'Do you make people produce by appealing to the altruism which was very much in short supply? Or do you make them produce by making use of their selfishness, which is in abundance?' he said in a recent interview."[155]

Uganda's spectacular comeback is due to economic liberalization, privatization, and investment promotion, all of which have been pursued vigorously probably more than anywhere else on the continent. As Museveni says about the free-market policies he has borrowed from the West:

> "There are still other problems in Europe, but the problem of shortages, of want, of need, has been somehow addressed."[156]

In fact President Museveni's ideas across the socioeconomic political spectrum have had a profound impact beyond Uganda's borders, altering African political thought. He has been hailed as Africa's leading statesman and a representative of the new generation of African leaders in the post-Cold War era. "His Socratic style has won Museveni a reputation as the continent's most self-consciously intellectual leader. And his success, especially in the

[155] Peter Graff, "Ex-Leninist Leads Uganda to Prosperity: Single-party; Rule Troubles Free-Market Admirers," in *The Boston Globe*, December 7, 1997, p. A-44.
[156] Yoweri Kaguta Museveni, quoted by Peter Graff, ibid.

field of economics, seems to speak for itself."[157] And Michael Southwick, former American ambassador to Uganda during Museveni's presidency, described Museveni as Africa's "best president apart from Nelson Mandela."[158] Other people simply refer to him as Africa's "other statesman," second only to Mandela.[159]

Political pundits across the continent also call Museveni an African Bismarck. Not only has he revived Uganda's economy; he has also been the major sponsor of the rebel movements in his region: He armed the Rwandan Patriotic Front which toppled the genocidal Hutu regime in Rwanda in 1994; he sponsored Laurent Kabila's rebellion which ousted Mobutu in Zaire in 1997; and he continues to arm and support the Sudanese People's Liberation Army in southern Sudan led by his friend and former classmate, Dr. John Garang, in its fight against Arab domination. As one diplomat based in East Africa put it:

> "It appears Museveni is the regional power broker who has emerged as a result of all this. He seems to be relishing his role."[160]

Museveni himself has acknowledged that his ideas are beginning to have an impact beyond Uganda. Referring to his own rebellion in Uganda which propelled him into power, he stated:

> "We were the first to overthrow a dictatorship, a black dictatorship. Our contribution is by way of example."[161]

Almost all the other African governments which have been overthrown have been toppled by soldiers of the national army; they are the ones who usually execute military coups. There have been only two exceptions so far: in Uganda and in Congo-Brazzaville. Museveni's fighters were rebels, not

---

[157] P. Graff, ibid.

[158] Michael Southwick, quoted ibid.

[159] James C. McKinley, Jr., "Uganda Leader Stands Tall in New African Order," in *The New York Times,* June 15, 1997, p. Y-3.

[160] An unidentified diplomat, quoted by J.C. McKinley, ibid.

[161] Museveni, quoted ibid.

regular soldiers, who fought the nation army, and won. A similar case happened in Congo-Brazzaville where the Cobra militia led by Denis Sassou-Nguesso fought the national army of President Pascal Lissouba for control of the capital, Brazzaville, and overthrew him after a four-month civil war. But unlike the Ugandan leadership overthrown by Museveni and his rebels, Lissouba was a democratically elected leader; Major-General Tito Okello, the Ugandan head of state toppled by Museveni's National Resistance Movement (NRM), was not.

Since Museveni came to power in 1986, he has been able to communicate his message to all segments of society, all the way to the grassroots, and it has resonated well. His ideology is simple and pragmatic. He bluntly states what most leaders don't say publicly, because they know they would be talking about themselves. He says, and rightly so, that for too long African politicians have duped the common people, manipulating tribal loyalties to perpetuate themselves in power and steal millions of dollars in foreign aid and from people's taxes. He contends that the real struggle on the continent is between corrupt leaders and the poor masses they exploit without the slightest compunction; it is a struggle the people must wage relentlessly in order to have leaders who are dedicated and accountable for their actions.

However, he is also quick to point out that most African nations are not ready for multiparty democracy. Such democracies, he explains, need a thriving economy and a strong middle class which can then form political parties based on issues, and not based on tribal and regional loyalties. He cites Uganda's past as an example, especially during the sixties and also after the ouster of Idi Amin, a period when political parties were no more than fronts for tribal interests. The result was ethnic conflict and bloodshed. That is the case throughout Africa where political parties are used by "national" leaders to grab power for their own tribes and tribal allies. Museveni emphatically states:

> "Multiparty democracy will come, but it will come when the society has got a social base for it. The problem here is you are talking about

> a multiparty democracy in a pre-industrial society. The society must be transformed. We don't have a middle class."[162]

On the economic front, Museveni is just as emphatic, saying that the engine for progress and social transformation must be private enterprise, not foreign aid. Private enterprises will fuel the economy and lead to the formation of a large middle class, which is itself necessary for economic development as a source of investment and for the establishment of issue-based - not ethnic-oriented - political parties which can then, as trans-tribal parties, compete in a truly multiparty democracy that transcends tribalism and regionalism.

Museveni also says it is very important that African countries must stop blaming colonialism for their problems and relying on foreign aid for economic development. It is a sentiment shared by other Africans, including Eritrean President Isayas Afwerki who has rejected IMF loans for his country, and the Nigerian economist Adebayo Adedeji who was Executive Secretary of the UN Economic Commission for Africa (ECA). As Adedeji stated in an interview in October 1983 when he was still Executive Secretary of the ECA:

> "Quite frankly, I think the African governments have to accept full responsibility for the state of the economies today. The time has passed when we should lay this blame at the doors of others. If we continue to do that, it means we are not responsible people."[163]

Therefore Africa's main problem is not an economic one; it is political, due to lack of good leadership in most cases, a point also emphasized by Adedeji. As he stated in an interview 13 years later with *The Economist* in September 1996:

> "What we confront in Africa is primarily a political crisis, albeit with devastating economic consequences."[164]

---

[162] Ibid.

[163] Adebayo Adedeji, in *Africa Report,* op. cit., p. 14.

[164] A. Adedeji, quoted in "A Survey of sub-Saharan Africa," in *The Economist,* op. cit., p. 4 of the survey.

Economic development is impossible without good leadership. And Africa has poor leadership mainly because of corruption. Most leaders treat the national treasuries as their personal bank accounts, to be emptied at will. Nor will Africa be able to develop without economic integration leading to the formation of an African common market, an idea espoused by Nyerere (and other leaders) for decades during which he also called for the unification of Africa as much as Nkrumah did. It is a vision Museveni shares. As James McKinley stated in his report from Kampala, Uganda, in *The New York Times* in June 1997:

> "Mr. Museveni, now 53, learned on Mr. Nyerere's knee. He studied in Dar es Salaam, Tanzania, becoming steeped in the older man's socialism... For Mr. Museveni, Mr. Mobutu (whom he helped overthrow) was the major obstacle to his dream of an African common market. He would like to see a collective of African nations - ruled by people with similar philosophies - with open trade between them and less dependence on the West. The idea goes back to Mr. Nyerere, who has said he always wanted to forge 'a United States of Africa.'"[165]

Nyerere expressed some of his views calling for a continental union in his article "A United States of Africa," published in "The Journal of Modern African Studies" back in March 1963.[166] A strong advocate of African unity, even after he stepped down from the presidency, he has consistently articulated his Pan-Africanist position in his other writings and speeches

[165] J.C. McKinley, "Ugandan Leader Stands Tall in New African Order," ibid. See also Julius Nyerere, "A United States of Africa," in *The Journal of Modern African Studies*, Vol. 1, No. 1, March 1963; and Nyerere, "The Dilemma of the Pan-Africanist," "Africa Must Not Fight Africa," and "A New Look at Conditions for Unity," in *Freedom and Socialism: A Selection from Writings and Speeches 1965-1967* (Dar es Salaam, Tanzania, Oxford University Press, 1968), pp. 207-217, 218-222, 291-300. See also p. 195: "Africa will only be secure in its freedom, and only allow real economic prosperity for its people, when the present multitude of small states are replaced by one internationally sovereign authority ('A United States of Africa')."

[166] Nyerere, "A United States of Africa," in *The Journal of Modern African Studies*, ibid.

through the decades. His article, "A United States of Africa," was published just three months before the African heads of state and government met in Addis Adaba, Ethiopia and founded the Organization of African Unity. President Nkrumah also had his book, "Africa Must Unite,"[167] published just in time for that historic meeting. Unfortunately leaders like Mobutu, who ruled what is probably potentially the richest and most strategically located country on the African continent, were a major obstacle to the realization of that goal, and the OAU ended up being no more than a prestigious debating club.

If Congo (then Zaire) had good leadership, and a solid infrastructure - roads, railways, communications and storage facilities and good shipping on the Congo River and other waterways in that vast country - the entire region of East-Central Africa would have been an economic powerhouse during all those years Mobutu was in power. Instead, for 32 years, he just let the country rot. The nation's infrastructure crumbled, and almost all the roads and railways - as well as schools, clinics, and factories - were reclaimed by the jungle. As Museveni put it:

> "Talk of the African common market is just a fable as long as you've got people like Mobutu... What is new now is that you are having more and more people (leaders) who are like-minded, of the same thinking, and once you have such people, they work together. The people are waking up. The people of Africa are waking up."[168]

They are indeed waking up. But they still have a long way to go in their fight against tribalism, tyranny, and corruption which are sapping so much of Africa's wealth and energy. Everything is going down the drain. As Howard French reported from Monrovia, Liberia:

> "Africa's most troubled countries are almost all fantastically rich in minerals, boasting combinations of alluvial diamonds, gold, tropical

[167] Kwame Nkrumah, *Africa Must Unite* (New York: Praeger, 1963). See also Nkrumah, *I Speak of Freedom: A Statement of African Ideology* (New York: Praeger, 1961).
[168] Museveni, quoted by J.C. McKinley, "Uganda Leader Stands Tall in New African Order," in *The New York Times,* ibid.

timber and oil. (But) the exploitation of these kinds of products rarely involves much of the systematic hard work that can bind a nation together and give it a productive ethic. The situation is more akin to prospecting and poaching by soldiers and mercenaries or other hired bands than it is to people coming together and building a country. 'The leaders of many African countries have just been raping their countries,' said one European aid official who spoke in the wake of the Brazzaville fighting, 'and we have been helping them do it, participating in it step by step, but pretending that it is none of our fault.'"[169]

It is for the new African leadership to avoid repeating the same mistakes; it is time for them to set their countries on the right course. Museveni in Uganda has shown that there is no secret formula to peace and prosperity, except common sense and commitment to the country's well-being. Uganda's spectacular success has now become a shining example for others to emulate. During Idi Amin's reign of terror and destruction, Uganda was in even deeper trouble than most countries on the continent. Amin left it in tatters. During much of the eighties, the country was still a wreck, almost in just as much trouble as it was during the seventies. But it got out of it. Why not the rest?

Uganda is also distinguished in another respect. It is the only black African country, besides South Africa, which manufactures weapons such as armored personnel carriers with the help of South Africa. According to *New African*:

"South Africa... has sent experts to run the Nakasongola arms factory, 100 miles north of Kampala, which was formerly run by the Chinese and North Koreans. At Nakasongola the South Africans are assembling their armoured personnel carriers which are being specially modified to fight the rebels of Joseph Kony's Lords' Resistance Army (in northern Uganda). The APCs (Armored Personnel Carriers) are already used extensively in the north. They

[169] Howard W. French, "Sure, Africa's Troubled. But There Is Good News: In Even the Successful Countries, Greed and Autocracy Threaten Stability," in *The New York Times*, June 15, 1997, p. E-16.

can travel at 60 mph on good roads. South African experts are also assembling long range artillery. Among them are the G-5 guns which can hit targets 40 kms away. They are also producing grenades and ammunition."[170]

Uganda's road to success has not been paved with gold. African countries with a lot of gold and other resources - Uganda does not have - have achieved less, the leaders being the reason why.

West of Uganda is the small nation of Rwanda which is still suffering from the horrendous tragedy that befell the country in 1994 when almost the entire Tutsi population was exterminated, a subject we have addressed in a different book, "The Modern African State: Quest for Transformation." Therefore we are going to concentrate here only on the economic aspect, as we will next with regard to Rwanda's neighbor, Burundi.

Rwanda is one of the poorest and most populated countries in the world; it is also the most populated in Africa, with 673 persons per square mile.[171] The country's problems of poverty and overpopulation are made even worse by soil erosion - due to leaching caused by heavy rains, poor farming techniques and cattle feeding - which imperils cultivation, on which the economy depends. Burundi's economic development is also impeded by lack of enough arable land for its large population in so small a country, and by its lack of access to the sea - and thus to foreign markets.

One solution to the problem of overpopulation is to open up the borders of all African countries so that the people can migrate freely, a solution proposed by Julius Nyerere. But it will take a "leap of faith," from nationalism to Pan-Africanism, for African countries to make such a bold move. Most of the leaders are too parochial in their thinking, concerned only about the well-being of their own tribes, and next their countries sometimes; they are not really concerned about Africa as a whole. Only a few like Nyerere, Mandela, Museveni and Jerry Rawlings - those are only a few examples - see Africa as an organic entity. But the solution Nyerere proposes

---

[170] "South Africa Arms for Uganda," in *New African*, op. cit., p. 32.

[171] "1997 Almanac," op. cit., p. 256.

is still worth trying. As Francis Deng, a former Sudanese foreign affairs minister states in "Needed in Africa: Elastic Borders":

> "The nations of Africa's Great Lakes region are still seized by the problems of Burundi and Rwanda... What the current situation calls for first is a radically different view of borders. In the past, neighbors and farmers and herders moved across borders in search of pastures and sources of water. Colonial state borders interfered with that relative freedom of movement. From being a constraint to population mobility, these otherwise artificial borders should be modified to allow freedom of movement and regional cooperation.
>
> Former President Julius Nyerere of Tanzania has proposed a similar idea. In his view, the crisis of Rwanda and Burundi is essentially one of overpopulation and land shortage. He proposes to make arrangements for countries of the region to open up and expand economic and political space for populations now squeezed within their present boundaries. Naturally, there will be resistance to this idea, but the situation calls for difficult choices.
>
> Either Africa continues to hold the colonial borders as sacrosanct and risk implosions and even disintegration, or Africans must modify state borders, widen the scope of participation, and make creative arrangements that would ease the tensions and foster regional economic and political cooperation...
>
> Statesmen must try to balance and reconcile the forces of fragmentation at the national level with the forces of integration at the regional level. These internal and external dynamics also dictate that within a given country, state sovereignty can no longer be defined negatively as a barricade against external involvement. It must be recast as primarily a positive concept of responsibility toward the citizens and all those falling under the jurisdiction of the state...

The international community can generate strategic thinking along the lines of the regional economic and security arrangements envisaged by President Nyerere."[172]

Because of the tragedy caused by the conflict in both Rwanda and Burundi, even the people themselves in those two countries, especially the Hutus who are dominated by the Tutsis, proposed a similar solution; saying they wouldn't mind moving to other parts of Africa and settle there permanently, but not anywhere outside the continent. They insisted that they wanted to live only in Africa. Some Hutus mentioned West Africa, while others started moving, saying they were walking all the way to Zambia, when humanitarian agencies under UN supervision started moving them out of Tanzania to send them back to Rwanda and Burundi. Unfortunately, there is not enough land in those two countries for all the people. And as we noted, Rwanda is the most heavily populated country in Africa.

The country's chief crops are bananas, cassava, sweet potatoes, pulses, sorghum, maize, fruits, vegetables, and yams. The principal cash crops are coffee, tea, and pyrethrum. Large numbers of cattle, goats, and sheep are also raised. Like in neighboring Burundi, most of the cattle are owned by the Tutsis, for whom they are a symbol of wealth and status more than a source of food or income.

Rwanda also has some minerals. Tin ore, wolframite, beryl, and colombo-tantalite are mined in significant quantities; and natural gas is produced at Lake Kivu. Gold is another important mineral, although it is not mined in large quantities.

The country's major exports are coffee, tea, and tin. Other important exports include wolframite which is a form of tungsten, and pyrethrum.

Those are significant resources - agricultural and mineral - which can help the country overcome poverty. Rwanda also has a good road network which can facilitate economic growth. But the country has no railroads critical to the transportation of much larger quantities of goods and exports. However, an international airport was opened at Kigali, the capital, in 1986 and could play

[172] Francis M. Deng, "Needed in Africa: Elastic Borders," in the *International Herald Tribune,* December 21, 1996, p. 6.

a major role in the import/export business of the landlocked nation if the centuries-old ethnic conflict between the Hutus and the Tutsis is contained or resolved. But like the rest of the countries in the region – including prosperous Uganda – and across Africa, Rwanda's future lies in the establishment of stronger economic ties with its neighbors, eventually leading to an economic union, a common market, and a common currency preferably on a continental scale.

Next we look at neighboring Burundi. Like Rwanda, Burundi is also one of the poorest and most populated countries in the world, and the second most populous in Africa – next only to Rwanda – with 553 people per square mile. Now compare that with Nigeria's population density of 291 per square mile. Also compare Rwanda's population density of 673 per square mile with Nigeria's. Both far surpass Nigeria. Yet Nigeria is the most populous country in Africa.[173]

Burundi depends almost exclusively upon coffee for its income; coffee accounts for about 90 percent of the country's exports.[174] Reliance upon this single commodity and the poor transportation infrastructure of the landlocked country are major obstacles to economic development. However, Burundi has even more natural resources than Rwanda. But like Rwanda, Burundi's soil is mostly eroded, although very fertile. Most Burundians live very simple lives, raising beans, cassava, maize, yams, bananas, groundnuts, and fishing in Lake Tanganyika.

In spite of the country's grinding poverty, the people have large numbers of cattle, goats, and sheep. Cattle hides and skins are also one of the major exports. In addition to coffee, Burundi's other important export crops are tea and cotton. Although the country relies almost entirely on agricultural exports to earn foreign exchange, it has other resources many African countries – and other elsewhere – don't have.

Burundi has several minerals, but they are now mined only in small quantities. And exploration for more minerals continues. Burundi's minerals include nickel, which is also found in large quantities just across the border in

---

[173] *1997 Almanac*, op. cit., pp. 160, 242 and 256.

[174] *1986 Reader's Digest Almanac*, op. cit., p. 517.

neighboring Tanzania; uranium, rare earth oxide, peat, cobalt, copper, unexploited platinum, vanadium, gold, kaolin, and tin.

All those minerals and the country's agricultural export crops of coffee, tea and cotton are more than enough to make Burundi rich. Unfortunately, Burundi's poor transportation system and its distance from the sea have been major obstacles to its economic development; more than 70 percent of Burundi's exports and imports go through Tanzania. Also Burundi has no railways, and less than 200 miles of paved roads.[175] And like its neighboring Rwanda, Burundi is wracked by ethnic warfare between the Hutus and the Tutsis, another major obstacle to progress.

Our next stop is further south. We go across Tanzania down to Malawi, another very poor country, yet one which is making remarkable progress in improving its economic situation. West of Malawi is Zambia, which we looked at in the first chapter, as we did Zimbabwe which lies south of Zambia.

Besides Malawi, the only other countries in sub-Saharan Africa which we have not looked at are Mozambique, Swaziland, South Africa, Lesotho, Namibia, and Angola. We are going to examine the economic potential of each one of them in that order, starting with Malawi.

Malawi is primarily an agricultural country, like the rest on the continent. It has a very low per capita income which can be raised substantially with the full exploitation of its resources. Malawi's principal crops are maize, cotton, millet, rice, groundnuts, cassava, beans, potatoes, sorghum, sugar cane, fruits and vegetables, grown mostly on small farms owned by individual farmers and families. The rest of the farmland is consolidated into large estates where tea, tobacco, sugar cane and tung oil are produced. The country's major exports are sugar, tobacco, groundnuts, cotton, maize, and coffee. Rubber is also another important export commodity.

Large numbers of poultry, goats, cattle, and pigs are also raised in Malawi. There is also a small fishing industry which has great potential for expansion since 20 percent of Malawi's total area is made up of Lake Nyasa (which is sometimes called Lake Malawi) one of East Africa's three Great

[175] Ibid.

Lakes, which like the other two is also one of the largest in the world. All three are freshwater lakes and have fish in abundance.

Forestry products are another important part of Malawi's economy; since the 1970s the forestry industry has expanded considerably. In terms of mineral wealth, not a lot of minerals are mined in Malawi. But there are substantial deposits of bauxite, and further exploration is underway for apatite and coal. Malawi also has limestone and uranium, making its list of minerals - bauxite, coal, uranium, limestone and apatite - an impressive one for such a poor country. With its combined resources of minerals and agricultural products - as well as an abundance of fish in Lake Nyasa and a variety of forest products including rubber and timber - there is no reason why Malawi should remain poor.

South and southeast of Malawi is Mozambique, another very poor country; in fact it was once the poorest countries in the world. Yet Mozambique is one of Africa's richest, in terms of natural resources.

The country has substantial mineral resources, but development of mining has been hindered by poor transportation and civil war through the decades since the country won independence from Portugal in 1975; and as a result of Mozambique's support for Zimbabwe nationalist guerrillas during the war for independence in what was then Rhodesia. Rhodesia won independence as Zimbabwe in 1980. The 20-year civil war in Mozambique between the rebels of the Mozambique National Resistance (RENAMO) and the FRELIMO government ended only recently in October 1992. The infrastructure was almost totally destroyed during the war.

In addition to an abundance of minerals, Mozambique also has substantial agricultural potential. There are also extensive hardwood forests, and palms grow widely along the coast and near the country's numerous rivers.

But in spite of the country's abundant wealth, the vast majority of the people live in abject poverty because the resources have not been fully exploited. In 1990, Mozambique was estimated to be the poorest country in the world.[176] The main cash and export crops are cashew nuts, sugar cane, copra, tea, cotton, timber, sisal, and groundnuts. Other crops include maize,

[176] *Columbia Encyclopedia*, op. cit., p. 1849.

sweet potatoes, millet, cassava, palm kernels, fruits and vegetables, mainly for domestic consumption. But palm kernels are also exported.

The livestock industry, especially the raising of cattle and goats, is also an important part of the country's economy. But expansion of the industry is severely limited by the tsetse fly. Forestry and fishing are also important economic activities which have great potential for growth. Mozambique is already one of the world's major exporters of shrimp, and with bigger investment, can greatly expand its fishing industry. The country has plenty of fish and other seafoods in its Indian Ocean territorial waters along its extensive 1,600-mile coastline; in Lake Nyasa one third of which falls within Mozambia's boundaries; as well as in the country's numerous rivers including the Zambezi, and the Ruvuma which also forms part of the boundary with Tanzania. The two rivers are some of Africa's biggest.

The extent of Mozambique's mineral wealth has not been fully determined, but it is believed to be extensive, as preliminary surveys show. The country's known minerals include coal, copper, bauxite, titanium, iron, tantalite, fluorite, gold, and diamonds. Mozambique is also believed to have petroleum and natural gas; several oil seeps have been found just across the border in Tanzania, and the same geological features extend south into Mozambique.

Mozambique also has enormous hydroelectric potential. Electricity from the giant Cabora Bassa hydroelectric project on the Zambezi River near Tete in west-central Mozambique is also exported to South Africa, generating substantial income for the poverty-stricken nation. The 3,600-megawatt capacity dam was completed on December 5, 1974, and is one of the largest in Africa. It is expected to play a critical role in the exploitation of the country's vast resources. Mozambique has another major hydroelectric plant on the Revúe River, one of the country's several main rivers. Mozambique also derives considerable revenue from handling some of the foreign trade of nearby countries, especially Swaziland, Zimbabwe, Malawi, Zambia, and Botswana, which go through its four main ports of Maputo the country's capital, Beira, Nacala, and Lumbo.

Mozambique also has a lot of potential to develop its tourist industry. The beaches on its 1,600-mile coastline attract thousands of tourists from neighboring South Africa and other countries every year. Fishing is one of their most important activities while vacationing on the sandy beaches. And competition with much more developed South Africa for tourists from other parts of the world will also help Mozambique to expand and modernize its tourist industry in order to stay in the business and earn substantial income.

South of Mozambique, between Mozambique and South Africa, is one of Africa's smallest countries: Swaziland. It is surrounded on three sides by South Africa. Although Swaziland is very small, it is also one of the richest countries on the continent. It has the third-highest per capita income on the continental mainland, after Libya (first) and Gabon and Namibia (tied second). Botswana is fourth, South Africa fifth, Congo-Brazzaville sixth, and Ivory Coast seventh.[177]

Once dependent on subsistence farming for its economy, Swaziland has become one of the most prosperous countries in Africa. British and South African investors - during apartheid in South Africa - helped develop iron mines, sugar refineries, a pulp paper mill; and sugar, pineapple, and orange plantations. An east-west railroad also was built across the country to carry exports to the port of Maputo, Mozambique.

Called "the Switzerland of Africa" (Switzerland is the Swaziland of Europe, of course), Swaziland attracts a large number of tourists each year to its gambling casinos, hotels, golf courses, and game preserves. And a lot of efforts have been made to diversify the economy in a country whose climate is highly suitable for agriculture. Average temperatures range from 60 degrees Fahrenheit in the mountains west to a mild 72 degrees in the subtropical lowlands in the east.

Swaziland is also traversed by four major river systems, which have vast hydroelectric potential and are increasingly used for irrigation; and has excellent agricultural and ranching land than most countries on the continent. The country's main crops are sugar cane, citrus fruits, pineapples, rice, cotton, maize, groundnuts, sorghum, and tobacco. Of all the fruits produced in the country, pineapples are the most important, followed by oranges. Cattle, a major export, and goats are also raised in large numbers. Forestry and lumbering are also a very important part of the economy. In fact the forestry and lumbering industry in Swaziland is far more developed than in most other African countries except, perhaps, the Ivory Coast, the most prosperous

---

[177] *1997 Almanac*, op. cit., pp. 157, 170, 171, 191, 223, 237, and 264.

country in West Africa. The forests of Swaziland's highveld yield wood pulp and timber which are produced by foreign concerns and account for about one-fifth of all export earnings.

Swaziland also has extensive mineral resources. They include asbestos, coal, iron, and diamonds which are already being extracted; and unexploited reserves of gold, beryl, silica, and barytes. Tourism is, of course, a thriving industry, one of the most successful on the entire continent, drawing tourists from all over the world to "the Switzerland of Africa."

Swaziland is, simply, one of the most well-endowed African countries in terms of agricultural and mineral resources as well as tourist attractions. And it could become one of the richest countries in the world in telescoped time if all of its potential is harnessed to the maximum to achieve economic growth. It is already one of the richest in the entire Third World.

Next, we look at South Africa, Africa's economic powerhouse. It has the largest gross domestic product (GDP) and is the most industrialized country on the entire continent. Nigeria, the richest black nation in the world besides South Africa itself, is a distant second in terms of GDP; and its manufacturing sector produces only one-seventh of what South Africa produces. According to *The Economist*:

> "South Africa possesses... a manufacturing sector seven times as large as second-place Nigeria's and two-fifths of the GNP of (the entire) sub-Saharan Africa."[178]

In terms of industrial capacity, South Africa is a First World nation with highly trained manpower in all fields including nuclear. And in terms of military might, it is the continent's super power. Its nuclear scientists produced Africa's first atomic bomb, first tested in 1979:

---

[178] "A Survey of Sub-Saharan Africa," in *The Economist,* op. cit. p. 6 of the survey. See also R. Stephen Brent, "South Africa's Economic Woes: Tough Road to Prosperity - Cry the Beloved Country," in "Foreign Affairs," March/April 1996, pp. 113-126; and John Chettle, "South Africa After the Miracle: Can South Africa Be A Normal State?," in *The National Interest,* No. 47, Washington, D.C., Spring 1997, pp. 64-75.

> "A flash of light detected by a U.S. satellite off the southern coast of South Africa on September 22, 1979, was interpreted by some nuclear scientists as evidence South Africa had tested an atomic bomb. However, the government denied doing so."[179]

In spite of the government's denial, the nuclear test was confirmed by several other observers.[180] Probably the best confirmation came several years later when Nelson Mandela became president of South Africa and announced that his country would not keep its nuclear weapons under the new dispensation.

Although the nuclear bomb was developed by the apartheid regime with the help of Israel - and the United States itself, frankly speaking, although it reported the nuclear test, to disassociate itself - to intimidate the rest of the African countries and hold them hostage, and even use the weapon against them, because of their strong support for the South African freedom fighters; the new multiracial democratic government of South Africa had as much right to keep the bomb in its arsenal just like any other country, had it chosen to do so. And all the other African countries even today have the right to have it just like the United States or any other world power does. And the reason is simple, however offensive it may be to the big powers: You have no right to tell us what not to have when you insist that you have the right to have what you say we cannot have.

Why don't the big powers abolish their nuclear weapons first - since they are so bad - before they ask others not to acquire or develop nuclear capability? They have no right to have those weapons for the same reason they say other's shouldn't have them. Yet the big powers get offended when they are told that, obviously because they are morally "superior" and therefore deserve to have all kinds of weapons of mass destruction: Get rid of your gun, but I am keeping mine so that I can point it at your head. That's their logic, of might is right. Equating military superiority with moral superiority – that is what is offensive. But acquisition of nuclear weapons by poverty-stricken African countries will, of course, be a waste of money and resources.

---

[179] *1986 Reader's Digest Almanac*, op. cit., p. 651.

[180] *The New York Times,* September 1979; "Africa," October 1979; *Africa Report,* November-December 1979.

Although South Africa no longer has nuclear weapons, it still remains a super power - and is the only super power - in the African geopolitical context, but for constructive purposes; not the way it was under the diabolical regime of apartheid when it was a destabilizing force on the continent and a threat to world peace. And it has the capacity, economic and technical, to facilitate economic development on a continental scale.

Fabulously rich in natural resources, South Africa leads the world in gold production, and also produces about a third of the world's diamonds. It also has large deposits of iron, coal, copper, tin, uranium, and many other minerals. It lacks only natural petroleum in terms of vital natural resources, but has undertaken large-scale production of petroleum from coal, thanks to its superior technology unequaled anywhere else on the continent and in most parts of the world.

The country also has enormous agricultural potential. South Africa's fertile farmlands produce large quantities of wheat and several other food crops, with a lot of it left over for export.

Until about 1870 the economy of the region – there was no country called South African then until the Union of South Africa was formed in 1910 - was almost entirely agricultural. With the discovery of diamonds in 1867, mining became the foundation for rapid economic development, which was accelerated by the discovery of gold in 1886. In the twentieth century, the country's economy was diversified so that by 1945 the manufacturing sector accounted for the largest share of the gross national product.[181]

But South Africa's agricultural sector also dwarfs those of other African countries in terms of output, although theirs account for more than 90 percent of the gross national product. This contrast shows how developed the South African economy is. The country's sophisticated farming techniques, including mechanization and the use of fertilizers, account for the difference.

South Africa's chief crops are maize, wheat, sorghum, potatoes, groundnuts, citrus fruits, apples, cotton, tobacco, sugar cane, and vegetables. Large numbers of dairy and beef cattle, sheep, goats including many Angora goats, and hogs are also raised. Wool is another major export. Fishing is also a very important industry. In fact South Africa has the largest and most

---

[181] *Columbia Encyclopedia*, op. cit., p. 2568.

sophisticated fishing industry on the continent. A lot of fishmeal is produced for domestic consumption and for export. Tourism is also a large industry, ranking South Africa together with Kenya, Tanzania, Zimbabwe, Zambia, Swaziland and Botswana among the leading countries on the continent involved in the tourist industry.

South Africa also has very good road and railway networks and sea ports unmatched anywhere else on the continent. It is also building a major hydroelectric and irrigation scheme, the Orange River Project, in the central part of the country which is expected to be completed in the year 2000. All that is going to accelerate South Africa's economic growth which is already far advanced than any on the continent.

But it is the country's mineral wealth for which South Africa is known round the globe, and which was responsible for its rapid economic growth. The name South Africa has become synonymous with gold and diamonds. The country's list of minerals is dazzling, and the quantity astounding. We look at the entire list.

South Africa is the world's largest producer of gold, diamonds, and chrome. The other minerals the country produces in large quantities include copper, iron, coal, tin, uranium, asbestos, platinum, silver, antimony, and manganese. South Africa is also rich in nickel, titanium, phosphates, and vanadium. And it has several other less well-known minerals.

South Africa is already one of the richest and most developed countries in the world, mainly because of its vast mineral wealth. But as we pointed out earlier, Congo, the former Zaire, has even more minerals than South Africa, and far greater agricultural potential. And collectively, the entire continent has huge quantities of a dazzling array of minerals, an enormous potential which, if fully exploited, could make Africa the richest continent on earth; that is without even taking into account its enormous agricultural resources.

Our next stop is within South Africa itself. Entirely surrounded by South Africa is one of Africa's smallest and poorest countries, Lesotho, formerly known as Basutoland when it was under British rule. The small kingdom has another distinctive feature: Lesotho is one of the very few places in Africa with ski resorts. It is a rugged, mile-high plateau country nestled amid the 11,000-foot peaks of the Drakensberg Mountains. Only about 10 percent of the land can be farmed. Temperatures average 45 degrees Fahrenheit in July and 70 degrees in January. Lesotho is also one of only three kingdoms which remain on the entire African continent. The other two kingdoms are Morocco and Swaziland.

Lesotho has few known natural resources and, because of its poverty, its destiny is inextricably linked with that of South Africa. About a fourth of the country's men travel to South Africa for several months each year to earn cash by working in the mines. Heavily dependent on foreign aid, Lesotho imports food and goods worth 12 times its exports, a frightening disproportion. An agricultural country, Lesotho is, in addition to foreign aid, also heavily dependent on livestock and food crops such as wheat, maize, sorghum, barley, beans and peas for survival. Poor farming techniques have also resulted in a shortage of good land.

But maize, sorghum, and wheat are extensively cultivated. Production, however, is inadequate for domestic consumption, and these staples must be imported from South Africa. Sheep are bred for wool, and cattle and Angora goats are also raised. Lesotho's mineral resources are limited to diamonds, which have been exploited on a large scale by foreign firms, especially South African, since the 1960s.

Lesotho has one of the highest literacy rates in Africa, but that has not been enough to spur economic development. The country's major exports are wool, cattle, mohair, diamonds, hides and skins, and baskets. But its economy is so tied to South Africa's that it uses the South African rand as its currency, although it also has its own currency, the loti. Just as its economy is tied to South Africa's, so is its growth. Lesotho cannot develop without fully integrating its economy with that of South Africa and the other neighboring countries as they have been trying to do for a number of years as members of the Southern African Development Community.

From Lesotho, we go west across South Africa to Namibia, one of the largest and richest countries which lies between South Africa and the Atlantic Ocean. The country was once known as South West Africa.

Together with Gabon, Namibia has the second-largest per capita income on the continental mainland, next only to Libya's. It is one of the world's leading diamond-producing countries and depends on diamond exports for nearly a third of its gross national product. Walvis Bay on the Atlantic Coast is the country's main port, and nearly 1,500 miles of rail lines connect the port to mining and ranching areas across the country, providing excellent transportation for export goods to the sea outlet.

The mineral sector accounts for most exports, diamonds and uranium being the leading commodities. Other important minerals exported include copper, lead, zinc, gold, marble and semi-precious stones. Besides minerals, Namibia's other major exports are fish, beef, cattle, and Karakul fur pelts. Livestock dominates the agricultural sector, and fishing is one of the most developed industries on the continent, as is Namibia's livestock industry: meat processing and fish canning are the country's two other main industries, besides mining.

Livestock, not crops, constitutes the backbone of the agricultural sector because of inadequate rainfall which makes it impossible to grow a lot of food and cash crops which could account for a large agricultural output. Goats and sheep are raised mainly in the south, and cattle in the north. Game animals are also raised. Agricultural income is derived mainly from Karakul pelts, livestock and dairy goods.

But, like neighboring South Africa, it is the mineral wealth for which Namibia is known. There is an extensive mining industry, run mainly by foreign-owned companies, and it generates substantial earnings; for example, in 1988, mining accounted for almost 73 percent of export earnings, and still contributes as much today. Here are all the major minerals produced by Namibia for export: diamonds, uranium, copper, lead, manganese, zinc, salt, lithium, silver, amethyst, germanium, vanadium, gold, semi-precious stones, and marble.

And although fishing remains a major industry, it also has had a negative impact in one area. Fleets owned by commercial companies, some of them foreign, operate extensively within Namibia's territorial waters in the Atlantic Ocean. But their unrestricted fishing has severely depleted the country's supply of certain types of fish.

Namibia also has a good transportation network which facilitates its economic growth. The central part of the country is served by roads and rail lines that are linked to the South African systems, thus linking together two of Africa's most successful economies.

Just north of Namibia is Angola which, besides South Africa, is the most economically potent force in southern Africa and one of the economic powerhouses on the entire continent. The country has vast mineral resources which include diamonds, iron, gold and petroleum; and huge coffee plantations which provide the second major export after minerals. Cotton and maize are also produced in large quantities. But that is only a short list of Angola's extensive natural resources. And because of its status as one of Africa's five richest countries in the sub-Saharan region - in addition to South Africa, Congo (formerly Zaire), Nigeria, and Ivory Coast - we are going to devote several pages to Angola for a comprehensive assessment of its vast economic potential.

Angola's huge potential for economic development spans the spectrum. The country has numerous rapids and waterfalls which are used for the production of hydroelectric power so critical to economic growth. The main rivers are the Cuanza and the Cunene. Northeastern Angola has densely forested valleys which produce hardwoods for export; and palm trees are cultivated along a narrow coastal strip where precipitation is heavy. Angola's substantial mineral, power, and agricultural resources give the country the potential to become one of the most developed countries in the world within the next generation (30 years) or so. But whether or not it will be able to exploit that, is an entirely different matter.

The agricultural sector is, so far, the most important part of the economy because the other sectors have not been fully developed. The mining sector is one of them, although it already generates substantial income, but not yet to the maximum of its potential. Among Angola's minerals, diamonds are the major export, besides oil. Oil has been produced and refined near Luanda, the capital, since the 1950s, and exploitation of large reserves off Cabinda began in 1968. Natural gas is also produced in large quantities. Angola also has large deposits of copper, manganese, and phosphates - in addition to diamonds, iron, gold and petroleum.

Livestock raising, especially sheep and goats, is also an integral part of Angola's economy. In terms of other agricultural products, not only is coffee the most important export crop; Angola is one of the world's biggest producers of the crop. Other crops grown include sugar cane, tobacco, sisal, bananas, cassava, rice, maize, groundnuts, palm kernels, pulses, fruits and vegetables. Some of them are for domestic consumption, and others for export - especially sugar cane, tobacco, sisal, palm kernels and oil. Fishing is also an important industry. A lot of the fish and other sea foods - from the Atlantic Ocean and the country's several large rivers - are canned for export as well as consumed locally or exported fresh.

Angola also has more industries than several other African countries. Its industries include railroad shops, foundries, cereal mills, fish and palm oil processing plants, meat and fish canneries, and enterprises that manufacture jute, cotton textiles, paper, chemicals, tobacco products, and tires.

Another important source of revenues for Angola is the Benguela railway, which carries minerals from the mines of Congo (former Zaire) and the Zambian Copperbelt, as well as other export goods from those two countries. Angola also has several shorter railways and a good road network. And its ports of Luanda, Lobito, and Namibe on the Atlantic coast, are among the best in Africa.

Angola is one of the largest countries in Africa, but also one of the least populated. It has only about 11.5 million people in a vast expanse of territory: 486,213 square miles. And its economy is vibrant, in spite of more than 20 years of civil war since 1975 which devastated the infrastructure. One clear sign of the strength of Angola's economy is the fact that the value of its exports far exceeds that of its imports almost five times, a rare achievement in most countries around the world.[182] And in 1996, its economy grew an astounding 9 percent,[183] surpassing the Asian "tigers" - Southeast Asian nations - by almost twice as much; their economies grew about 5 percent during the same period.

Foreign investment is expected to play a major role in Angola's economic growth during the coming years. One of the country's most attractive features for foreign investors, besides its huge economic potential, is the fact that Angola is part of southern Africa which is already the most powerful economic bloc on the continent. Organized as the Southern African Development Community (SADC) comprising 14 countries, it has the largest number of some of the richest countries in Africa: South Africa, the Democratic Republic of Congo (former Zaire), Angola, Botswana, Zimbabwe, and Swaziland, all of them endowed with vast mineral resources and huge agricultural and hydroelectric potential; they are also among the most industrialized on the continent. South Africa's membership in the economic

---

[182] Ken MacKenzie, "Angola At A Glance," in the *International Herald Tribune,* May 14, 1997, p. 18.

[183] Ibid. See also Lynne Duke, "Africa: A Sign of Hope Amid the Turbulence: Economic Growth Catches Attention," in the *International Herald Tribune,* August 16, 1997, pp. 1, and 4.

community, as the richest and most industrialized country on the continent, boosted SADC's wealth enormously. And when Congo was promptly admitted as a member in 1997, the economic community got another enormous boost in potential wealth which was already vast.

Southern Africa has a combined gross domestic product (GDP) of $150 billion, and 130 million people[184] - a huge consumer population. The Southern African Development Community (SADC) was formed in 1992 by Angola, Botswana, Lesotho, Malawi, Mozambique, Namibia, Swaziland, Tanzania, Zambia, and Zimbabwe. Post-apartheid South Africa joined in August 1994; Mauritius became the 12th member in 1995; and Congo the 13th in 1997 and Seychelles the 14th member in 1998. The vast economic potential of the community can also be looked at in terms of percentage: SADC countries account for 40 percent of Africa's population, 81 percent of the continent's GDP, 81 percent of Africa's imports, and 80 percent of the continent's exports.[185] Much of that is due to South Africa's membership.

According to the Africa Institute of South Africa, in 1992 South Africa alone accounted for 78.4 percent of the combined GDP of the SADC member countries; while the rest of the members had a combined percentage of only 21.6 percent. During the same year, South Africa alone also had 41.4 percent of the combined GDP of all the sub-Saharan countries, leaving the rest of them with a combined total of 58.6 percent. In other words, South Africa alone had almost half the entire GDP of sub-Saharan Africa.[186]

SADC replaced the Southern African Development Coordination Conference (SADCC), which was formed in 1980 mainly as an attempt to reduce the region's economic dependence on apartheid South Africa. The emergence of democratic South Africa changed the political objectives of the member countries - which was to isolate the apartheid regime as a pariah on the continent - but the new organization's (SADC's) objectives remain the same:

---

[184] Erik Ipsen, "Southern Africa Strives for New Free-Trade Zone," in the *International Herald Tribune,* October 25, 1996, pp. 1 and 12.

[185] K. MacKenzie, "Southern Africa: Dynamic Market is Expanding," in the *International Herald Tribune,* May 13, 1997, p. 18.

[186] Africa Institute of South Africa, 1992 Report, cited in "A Survey of sub-Saharan Africa," in *The Economist,* op. cit., p. 6 of the survey.

- Boosting Southern Africa's general economic independence;
- Building regional integration and trade;
- Mobilizing support for national and regional projects.

In August 1996, SADC heads of state signed an agreement aimed at creating a regional free-trade area. Such free-trade policy for the entire subcontinental region of southern Africa is intended to reduce and eventually eliminate all import tariffs among the member states over a period of 8 to 10 years. SADC member countries also plan to establish a southern African power pool which would enable the members to benefit from cheap electricity produced in South Africa and, ultimately, Angola which may one day replace South Africa as the region's main energy supplier once new hydroelectric projects are completed. Angola has about six major rivers, that's including its two most well-known ones: the Cuanza and the Cunene.

More ambitious plans by SADC member countries include the establishment of a regional development bank, a common currency, and a regional parliament; for example, before the collapse of the East African Community in 1976, Kenya, Uganda, and Tanzania had a regional parliament known as the East African Legislative Assembly which convened in the countries' three capitals once a year on rotational basis, but it had no functional apparatus to enforce its decisions; the members were free to honor those decisions or not. But SADC members intend to make their subcontinental parliament more functional. And some of the steps they have taken in other areas, for example, defense, point in that direction.

As a step towards even stronger regional ties in southern Africa, SADC defense ministers voted in 1994 to create a regional rapid-deployment peacekeeping force to contain conflict between member states. One would hope that the peacekeeping force would also intervene in domestic crisis of member countries to reverse coups executed against democratically elected leaders as South Africa and Zimbabwe did in Lesotho in 1994 when they forcibly intervened and restored constitutional authority; and as the West African peacekeeping force, known as ECOMOG, did in Sierra Leone in 1998. Nigeria, in spite of its military dictatorship at home which deserved condemnation and ostracization by the international community, should in this particular case be highly commanded for taking the initiative against

Sierra Leone's military junta, and kicking it out of power; thus paving the way for the return of the country's democratically elected leader, President Ahmad Tejan Kabbah, who was overthrown in May 1997. It is encouraging to note that South Africa and Zimbabwe have already set precedent with regard to that problem, with their intervention in Lesotho to restore legitimate government.

One of the countries which, because of its vast resources, will play a critical role in achieving all the SADC objectives outlined here, is, of course, Angola, the third-richest member in the Community after South Africa and Congo; in fact it is not very far behind these two economic giants - South Africa and Congo - in terms of wealth, as a comprehensive assessment of Angola's economic potential clearly shows.

Producing nearly 700,000 barrels of oil a day, worth $4.5 billion annually, Angola is the second-largest oil producer in sub-Saharan Africa, next only to Nigeria. Crude oil accounts for 90 percent of the country's total exports, more than 80 percent of government revenues, and 42 percent of the gross domestic product (GDP).[187]

About 15 foreign companies have invested more than $8 billion in Angola's oil industry, and they all reap huge profits. All the big-name oil companies are in Angola. They include AGIP, Chevron, Elf Aquitaine, Exxon, Occidental Petroleum and Texaco. Ever since production began in 1955, the oil companies have maintained a continual flow of oil, in spite of the guerrilla warfare by the freedom fighters from 1961-75, and the civil war that raged on thereafter for two decades (from 1975-1994) between UNITA and the MPLA government. Unfortunately, before independence in 1975, none of the oil profits went to the indigenous people of Angola; they all went to the Portuguese Angolans who were the colonial masters, and to the oil companies. Fortunately, the country still has immense reserves of oil.

As production continues, so will output which is expected to reach one million barrels of oil a day by the year 2000. The country's recoverable reserves are estimated to be about 4 billion barrels. But Angola has more oil

[187] K. MacKenzie, "Angola: Oil Success Story Continues Apace," in the *International Herald Tribune,* May 14, 1997, p. 19.

than that, as new discoveries show. Exploration finds new reserves at the same rate as oil companies deplete old ones.[188]

In 1996, Angola earned distinction in the history of oil exploration. According to the *International Herald Tribune*:

> "In July last year (1996), Elf announced the discovery of what is reported to be the biggest oil field in the southern hemisphere."[189]

Foreign companies continue to invest substantial amounts of capital in Angola's oil industry and exploration, and they are getting very good results. For example in 1997, Chevron, which has been operating in Angola for more than 40 years, discovered four new offshore fields with 300 million barrels of recoverable oil. Between 1994 and 1998, Chevron invested $2.8 billion to develop deep water oil wells off the coast of Angola. Such a large investment is definitely a sign of confidence investors have in Angola's oil industry - and economy in general. Texaco, which has been in Angola for more than 25 years, invested $600 million in 1998 to develop new oil fields.[190]

Oil production began in two different parts of Angola, and in different years: it began onshore in 1955, and off the coast of Cabinda in 1968. About two-thirds of current reserves are off the coast of Cabinda, and most of the rest are off the coast of Soyo in the northwestern province of Congo (former Zaire); Cabinda borders Congo. This location of oil reserves in the coastal areas of the northwestern part of Angola, mostly offshore, helped the oil industry escape the devastation that the civil war inflicted on most of the other sectors of the economy virtually everywhere else across the country; it was total war. But the phenomenal increase in oil production through the years has been a great boost to Angola's economic growth, despite the ravages of war, and has compensated for much of the loss sustained during the conflict. Production rose especially after 1982. In 1992, it had reached 549,000 barrels a day, more than four times its 1982 level. In 1995, the

---

[188] Ibid.
[189] Ibid.
[190] Ibid.

average production level was 650,000 barrels a day; in 1997, 700,000 barrels a day; and is expected to reach 1 million barrels a day by the year 2000.[191]

Angola also has vast quantities of natural gas. About half the gas produced in association with oil is flared, and most of the rest is used to boost oil production in oil fields, but Chevron operates facilities in Cabinda for extracting a propane/butane mix from gas. Exports, in the form of liquefied petroleum gas, are estimated to have totaled 1.27 million barrels a day in 1994. And because the country also has vast hydroelectric potential, consumption of refined petroleum is lower than it normally would have been - for example it was 15,600 barrels a day for the whole country in 1993. That is because Angola relies on its substantial hydroelectric resources from its several major rivers, not on oil, for generation of electricity.[192]

In terms of minerals, Angola was, before 1975, the world's fourth largest producer of diamonds. That was before the civil war erupted following independence that year. The industry almost collapsed, especially between 1975-76 immediately after independence, but it has since recovered, although not fully, because of insurgency activities by UNITA which through the decades also controlled vast tracts of land producing diamonds, denying the legitimate MPLA government substantial amounts of income. UNITA mined and sold the diamonds to finance its military campaign, most of the diamonds were sold through Zaire when Mobutu, a strong supporter of UNITA, was in power. However, by mid-1997, UNITA was still in control of several large diamond mines. Combined production, official and unofficial, remained high and was expected to increase because of the country's large reserves of the mineral:

> "At present (1997), official and unofficial diamond production is estimated to be worth $700 million a year. Angola's alluvial reserves total between 40 million and 130 million carats; in addition, volcanic pipes called kimberlites hold an estimated 180 million carats. The new government program aims to produce more than 2 million carats of diamonds annually... (But) the official figures for diamond

[191] Ibid.

[192] Ibid.

> production and exports do not take account of smuggled diamonds. Some estimates put unofficial diamond exports at almost $500 million in 1992."[193]

The first diamonds were found in Angola in 1912. The diamond industry during the colonial period was dominated by Portuguese and Belgian financial interests who founded the Companhia de Diamantes de Angola (DIAMANG), a company which had almost exclusive monopoly of the business. Diamonds were Angola's major export until the coffee boom in the late 1940s and the rise of the oil industry supplanted them. However, diamond production remained high and reached 2.4 million carats in 1971. Although the industry almost collapsed soon after independence, it made gradual recovery, and in 1980 produced almost 1.5 million carats. But the civil war again hit the industry hard, so that by 1986 output was down to 266,000 carats. Production went up again, gradually, reaching 1.24 million carats in 1992.[194]

However, at the end of 1992, UNITA occupied the main mining areas in the Cuango valley, reducing official production substantially, down to a mere 46,000 carats in 1993.[195] The MPLA government eventually took over all the major mining centers, and Angola's future looks very bright, as it sparkles with brilliance from a dazzling assortment of minerals in what is potential one of the richest countries in the world:

> "With substantial deposits of gold, iron ore, phosphates, manganese, copper, lead, quartz, gypsum, marble, black granite, zinc and several other metals (including diamonds of course), Angola has been described as one of the world's biggest and least developed mineral treasure troves."[196]

---

[193] K. MacKenzie, "Angola: Diamonds Move Back Into Light," in the *International Herald Tribune,* ibid., p. 19.

[194] Ibid.

[195] Ibid.

[196] Ibid. See also Lynne Duke, "Africa: A Sign of Hope Amid the Turbulence: Economic Growth Catches Attention," in the *International Herald Tribune,* August 16, 1997, pp. 1 and 4; and Stephen Buckley, "Some Places the Boon of Globalization Forgot: Africa - Investors Skip the Sub-Sahara and Its Many Flaws," in the *International Herald Tribune,* January 2, 1997, pp. 1 and 4.

Add to all that the country's vast petroleum and natural gas reserves, its huge agricultural and hydroelectric potential, and a large fishing industry with catches amounting to 600,000 tons annually.[197] Angola is, undoubtedly, destined to become a major economic power in the entire Third World and a force to be reckoned with in the global arena.

We have looked to all the predominantly black countries in sub-Saharan Africa on the continental mainland. That is a total of 40 countries - out of a total of 53 on the entire continent including the island nations - which constitute about 70 percent of the continent's population. They are among the poorest in the world. Yet they are also among the richest because of their enormous economic potential, individually and collectively.

But that is only potential. Their real gross domestic product is the lowest in the world, even when looked at collectively. First, we look at it individually:

> Angola $6.1 billion; Benin $6.7 billion; Botswana $4.3 billion; Burkina Faso $6.5 billion; Burundi $3.7 billion; Cameroon $15.7 billion; Central African Republic $2.2 billion; Chad $2.8 billion; Republic of the Congo (Congo-Brazzaville) $6.7 billion; Ivory Coast $20.5 billion; Djibouti $500 million; Equatorial Guinea $280 million; Eritrea $1.8 billion; Ethiopia $20.3 billion; Gabon $5.6 billion; Gambia $1.00 billion; Ghana $22.6 billion; Guinea $6.3 billion; Guinea-Bissau $900 million.
>
> Kenya $33.1 billion; Lesotho $2.6 billion; Liberia $2.3 billion; Malawi $7.3 billion; Mali $5.4 billion; Mozambique $10.6 billion; Namibia $5.8 billion; Niger $4.6 billion; Nigeria $122.6 billion; Rwanda $7.9 billion; Senegal $12.3 billion; Sierra Leone $4.5 billion; Somalia $3.3 billion; South Africa $133 billion; Swaziland $3.3 billion; Tanzania $21 billion; Togo $3.3 billion; Uganda $16.2 billion; Zaire (renamed Congo) $18.8 billion; Zambia $7.9 billion; and Zimbabwe $17.4 billion.[198]

---

[197] K. MacKenzie, "Angola," in the *International Herald Tribune,* May 14, 1997, ibid.

[198] "1997 Almanac," op. cit., pp. 145-297.

That is a mere $459.090 billion, total GDP, for all the 40 black African countries, which is less than Brazil's GDP of $677 billion, a developing country itself; and less than Indonesia's GDP of $619.4 billion,[199] a country which in 1965 was poorer than Nigeria, yet today dwarfs both Nigeria and all the rest of the black African countries - combined!

Individually, almost all of them are non-viable states: they do not have a large population base; a large domestic market; adequate transportation and communications and storage facilities; and enough trained manpower, all combined, needed to achieve economic growth. For example, a large population base by itself is not enough to fuel economic growth - in fact it can sometimes retard progress: too many mouths to feed, with so little to eat.

Therefore one thing becomes clear. African countries cannot sustain economic growth, let alone achieve economic development and conquer poverty, unless they integrate their economies on regional and continental basis. The 16-member Economic Community of West African States (ECOWAS) and the 14-member Southern African Development Community (SADC) are the two most successful regional groups pursuing this goal. It is for the rest of the countries on the continent to form their own economic blocs or forge links with these two in order to establish an African common market and a fully integrated economic and monetary union with a common currency, and end Africa's dependence on foreign aid which is both humiliating and counterproductive. It perpetuates dependence and makes a mockery of African independence.

[199] Brazil and Indonesia, in *1997 Almanac*, ibid., pp. 157, and 205.

CHAPTER FOUR

THE STATE AS A FUNDAMENTAL DYNAMIC IN AFRICA'S ECONOMIC PERFORMANCE

THE MODERN AFRICAN state has not done very well as a dynamic for social change because of its poor economic performance. It has been more static than dynamic because it has stifled individual initiative by dominating the economy, and also because in most cases it is a corrupt institution whose failure is writ large on the African economic landscape, telescoped into appalling statistics.

It is a sad commentary that the total gross domestic product (GDP) of all the 40 black African countries combined is dwarfed by that of a single country, Indonesia, which in 1965 was poorer than Nigeria, and was itself a colony that won independence roughly around the same time that African countries did: during the post-World War II era.

It is just as sad, probably even more so, when we look at the dismal performance of the black African countries from another perspective: more than half of their total GDP is contributed by only two countries, South Africa and Nigeria, whose combined GDP is $255.6 billion out of a total of $459.090 billion for the entire sub-Saharan region. That means a total of 38 black African countries - almost the entire region - have a combined gross domestic product of merely $203.49 billion (almost $203.5 billion), which is about a third of Indonesia's: a dismal statistic.[200]

[200] *1997 Almanac* (New York; Houghton Mifflin, 1996), pp. 145-297.

But unlike in the past when it was fashionable for many Africans to blame colonialism and imperialism for almost all the problems their countries faced after they won independence, an increasing number of them today, especially those of the younger generation, insist on accountability within Africa itself; as they apportion guilt accordingly, instead of blaming colonialists and imperialists for the perpetual misery – due to tyranny and corruption, poverty and disease - hundreds of millions of Africans have to endure all their lives.

To these millions, independence is an abstract ideal which has yet to be translated into concrete reality, as they remain mired in poverty, and continue to be ravaged by disease, while billions of dollars in foreign aid, and taxes paid by the toiling masses are being stolen and squandered by unscrupulous politicians and their cronies. It is clear where the problem lies: it lies within, not without. And the people of Africa are now beginning to speak up more and more against corrupt politicians, even risking their lives by doing so. As Ernest Aning bluntly states:

> "Millions of dollars are stashed away by corrupt leaders, their families and cronies... The message is the same in Zaire, Tanzania, Kenya, Nigeria, Sierra Leone, Burkina Faso, Gambia, Ghana, etc. Development in Africa has stagnated over the years due to turncoat politicians and soldiers who have perpetuated themselves in office by manipulating the system.
>
> We find ourselves asking: Where did all the good people in Africa go?... What happened to the foreign exchange and the loans given for development projects? Some of these funds find their way right back in donor countries, stashed in coded accounts.
>
> Who do you call in Africa when you see waste and embezzlement? Nobody! Our courts are under the thumbs of the leaders. So what is the solution? Maybe we should all start to look around and ask questions about why there have been no additional hospitals, clinics, schools, roads, jobs or any change in our economic lives over the last two or three decades.
>
> We should look at Thailand, South Korea, Indonesia, Singapore, Malaysia and all these countries that were just like us not too long ago. What are they doing, or better put what did they do, to change

things? What did their governments do to achieve all these successes?...
In Africa, the average Joe goes into politics by any means possible to steal as much as he can. We've reached a point where the people can no longer be aloof... (But) today, well-meaning citizens stand and watch because intimidation has become too real and life-threatening."[201]

And as Maxwell Oteng, another Africa, also states:

"A greater part of the blame on the present economic woes in our various countries should be apportioned to internal causes, especially bad political leadership. The Mobutus had a very good chance to push us away from being perpetual producers of raw materials to producers of value-added goods which would have given us control over our products. Instead what did they do? ... Until recent years, Malaysia was an agriculture-dependent primary producer like us, but it diversified the economy and encouraged local production of goods."[202]

And in the words of yet another African, Simbowe Benson:

"Mobutu's hour of reckoning has finally come. And he deserves no sympathy! For three decades, he has run Zaire as his personal fiefdom, culminating in mismanagement and institutional corruption. Zaire is a rich country... Now this rich nation has been reduced to penury while Mobutu and the Western business interests he fronts for have grown rich at the expense of the people. Laurent Kabila and his Alliance for Democratic Forces deserve our full support in their effort to unseat Mobutu and his sick regime."[203]

---

[201] Ernest Aning, "Let's Tackle the Turncoat Politicians First," in the *New African*, No. 352, London, May 1997, pp. 6-7.
[202] Maxwell Oteng, "What About the Mobutus?," in the *New African*, ibid., pp. 4 and 6.
[203] Simbowe Benson, "Mobutu Deserves No Sympathy," in the *New African*, ibid., p. 6.

Those are only three voices. But they express a collective sentiment shared across the continent. Corruption is destroying Africa. Even many investors, including local ones, are scared to invest in Africa, for a number of reasons of course, but corruption is one of them. African countries are also economically underdeveloped, technologically backward, and politically unstable. Any one of those reasons is enough to discourage investors. As Herman Cohen, the American assistant secretary of state for African affairs under President George Bush, stated:

> "(Africa) does not provide the climate for investment and economic growth. Not only do foreign investors worry about the safety of what they're going to put in, but local people have the same problem. When I went to Ghana recently (1989), they asked why American investors aren't coming in. And I said, how come Ghanaian investors aren't investing? They said they're waiting for the Americans to show that we have confidence."[204]

During the last several years, international trade, foreign investment and increasing technology have transformed the global economy and continue to improve the lives of hundreds of millions of people in the Third World. But this improvement has taken place mostly in Asia and in some parts of Latin America, alleviating poverty. Africa is the only underdeveloped region that has been almost completely left out. Hundreds of millions of her people have become poorer through the years, and there seems to be no way out of this vicious cycle of poverty and misery.

Political chaos, corruption, wrong economic policies, lack of infrastructure - poor transportation and communications and storage facilities - and a host of other problems including lack of skilled labor due to low levels of education, and poor health services which have led to diminuation of the labor pool because of frequent and long-term illnesses; all those problems collectively are the reason why African countries are in the deplorable condition they are in today, an entire generation after independence.

---

[204] Herman J. Cohen, interview, "Forging A Bipartisan Policy," in *Africa Report,* September-October 1989, p. 19.

In fact most of them were better off during the first decade of independence during the sixties than they are today. Besides the Congo and a few other hot spots, they had less chaos then than they do today, and they had more to eat then than they do today. Some of these countries even exported food during those days. Yet they had plenty left for the people to eat and sell on the domestic market. And almost all of them exported food decades before the sixties. As Dr. Robert Gardiner, the internationally renowned Ghanaian economist who was the first Executive Secretary of the UN Economic Commission for Africa, stated at the 15th Session of the UN Economic and Social Council in Geneva, Switzerland, on July 12, 1968:

> "Africa, Asia and Latin America were all net grain exporters thirty years ago, when the total grain outflow from these regions was taking place at an average annual rate of 11 million tons. In the 1940s, the developing regions became net importers; and by 1965, developing Africa was importing 4 million tons of cereals more than it exported."[205]

Today, almost 40 years after independence, almost all African countries not only import a substantial amount of food; many of them depend on food donations from other countries for sheer survival. Even other developing countries sometimes donate food to Africa, although they are not rich themselves. But they are still better off than most African countries. Yet they were just as poor as their African counterparts a generation ago. Some were even poorer. Not only are they richer today; they are also far more technologically advanced than almost all the African countries. Even simple technology has bypassed Africa; and where such technology is available, it can still be a battle to get things done, as this case illustrates:

> "For years, customers could not call Kwabena Afari, a pineapple exporter, directly in Aburi, his hometown 65 miles north of here

[205] Robert K.A. Gardiner, "Economic Commission for Africa," his address at the 15th Session of the UN Economic and Social Council, Geneva, July 12, 1968; reprinted in Colin Legum and John Drysdale, "Africa Contemporary Record: Annual Survey and Documents 1968-1969" (London: Africa Research Ltd., 1968), p. 746.

> (Accra). His clients first had to call this city, Ghana's capital. Then someone here would call the Aburi post office. Then a post office messenger (from the Aburi post office) would go to Mr. Aburi's home (usually walking, or on a bicycle). If anything went wrong, and it frequently did, he might not receive the message for days. 'Customers were complaining,' said Mr. Afari, 46, who recently bought a cellular telephone. 'My guy in Turin (Italy) got fed up. He said, 'I can't work with you any more. It is hard to communicate.' Mr. Afari's struggles are an example of what ails sub-Saharan Africa... As a great wave of trade and foreign investment transforms the global economy... sub-Saharan Africa has been left behind."

That is something Africans themselves admit. In fact things are worse than that. Africa has not even entered the race for a share of the global economy, which goes to the swiftest; those who attract foreign investors and have the upper hand in technical skills African's don't have, creating a climate conducive to foreign investment. As Lucia Quachey, head of the Ghanaian Association of Women Entrepreneurs, put it:

> "It's not that we have been left behind. It's that we haven't even started."[206]

In fact Africa has fallen so far behind that it really has nowhere else to go, but forward, even if it's at a snail's pace, while others are flying. Statistics tell the story, and it is a sad one through the years. They paint a gloomy picture of Africa's socioeconomic status, yet a realistic one. In its report entitled "ECA and Africa's Development, 1983-2008," the Economic Commission for Africa (ECA) has the following to say:

> "In 1980, the average per capita income of the African region was only $741 compared with a per capita GNP of $9,684 in the

[206] Lucia Quachey, quoted by Stephen Buckley, ibid.

industrialized countries. But this crude measure says little about the sad realities of life in Africa."[207]

Then the report goes on to depict an even more appalling statistical profile of Africa's socioeconomic plight:

- 70 out of every 100 Africans are either destitute or on the verge of poverty.
- Only 1 in every 4 Africans has access to clean water.
- Of the 33 million people added to the work force during the 1970s, only 15 percent found remunerative employment.
- Per capita income has risen more slowly in Africa than in any other part of the world in the last 20 years.
- Africa's population is expanding at a rate of 2.8 percent annually, while food production is expanding at 1.5 percent.
- In 1980 Africa spent $5 billion importing 20.4 million tons of grain, excluding substantial freight costs.
- In 1980, the average African had 12 percent less home-grown food than in 1960.
- Africa's potential arable land is estimated at 4.2 acres per person, yet only 1.4 acres per person are currently being used.
- Africa's average food production per acre is about half of the world's average.[208]

In his introduction to the report, ECA Executive Secretary Adebayo Adedeji said if the current trends continue for 25 years, which means until the year 2008, Africa's socioeconomic situation would be "horrendous". Sadly

---

[207] "ECA and Africa's Development, 1983-2008," cited in "Africa: A Statistical Profile," in *Africa Report,* September-October 1983, p. 58.

[208] "ECA and Africa's Development, 1983-2008," ibid; "Survey of Economic and Social Conditions in Africa" (E/ECA/CM. 9/5), UN Publications (New York: United Nations, 1983); "World Development Report, 1983" (Washington, DC: World Bank, 1982; New York Oxford University Press, 1982). See also *Demographic Yearbook for 1983* (New York; United Nations, 1982).

enough, we are almost there and, in many respects, Africa is no better off than she was back in 1983 when the ECA report was issued.

Nevertheless to avert the catastrophe the ECA, back then, called upon massive reforms across Africa's socioeconomic spectrum, and in international relations as well. To reverse the negative historical trends, the Commission called for the industrialized nations to live up to their commitment of devoting 0.7 percent of their gross national product to development assistance for African countries, a pledge made to other Third World nations as well; it also exhorted African nations to manage their own resources better in order to fuel an "industrial takeoff." Warning African countries about the devastating effects of their dependence on imported food, the ECA report recommended changes in agricultural pricing – which discourages African farmers and peasants from producing a lot of food since they are not paid much for it when they sell it on the domestic market; it also recommended changes in land-tenure practices. Both of those changes were recommended as an incentive to increased food production.

But the ECA report proposed nothing new in terms of solutions. However, in emphasizing the darker side of Africa's socioeconomic predicament, with grim statistics, the report left no doubt that Africa faces enormous problems just to be able to survive at the subsistence level, let alone develop.

In fact ominous trends to where Africa was headed were evident as far back as the 1960s. During that decade, in the initial euphoria of African independence, economic growth in African countries was very slow and generally below the modest target established by the UN General Assembly for the newly independent nations. Even then, Africa had the largest number of the poorest and least-developed countries as it still does today. Its economic growth was also the lowest compared with the other developing regions of the world, mainly Asia and Latin America. Computed in 1960 prices, African total output grew by 3.4 percent per year from 1960-66; and per capita income grew by a mere 1 percent annually during the same period.[209]

---

[209] Cited by Robert Gardiner, in *Africa Contemporary Record*, op. cit., p. 745. See also Arthur Lewis, "Development Planning," in *The Legon Observer*, Legon, Ghana, May 24, 1968.

As a result of such retarded economic growth, the poverty and misery which were so common across the continent at the beginning of the decade, continued virtually unabated during the succeeding years. Africa's poor economic performance during that decade was also highlighted by stark contrast as it has been through the years since independence. Higher growth rates in other developing regions have served to sharpen the contrast between Africa's plight and the relatively better conditions which prevail in many other parts of the Third World; for example, Mozambique is not Guyana nor is Niger the same as Trinidad in terms of economic conditions, although they are all Third World countries. There are poor countries, and there are those that are the poorest of the poor.

Unfortunately, the strategy African countries - hence the modern African state - adopted to pursue economic development was more externally - than locally-based. They counted a lot on foreign aid to fuel their economies. And that was a tragic failure by the modern African state practically in every country across the continent. We cannot depend on the goodwill of the industrialized nations to develop Africa. To a very large degree, their very prosperity depends on perpetuating the status of African countries - and other underdeveloped regions of the world - as plantation economies for the provision of cheap raw materials to the industrialized world, and as a source of cheap labor for the manufacture of consumer goods for the metropolitan countries. It has now become common practice for companies in the industrialized world to transfer some of their operations or relocate to Third World nations in order to take advantage of the virtually unlimited reservoir of cheap labor.

This asymmetrical relationship between the industrialized and underdeveloped countries also guarantees markets in the Third World for manufactured goods from the metropolitan nations. African countries have, through the years, been flooded with goods from other nations instead of encouraging the growth of their own local industries for the manufacture of import-substitution items. The modern African state discouraged such entrepreneurship because it dominated the economy through nationalization of most businesses, thus excluding local entrepreneurs and investors; and also squandered the nation's resources which could have been better spent to achieve economic growth and industrialization. And this served the industrialized nations well, since it meant African countries would remain primary producers of raw materials for the industrialized world and continue to be a dumping ground for its cheap manufactured goods.

That is what they still are today, and any talk of a new international economic order to redress the imbalance is sheer wishful thinking. Rich nations dominate the world economy - hence the world market. They are not interested in changing the pricing system, to their detriment, in order to enable Africans to have control over the prices of the goods they produce and sell on the global market. That is not how the profit system works; not at the national level or at the international level. You can't reform the price system for the benefit of the underdog because the only way it is meant to work is to serve the interests of the rich and the powerful, be it the industrialized nations vis-a-vis the underdeveloped countries of Africa or the local retailer vis-a-vis peasant customers who buy sugar and cooking oil from him.

Businessmen, individuals or nations, are not in the business of reducing their own profits; they are in the business of making more and more, not less. And the international economic system, controlled by rich powerful nations, is based on the exploitation of the weak raw-material producing countries. Therefore it cannot be reformed to benefit the exploited. The contradiction is obvious. For example, when African countries and other Third World nations called for a new international economic order to transfer some of the wealth from the rich to the poor nations, the former American ambassador to the United Nations Daniel Patrick Moynihan bluntly responded: "That's looting." And he said it on American national television which was as effective in transmitting his message as if it were an international medium.

So we are on our own. What African countries need to do is increase trade among themselves and establish an African common market on which they can even sell their own manufactured goods to each other which may not be competitive on the world market.[210] Africa's infant industries are simply not yet ready to compete on the world market flooded by manufactured goods from the industrialized nations. Had this strategy been pursued from the beginning soon after independence, African countries would not be in the situation they are in today.

---

210 See, for example, the "East African Community," in *Africa Research Bulletin*, Vol. V, London, 1968, pp. 13, 1164, 1193-95; *Africa Contemporary Record*, pp. 776-777. See also *The Nationalist*, Dar es Salaam, Tanzania, November 16, 1968.

But instead, they sought wider markets – outside Africa – for their primary commodities, as well as unimpeded access to customers in the industrialized nations to try and induce them to buy African semi-manufactured and even a few manufactured goods which, unfortunately, were no match for those produced in the developed countries. They also sought the transfer of resources and technology - to Africa - which would have amounted to about 1 percent of the gross national product of the developed nations per year. To their dismay, they found out that the industrialized nations erected tariff barriers against African imports, except for those goods they really needed and could not produce themselves. The governments of the developed countries also subsidized exports from their own producers - farmers and manufacturers - giving them a competitive edge over African commodities. And in most cases, the industrialized nations did not honor their commitment to contribute 1 percent of their gross national product to the international fund set up to finance economic development in Third World countries. They still don't today.

Behind all these strategies and policies was the modern African state which has since independence been the fundamental dynamic in Africa's economic development; without any input from local entrepreneurs, since the state discouraged the growth of the private sector, and without any input from the opposition, of which there was virtually none since the state tolerated no dissent, all of whom could have proposed alternative economic policies which could have saved Africa from economic ruin. That is still the case today in most countries across the continent, as the state continues to muzzle the opposition while only paying lip service to democracy, and only grudgingly implementing free-market policies intended to dismantle state monopoly over the economy and replace it with the private sector as the engine for economic growth. The state still wants to maintain monopoly despite its tragic failure as the catalyst for economic progress.

The role the opposition could have played here - pointing in the opposite direction as the best route to economic development, and demanding accountability from those in office - cannot be underestimated; even if such opposition had been allowed to flourish and present alternative policies within the ruling party itself, while maintaining the one-party system especially during the early years of independence for the sake of national unity which could have cracked along ethnic and regional lines under "multiparty" - read, multitribal - democracy many people were demanding soon after the young African nations emerged from colonial rule.

But that does not mean the one-party state should have, as it did in most African countries, snuffed out the opposition, muzzled the press, and discouraged cross-fertilization of ideas in public forums, just for the sake of "national unity." Had the people been allowed to freely express their views without fear of retribution and instant justice from the nation's security forces, and to publicly challenge government policies and present alternative policies even without the existence of an official opposition in parliament, almost all African countries would have adopted free-market policies soon after independence, and their economies would not be in tatters today. They have now adopted those policies - one generation too late. Freedom of speech is a natural right, and difference of opinion part of human nature. As one Ugandan professor at the renowned Makerere University in Kampala, Uganda, who asked that his name not be used, put it somewhat differently in an interview in 1998:

> "Don't tell me democracy is a Western concept. It's a market concept. Don't tax me and say I should not question you."[211]

But there were also other problems during the sixties and later on through the decades which retarded Africa's economic growth; again, thanks to the ubiquitous presence of the modern African state, directing virtually everything instead of allowing the people to micro-manage their own affairs and letting the invisible hand of laissez-faire also play a role in pursuit of economic development. However, some of those problems also had their own momentum due to the underdeveloped nature of the African economies and would still have impeded progress even if the state had played only a peripheral role in directing economic development. But the problems were also fueled by unwarranted intrusion by the state, misguided policies, and waste of resources through theft and mismanagement by government officials and their auxiliaries.

---

[211] Quoted by Lara Santoro, "West Cheers Uganda's One-Man Show: This Month, Clinton will Visit a New Type of African Strongman, Yoweri Museveni," in *The Christian Science Monitori*, March 2, 1998, p. 6.

However, it is also very important to remember that, although the modern African state failed to fuel economic development through state enterprises, its failure should also be looked at in its proper historical context. There would have been no economic development in Africa at all without state involvement and enterprise. In the absence of an indigenous private sector, and there was hardly any, it was only the state in the young African nations which had the money – from export commodities, taxes, and foreign aid and investments – to launch and finance economic development projects and invest in the economy. Equally important to remember is the fact that when African countries won independence, the first thing they had in mind was the consolidation of the nation-state - no country can survive under a weak government and without national unity - and the provision of education and health services (building schools and clinics and hospitals), as well as the building of infrastructure: mainly roads and railways, bridges and ports, communications links, power plants, storage facilities, and much more. They were all essential projects, as they still are today. But they were not productive right away. They absorbed more funds and other resources than they yielded benefits during those early days of independence. It was years before African countries could see the results, and not all positive.

Agriculture was, of course, the backbone of the economy in all African countries, as it still is today. But unfortunately, between 1960 and 1966, agricultural production grew more slowly than the other sectors of the economy in most African countries. In 1960, the agricultural sector accounted for almost 40 percent of the gross domestic product of Africa; and during the next six years, the value added to total output by agriculture increased at a dismal rate of 1.3 percent per year.[212]The low level in agricultural production explains, more than anything else, why incomes grew so slowly in African countries during that period. And it is easy to understand why agricultural output was so low, as it still is today.

In most parts of Africa, most of the food and export crops are produced in very old-fashioned ways; "primitive" is the word others use, although we don't because of its derogatory connotation in this context. But it is true that

---

[212] Robert Gardiner, "Economic Commission for Africa," in *Africa Contemporary Record*, op. cit., p. 746.

farming techniques in African villages, where most of the crops are grown, have remained relatively the same probably for hundreds of years, severely limiting agricultural production mostly to the subsistence level. Such low yield can guarantee only one thing: economic stagnation. And also, very unfortunately, such output has not kept up with population growth and increasing urbanization. Even the peasants themselves don't always have enough food for their own families, let alone for urban dwellers. One of the devastating consequences of such low production is hunger. Food shortages across Africa through the years since independence has forced African countries to import and even beg for food without which there would be mass starvation. Yet all these are primarily agricultural countries which should be exporting food instead.

Income levels have equally stagnated or climbed very slowly through the decades, so that by the late 1990s, almost half the entire population of Africa - and not all that half is a wageless peasant population - was living on less than $1.00 a day. That is almost 400 million people. As Stephen Buckley reported from Africa in 1997:

> "About 40 percent of Africa's people live on less than $1 a day. From 1989 to 1992, nearly half of the continent's countries suffered negative economic growth rates. Only in the last two years have there been signs of an upturn as such countries as Ghana, Mozambique, Tanzania and Uganda pursue free-market policies; regional growth may have reached 5 percent last year, according to the International Monetary Fund. Still, in the last 20 years, per-capita income has crawled upward by roughly $70 in Africa, compared with a $900 jump in East Asia."[213]

As Africa's population continues to grow at a phenomenal rate, at least 20 million more people every year, there is an imperative need for African countries to improve agricultural production and marketing in order to increase output and income especially for those living at the subsistence level.

[213] Stephen Buckley, "Africa: Investor Interest and the Boon of Globalization Skip Sub-Saharan Countries With Their Flaws in Politics and Infrastructures," in the *International Herald Tribune*, January 2, 1997, p. 4.

As you increase the purchasing power of the vast majority of the people, who are mostly peasants and workers, you also improve prospects for industrialization which is impossible and meaningless without a large domestic market for manufactured goods.

An improvement of the agricultural economy will also increase the labor pool for industry (by producing enough food for the urban dwellers where factories and the workers are) and expand other sectors of the economy whose growth depends on the existence of a vibrant agricultural sector in pre-industrial societies such as Africa. The industrial sector in most African countries is still very small, not very much different from what it was during the sixties, despite its steady growth in some parts of the continent through the years, for example in the Ivory Coast, Ghana, Nigeria, and Kenya, which are some of the most industrialized countries in black Africa, at least by African standards; by international standards, they are not industrialized at all. Between 1960 and 1966, the contribution of manufacturing production to total output in Africa as a whole grew at an annual rate of 4.2 percent. However, by 1966, the manufacturing sector accounted for less than 12 percent of Africa's gross domestic product.[214]

Some of the major obstacles which impede industrialization in Africa are the very ones which retard economic growth: lack of investments; a weak infrastructure; shortage of energy supplies in spite of the fact that Africa alone has 40 percent of the world's hydroelectric potential, the largest of any continent, which unfortunately is underutilized; low levels of technical skills; and the limited scope of domestic markets. For example, in terms of market potential, in 1968, 30 African countries had each a total population of less than 5 million. Some even had less than 1 million. That is in a continent of 53 countries. Compounding the problem was the fact that these small populations were spread over vast expanses of territory, called countries of course, whose per capita and aggregate purchasing power was almost negligible in terms of sustaining a large domestic market for both agricultural and industrial products.

But even if all these problems, besides inadequacy of population, were eliminated overnight, most of the African countries simply did not have large

---

[214] Robert Gardner, "Economic Commission for Africa," in *Africa Contemporary Record*, ibid.

domestic markets to justify large-scale investment in industrialization without coordinating their activities to pursue industrial projects at the regional level. Today they have larger populations, of course, but still not large enough individually to achieve rapid economic growth and industrialization. It is only through regional integration that they can do that.

A regional grouping is in a much stronger position to attract larger investments, especially from foreign investors who have the largest amount of capital, because of its large size for a domestic market and provision of raw materials. An integrated region is also in a much stronger position to form common services and taxation systems and build a solid infrastructure at the regional level, all of which are vital for rapid economic growth. In the absence of massive foreign aid, such growth is possible only when the private sector is allowed to flourish and operate as the main engine of progress. And it is possible to achieve such progress on a continental scale because of Africa's enormous potential wealth, unequaled anywhere else in the world, a fact conceded by outsiders as well, who have great interest in the continent. As Chedly Ayari, president and director general of the Arab Bank for Economic Development in Africa (BADEA), stated in 1983:

> "Let us not forget that by helping Africa to develop, we also help ourselves, our children, and grandchildren. Africa is the poor rich man. There are huge potential resources to be developed for the benefit of Africa as well as mankind as a whole. Hydroelectric potential is one such resource... which accounts for some 40 percent of the world's total... But the continent also contains 97 percent of the world's chrome, 85 percent of the platinum, 64 percent of the manganese, 25 percent of the uranium, and 13 percent of copper, not to mention bauxite and lead, 20 percent (so far, but more oil wells are being found) of the oil traded in the world – excluding the United States and the Soviet Union, 70 percent of the world's cocoa production, 33 percent of its coffee output, and 50 percent of its palm oil production. And the list is far from complete."[215]

[215] Chedly Ayari, "What Strategy for Africa's Development?," in *Africa Report,* September-October 1983, pp. 11 and 9.

The list is indeed far from complete. Africa also has most of the world's reserves of gold and diamonds and other minerals - including strategic minerals vital to the defense industry of the United States and other Western countries especially the other nuclear powers – Britain and France, as well as non-nuclear Germany which is also the most powerful country in Europe. As Antonio-Gabriel M. Cunha and Joanne Donnelly state in "Defusing Africa's Debt":

> "Africa's importance to the industrialized world has for the most part been understated. In addition to being a key supplier of industrial raw materials and soft commodities - like coffee, cocoa, sugar, and cotton - Africa is a primary supplier of strategic and precious metals - cobalt, chromium, tantulum, vanadium, manganese, platinum, and gold - for which the only real alternate source is the Soviet Union."[216]

Another vital resource also critical to the survival of the industrialized nations Africa has is oil. The continent has huge reserves of oil as well as natural gas. But like all the other resources from the continent, Africans don't get what they really deserve when they sell their oil and natural gas to metropolitan countries. They are grossly underpaid. Oil companies and other multinational corporations which exploit Africa's vast natural resources give all kinds of excuses to "justify" the cost of their operations, claiming it costs more money to extract resources from Africa than it does anywhere else; which is simply not true.

They say all that so that they can pay Africans only a paltry sum while they scoop up the largest share. They also take advantage of the weakness of African countries to exploit them, which wouldn't be the case if the countries were united into a number of large federal states or as highly integrated units on regional basis to protect and promote their common interests. That is one of the biggest tragedies of the modern African state: its inability to protect the interests of its own people against outside powers who are only too happy to

---

[216] Antonio-Gabriel M. Cunha and Joanne Donnelly, "Defusing Africa's Debt," in *African Report*, September-October 1983, pp. 17-18.

take advantage of this weakness, which a number of African leaders themselves take advantage of, when they team up with foreigners to exploit their own people. The huge income from oil, and this is only one example, would have done a lot to develop Africa if African countries got their rightful share of the immense wealth. As Howard Schissel states in "What Prospects for the Oil Industry?":

> "Projections for Africa to the year 2000 indicate the potential discovery of another 7 billion tons of oil and 350 billion cubic meters of natural gas... Africa's ultimately recoverable remaining oil resources, at 41 billion tons, far surpass the 26.3 billion tons estimated for North America and the 18.6 billion tons in Latin America. At the 1982 production rate, the resource life of Africa's oil is close to 200 years, while it is just over 50 years in Latin America and 47 years in North America...
>
> African oil-producing states have sought over the past years to gradually wrest a greater share of the immense wealth extracted from their subsoils away from the Western oil groups and play a more prominent role in the development and exploitation of their own hydrocarbon resources. Western oil corporations defend their high profit margins in Africa on the grounds that the continent is a high-risk area. A closer evaluation of the facts reveals that Africa presents no higher risks than other Third World regions, or in fact the industrialized world. Indeed, political pressure is stronger on oil firms operating in the North Sea than in the Gulf of Guinea...
>
> Another argument commonly put forward in industry circles is the high cost of operations in Africa due to lack of infrastructure and the distance from home bases. In this respect, difficulties are perhaps greater in Alaska or northern Canada, but few oil groups complain about conditions there. By the same token, climatic conditions and technological headaches are much worse in the North Sea than along western and central Africa's continental plateau. Moreover, the geological risk factor in Africa is extremely low, with the rate of

discoveries relative to the number of wells drilled among the highest in the world."[217]

In spite of all that empirical evidence, oil companies contend that political and geographical factors have all conspired against Africa, making it the highest-risk area in which to operate. Based on the evidence presented here, they should be paying Africans a lot more than they are paying them now, because it is safer and cheaper to extract oil out of Africa probably than it is anywhere else.

They were pumping oil out of Nigeria and Angola when civil wars were going on in those countries. The two conflicts were among the bloodiest in the continent's history. Yet the two countries were among the safest for the oil companies to work in because they had full security protection from government troops – for one simple reason: the governments themselves needed the money, especially during those terrible crises, and did not want to risk any interruption in the flow of oil which was - and still is - their biggest source of income. Even the secessionist Biafran forces in Eastern Nigeria did not attack the oil installations or disrupt the oil business in that region, in spite of the fact that the Nigerian federal military government was getting a huge income from the sale of oil which it used to prosecute the war against them.

So where is the high-risk factor in African oil-producing countries for which American and European oil companies are charging Africans so much money? African oil is even of much higher quality than that obtained elsewhere. Yet Africans are paid only "pennies" by comparison. And more is still being discovered in large quantities everywhere across the continent. Poverty-stricken Chad, once considered a hopeless case because of its lack of abundant natural resources, is destined to become one of the richest countries after the recent discoveries of large oil reserves in that country. Yet it was once the poorest countries in the world. Even oil-barren East Africa has excellent prospects of finding oil. For example, several oil seeps have already been found in Tanzania. Also large reserves of natural gas were found in the

---

[217] Howard Schissel, "What Prospects for the Oil Industry?" in *Africa Report,* ibid., pp. 44, and 45.

country during the 1980s, and exploration for more hydrocarbons continues. Mozambique is another excellent prospect. Already mineral-rich, the country is also believed to have oil. As Schissel says about the continent's prospects and challenges that lie ahead:

> "Because African crudes tend to be of the light, low-sulfur variety, they are generally much sought after by buyers in the industrialized world.
>
> From the exploration point of view as well, Africa is well placed. Between now and the year 2000, it will be possible to discover on the continent new oil reserves totaling 121 billion barrels and 480 trillion cubic meters of natural gas ... (and) discovery costs in West and Central Africa are almost as low as in the Persian Gulf. A comparison of discovery costs conducted by the Geneva-based Petroconsultants shows that at 40 cents a barrel, Africa has an advantage over North America, where costs vary between 50 and 60 cents a barrel, the Far East at 90 cents, and South America at $1.40.
>
> The great challenge for the nascent African oil industry lies in producing countries winning a greater share of the benefits derived from the extraction of hydrocarbons from their subsoils. (But) procuring a larger portion of the oil wealth and greater autonomy in their relations with giant multinational oil companies will be a difficult uphill struggle for Africa. It takes, for instance, several decades to train a sufficient number of technicians, engineers, and commercial agents to make the dream of a viable national oil industry a reality for African states...
>
> There is (also) considerable room for cooperation between African nations in the oil sector. Already Algeria is at work drilling for oil and gas in Tanzania's offshore area. This, however, remains an exception to the rule. The vast sums required for exploration and development activities means that Africa will be dependent on the Western oil industry for many decades. But this does not imply that African states cannot win a fair deal in their relations with Western oil groups. According to Nicolas Sarkis, director of the Paris-based Arab Petroleum Research Center and adviser to several African oil-producing states, African countries must demonstrate a political will

> to measure up to powerful oil companies... 'It is (also) necessary,' remarks Sarkis, 'that African oil producers... form regional alliances with other producers to strengthen their bargaining positions.'"[218]

It applies to other products as well, not just oil. African countries selling the same commodities need to form alliances which could give them some leverage on the world market, especially against the industrialized nations which dominate the world economy.

But oil is, undoubtedly, one of their biggest single commodities which could bind them together into a cohesive bloc capable of negotiating with other countries from a position of strength. And the good news is that more oil is being found in substantial amounts in different parts of the continent which could give Africans even more leverage in their negotiations with outsiders.

So far there are 20 African countries which have oil. That is the largest number of any continent. They are found in all parts of Africa, from north to south, east to west: They are:

Egypt, Libya, Tunisia, Algeria, and Morocco in North Africa; Nigeria, Cameroon, Ivory Coast, Ghana, Benin, Senegal, Guinea-Bissau and Equatorial Guinea in West Africa; Chad, Gabon, People's Republic of the Congo (Brazzaville), and the Democratic Republic of Congo (Kinshasa) in Central Africa; Angola in Southern Africa; and Somalia and Eritrea in East Africa. Tanzania and Mozambique in East Africa are also potential sources of oil, according to recent surveys.

Africa also has the largest amount of minerals in the world. Many African countries have substantial amounts of different kinds of vital minerals, and almost all of them have a variety in varying quantities. Africa also has some of the largest reserves of natural gas found in several countries, from Ethiopia to Nigeria, Tanzania to Angola, Burundi to Cameroon, Ghana to Algeria, Egypt to Ivory Coast. The list goes on.

Simply put, Africa is, potentially, the richest continent. Tragically, it is also the poorest due to a combination of factors as we have shown in this study. But Africa's plight does not have to be permanent.

---

[218] Ibid., p. 47.

The effort has to start in Africa itself on regional basis to integrate the continent as whole, instead of being so dependent on outsiders both in terms of trade and economic aid. African countries do very little trade among themselves. They also have very few transportation and communications links between them.

Because of the continent's colonial past, the transportation system African countries inherited at independence was oriented towards export and import trade. They were also intended to serve colonial powers in their own areas. There was no road, railway or telecommunications network linking several African countries together as one region. Where some of those links existed, it was mainly between countries under the same colonial power. For example Kenya, Uganda, and Tanganyika had a common market, a common currency, and common services under the East African Common Services Organization. The common services were the East African Railways and Harbours Corporation which also included the road network; the East African Posts and Telecommunications Services; and the East African Airways. The East African Currency Board issued a common currency. And there was, of course, the East African Common Market. As Walter Elkan states:

> "The three mainland territories of East Africa, Kenya, Uganda and Tanganyika - all of them administered by Great Britain - were associated in three ways.
>
> First they constituted a common market with a more or less uniform external tariff, 'revenue raising' rather than 'protective' in intent. Within East Africa there was virtually free trade both in goods imported from abroad and in goods produced in the region.
>
> Secondly, they were associated by a common currency issued by the E.A. (East African) Currency Board and freely convertible into sterling with which it stood at par. There were no restrictions whatever upon the movement of money and since the commercial banks were all – with one exception – subsidiaries or branches of banks whose headquarters were in London, the whole system could be viewed as in a sense part of the British system with its apex in the Bank of England rather than in East Africa.
>
> Thirdly, they shared a number of common services which were jointly administered by the E.A. High Commission, later reorganized and

> renamed the East African Common Services Organization (EACSO). Some of these, the railways, posts and airways, were described as 'self-contained' because they were financed from their own revenues. The others, called the General Fund services, which included the collection of direct and indirect taxes and the provision of a number of agricultural, medical and other research services, were financed partly by the British CD&W funds and various overseas foundations, and partly by the three East African Governments. The High Commission also administered a number of other matters on which the three (colonial) territories tried to act in concert."[219]

In fact East Africa was the most integrated region in British colonial Africa. Yet it was not economically linked with the other neighboring countries, some of which were under different colonial powers. For example when Tanganyika was under British rule, it had no commercial or transportation and communications links with Portuguese Mozambique; very little with Belgian Congo, and only limited commercial ties with Burundi which, like neighboring Rwanda, was also under Belgian rule. The ties with Burundi were due to the fact that most of that country's exports and imports went through Tanganyika, as they still do today through Tanzania.

But colonial Tanganyika hardly had any trade links with Rwanda; virtually none with Nyasaland (which is Malawi today), except some transportation links via the ferry service on Lake Nyasa, in spite of the fact that both countries were under British rule. Tanganyika also hardly had any commercial ties with neighboring Northern Rhodesia (now Zambia), another British colony. Instead, Nyasaland and Northern Rhodesia, together with Southern Rhodesia (Zimbabwe today), belonged to what was then called the Central African Federation, another British creation. Yet the federation had

---

[219] Walter Elkan, "East African Community," in *Africa Contemporary Record,* op. cit., pp. 13-14. See also Arthur Hazelwood, editor, *African Integration and Disintegration* (Oxford: Oxford University Press, 1967), esp. chap. 3; A. Hazelwood, "The Treaty of East African Co-operation," in the *Standard Bank Review*, London, September 1967; Philip Ndegwa, *The Common Market and Development in East Africa*, East African Studies No. 22 (Nairobi, Kenya: East African Publishing House, 1965); and Peter Robson, *Economic Integration in Africa* (London: Allen & Unwin, 1968), esp. chap. 4.

no formal, or even informal links, with the three British territories of East Africa: Kenya, Uganda, and Tanganyika. It was more oriented towards apartheid South Africa.

That was the nature of the relationship among African countries during colonial rule. The continent was fragmented in more than one way, although the colonial boundaries by themselves were bad enough. And when the modern African state came into being at independence, it, unfortunately, did little to facilitate regional cooperation. In fact, it was during the post-colonial era that Africa witnessed the collapse of the East African Community which could have fostered economic growth at the regional level for the benefit of the three countries involved – Kenya, Uganda, and Tanzania – and for Africa as a whole. It would have been a regional economic powerhouse.

Therefore like in all the other African countries, the task of economic development had to be carried out by individual states within their own boundaries after the Community collapsed; which turned out to be an almost impossible task for such economically non-viable states without strong regional cooperation. Almost all African countries are non-viable economic and political entities. Besides lack of regional cooperation, all African countries faced other major problems after independence. As Adebayo Adedeji states:

> "These countries today are faced with major economic crises. We are now increasingly dependent on food imports. We have energy crises for the majority of the member states that are non-oil producing. We have balance of payments problems and debt burdens. We are in a way the victim of the international economic community because, as a result of colonialism, we inherited economies that were utterly dependent on the international economic community. We made the mistake of not cutting the link as soon as we became independent. We continued with the same mix of policies that we inherited – producing for export and import substitution industry. But we now know that this has not only failed to help us, but it has aggravated our very poor position."[220]

[220] Adebayo Adedeji, interview, *Africa Report,* September-October 1983, pp. 13-14.

Undue emphasis on production of export crops - coffee, tea, sisal, tobacco and others - left Africa hungry through the years. African countries should have emphasized food production first, as soon as they won independence. They did exactly the opposite. It is true that they need foreign exchange earned from export commodities. But what good does it do when they end up spending the foreign exchange they just earned to buy food from overseas - at an even greater cost than what they earn from export crops - they themselves could have produced on their own soil? The independent African states themselves, not the colonialists who have long been gone, are now responsible for having their priorities in the wrong order: export crops first, food last, instead of the reverse being the case. Even today, African economies are still oriented toward export production - to serve outsiders - instead of being geared toward food production to feed their own people.

Unfortunately, African exports themselves have not done well on the world market. They are not in the high demand, they fetch low prices, and are easily substituted in the industrialized nations by local products - a lot of them synthetic. Yet these are the very nations Africans expect to be their biggest customers. But they are not buying much from them. So Africans are stuck with their commodities or they end up selling them at very low prices. That alone is a very compelling argument for the establishment of an African common market on which Africans can sell their products to each other even for better prices; instead of waiting for outsiders to buy their products, for which they won't pay, or pay very little for them.

Even Africa's industrialization depends on outsiders, not only for capital investment and technical skills but also for the provision of raw materials. With regard to the first two, Africa will probably have to depend on foreigners for a long time to come. They are the ones who have the capital to invest more than Africans do; they are also the ones who have the technical skills Africans don't have. But in terms of raw materials, African countries can do far better than what they do now. And African governments - synonymous with the modern African states - are the ones who are at fault because they are the ones who formulate policies and strategies for national development including industrialization.

Why do they import raw materials when Africa produces all kinds of raw materials which can used by the industries on the continent? Most of the industries in Africa use imported raw materials. Yet their operations could be adapted to use local materials and produce goods in abundance from domestic resources. That is almost exactly the same contradiction Africans face with regard to food. Africa is an agricultural continent which could be producing enough food to feed its own people - yet Africans import food. Such dependence on imported food has even changed the eating habits of millions of Africans - they want to eat the kind of food their countries cannot produce because of the difference in climate. Food grown in America, Europe and Australia, continents which have a temperate climate, cannot grow in Africa's tropical climate. Dependence on imported food has also affected agricultural production. Some people don't want to grow enough food crops because they are waiting - and expect - to be given food donations; while there are those who don't grow enough because they don't want to eat African food anymore. They are tired of cassava and want wheat instead. It is the same situation with raw materials for Africa's industries. Many Africans may be shocked when they learn how high the percentage is, of imported raw materials, African industries use. As Adedeji points out:

> "Eighty percent (which is not very far from 100 percent) of the industries in Africa depend on imported raw materials and this is a raw material-producing continent. This is an agricultural continent. That is the greatest contradiction we face... We have created enclaves of modernized sectors that really have no linkage with the rest of the economies. In the production of beer, for instance, every raw material except water is imported, because we do not produce malt, barley, etc. Again (like in the case of food) it is a question of adapting. Why can't we adapt our own products? We must have industry based on the use of our own raw materials... The result is that what should have been a savings of foreign exchange becomes instead a great demander of foreign exchange (to pay for imported raw materials, which Africa wouldn't have to, if she used her own raw materials). And when you are short of foreign exchange, industries close down because you cannot purchase raw materials or spare parts."[221]

---

[221] Ibid., p. 16.

In spite of Africa's vast amount of natural resources, industrialization across the continent has proceeded at a very slow pace even in recent years. Foreign investments, a vital component of Africa's industrialization strategy, have not poured into the continent - although it is potentially a highly lucrative market - but have, instead, been diverted elsewhere. Not all foreign investors have ignored Africa, but a substantial number of them have. And if investment figures are a good statistical indicator of where the continent may be headed, it is highly probable that Africa will remain on the periphery of the global economy for many years to come; unless the continent moves en masse as an integrated whole into the mainstream of the world economy, and not as a fragmented region of dozens of non-viable states whose weakness and instability not only discourages but also scares away investors. Investment figures tell the sad story.

Since 1988, foreign investors have invested more than $400 billion in developing countries.[222] Yet only a trickle of that has gone to Africa. Trade in most parts of the world, including business transactions between developing nations in Asia and Latin America, has grown enormously since 1988. Yet African countries are still desperately struggling to find customers for their agricultural products and manufactured goods on the world market. Collectively, Africa receives only 3 percent of the total foreign investment directly invested in the Third World.[223] The rest of it, a staggering 97 percent, is poured into Asia and Latin America.

Africa's miniscule share could diminish even further. For example in 1995 alone, according to the United Nations, the amount invested in Africa dropped by 27 percent, a frightening figure for a region which is already not getting much investment. In terms of dollars, the amount dropped down to $2.1 billion. That was the total amount invested in the whole continent, which was less than what China received in only two months.[224] And most of that

---

[222] Stephen Buckley, "Africa: Investor Interest and the Boon of Globalization Skip Sub-Saharan Countries with Their Flaws in Politics and Infrastructure," in the *International Herald Tribune*, January 2, 1997, p. 4.

[223] Ibid.

[224] Ibid.

money was invested in South Africa, which always gets the lion's share of the foreign investment going to Africa.

And it is easy to understand why Africa does not attract many investors as we explained earlier; it is for the same reasons why the continent is not industrialized: lack of infrastructure and a large domestic market which would justify large foreign investments are some of the major reasons. It makes little sense for a foreign manufacturer to build a manufacturing firm in Malawi or Mali to make refrigerators when only very few people in either of those two countries can afford to buy them. And that applies to almost all of the countries across the continent except South Africa. As John Koo, president and chief executive officer of the giant Korean manufacturer LG Electronics, stated in 1997:

> "With Africa, we have a problem making investment decisions and we don't have a solution at the moment."[225]

Africa's inability to find enough investment from foreign countries has been made much worse by the reduction in foreign aid African nations have depended on so much since independence. The end of the Cold War has aggravated the situation. The Soviet Union is dead. Therefore there is no more competition between the two former ideological foes - capitalist West led by the United States and communist East led by the Soviet Union - for client states in Africa they used to entice with money. The amount of aid from donor countries and multilateral institutions to Africa dropped from $17 billion to $15 billion between 1990 and 1994. As President Henri Konan Bedie of the Ivory Coast put it:

> "We see certain countries going through budgetary difficulties that want to back away from offering development aid. They say everything ought to be referred to the private sector. If you wait until the private sector comes to build primary schools for children, I think you could wait a long time."[226]

---

[225] John Koo, quoted ibid.
[226] Henri Konan Bedie, ibid.

Military coups through the years since the sixties soon after independence, and civil wars that have ravaged the continent for decades, have made the situation worse. Since the first military coup in sub-Saharan African which took place in Togo on January 13, 1963, resulting in the assassination of President Sylvanus Olympio, 92 military coups have been executed; the latest being in Comoros in May 1999. That is an average of at least two coups almost every year since 1963. In most of those years, more than one government has been overthrown, sometimes within the same country. For example, two governments were overthrown in Nigeria in 1966; and three governments, including one civilian, were overthrown within the same month in Sierra Leone in April 1968.

In addition to military coups, more than 30 civil wars have been fought on the African continent since the sixties. That is an average of one every year. They are still raging today, including the biggest one in Congo (former Zaire) where seven African countries sent troops in August - September 1998 to support one side or the other. Angola, Zimbabwe, Namibia, Chad, and Sudan intervened to support President Laurent Kabila fight Tutsi-led rebels with their allies - Rwanda, Uganda, Burundi - who launched a rebellion to try and overthrow him. The war threatened to involve more countries and escalated towards the end of 1998 when Kabila's allies intensified their offensive. There are also separatist tendencies, some violent, for example the war in Senegal, although the conflict has been going on for almost two decades in a subdued way and has therefore remained unnoticed by the outside world:

> "Violence and political turmoil erupted in the West African nation of Senegal (during the first week of March 1998). A sneak attack by Army troops reportedly killed at least 50 people near Zinbuinchor in the province of Casamance, where separatists have been waging a 15-year war for independence. The rebels accuse the government in Dakar of ignoring the province, which is cut off from most of the country by the small nation of Gambia (the province, close to the

> Atlantic Coast, is surrounded on three sides - east, north and west - by Gambia)."[227]

Senegal also has always had border disputes with Mauritania involving parts of southern Mauritania. The differences over territorial claims have now and then erupted into military conflict between the two countries as late as the 1990s. Nigeria and Cameroon have also been involved in territorial disputes which led to fighting in 1996. The two countries also almost in fought in 1981:

> "'Nigerians and Cameroonians are brothers,' but the latter are trying by provocation to win control of an oil-rich area on their common border that almost caused a shooting war in 1981, the World Court was told. The court heard Nigeria's arguments in the long-running dispute over the Bakassi peninsula Monday (March 2, 1998); Cameroon's turn comes Thursday. Skirmishes were fought there in 1996."[228]

Not every African country is on fire. Nigeria is not burning, nor is Cameroon, despite their border dispute. Both countries continue to attract large foreign investments as they have through the years. Also Senegal is not wracked by civil war besides the conflict going on in its secessionist province. But the conflicts are unsettling enough for some potential investors who would rather turn elsewhere where there is no fighting at all. That does not mean Africa is a very high-risk area in which to invest. But it is a fact that there are many civil conflicts across the continent, and there are many countries which are politically unstable even if they have not yet exploded like Rwanda, Burundi, Somalia, Liberia, and Sierra Leone did. Perception matters even if it is not reality in all cases. Therefore it is easy to understand why many investors are not very enthusiastic to invest in what is generally perceived to be a highly volative continent.

---

[227] "The Christian Science Monitor," March 9, 1998, p. 2.
[228] "Nigeria/Cameroon," in *The Christian Science Monitor*, March 3, 1998, p. 2.

Then there is the question of leadership. Most of the leaders across the continent are corrupt, demanding huge kickbacks from investors and stealing outright from their own people and whatever they can scoop out from foreign aid. As Ghanaian economist George Ayitteh, who teaches at The American University in Washington, D.C., stated in 1997:

> "(Africa's economies will be crippled) as long as you have these mafia governments, these predatory states. In Nigeria, in Zaire, all over the continent, the people in government are just looters."[229]

They also perpetuate themselves in power so that they can continue to steal. Yet they are the very people who constitute the modern African state which is the fundamental dynamic in Africa's economic performance. Unfortunately, in most cases, they have accomplished exactly the opposite. As Professor Ayitteh stated on another occasion a few months earlier in *The Wall Street Journal*:

> "Africa's economic performance has lagged persistently behind that of other Third World regions, despite receiving more than $300 billion in foreign aid since 1960. Crumbling infrastructure, senseless civil wars, political instability, high taxes, rampant inflation, runaway government expenditures, unstable currencies and high-level corruption have all conspired to stunt Africa's economic growth and render the continent unattractive to foreign investors. According to the World Bank, in 1995 a record $231 billion in foreign investment flowed into the Third World. But Africa's share was a paltry $2 billion or 1 percent. Even Africa's own kleptocrats avoid the continent. The UN itself estimated that $200 billion - or 90 percent of Sub-Saharan Africa's GDP - was shipped to foreign banks in 1991 alone.
>
> The secrets of economic growth are known: rule of law, private property rights, pro-market and pro-trade policies, investment in human capital and creating an entrepreneurial environment. But

[229] George Ayitteh, quoted by Stephen Buckley, op. cit.

> Africa's problem is the predatory state itself - government hijacked by gangsters and con artists, who have turned the state sector, instead of the market, into the arena for private wealth accumulation. The underlying ethic is self-aggrandizement and self-perpetuation in power. The richest people in Africa are heads of state and their ministers. Helping the poor, promoting competitive economic growth and reforming the state are anathema to the ruling elite. If pressured, they adopt temporary, cosmetic 'reforms' that ensure a continued flow of Western aid. But most Africans understand this reform posturing as the 'Babangida boogie': one step forward, three steps back, a sidekick and a flip to land on a fat Swiss bank account."[230]

But reform is not impossible, Ghana under the leadership of Jerry Rawlings being one example. Rawlings overthrew President Hilla Limann's democratically elected government on December 31, 1981, declaring that it had bought Ghana "total economic ruin."[231] He was right about that. Under Dr. Limann, an economist, Ghana was paralyzed by crippling inflation and other economic problems. Rawlings froze prices in an effort to bring under control inflation that had been running at an annual rate of 116 percent.[232] By the early 1980s, it had shot up to 123 percent.[233] But the coup Rawlings executed to oust President Limann was also the bloodiest in Ghana's history and one of the most violent in Africa which caused a lot of social unrest. Several hundred people were killed and Limann and more than 200 former officials were imprisoned. Also thousands of Ghanaians fled to neighboring countries.[234] The exodus continued. By the early 1980s, more than 1 million Ghanaians had fled to other West African countries such as Togo, Ivory

[230] George B.N. Ayitteh, "The UN's Shameful Record in Africa," in *The Wall Street Journal*, July 26, 1996, p. A-10.

[231] Jerry Rawlings, quoted in *1986 Reader's Digest Almanac and Yearbook* (Pleasantville, New York: Reader's Digest Association, Inc., 1985), p. 564.

[232] *Reader's Digest Almanac and Yearbook*, ibid.

[233] S. Buckley, *Africa: Investor Interest and the Boon of Globalization Skip Sub-Saharan Countries with Their Flaws in Politics and Infrastructure*, op. cit., p. 4.

[234] *1986 Reader's Digest Almanac*, ibid.

Coast, and even as far away as Nigeria. People were hungry, shops were empty, and inflation and unemployment reached unprecedented high levels.[235]

Ghana's economy suffered another severe blow when Nigeria expelled 500,000 poverty-stricken Ghanaians in 1983. Loans from the World Bank and the International Monetary Fund helped the country begin a modest recovery in 1984-85. But yet another blow came in May 1985 when Nigeria forced another 300,000 Ghanaians out of the country and sent them back to their native land. To help finance their repatriation and resettlement, Ghana's government forced the returning Ghanaians to pay import taxes on their goods or have them confiscated and auctioned.[236]

Yet in spite of all these economic crises, Ghana remained intact and gradually recovered. In less than 10 years by the early 1990s, the country's economic growth rate was an impressive 5 percent per year, and inflation was down 10 percent from an astronomical 123 percent. In fact as early as 1989, Ghana had made tremendous progress, an achievement which was also acknowledged by the United States, a country which did not have good relations with Rawlings' regime yet continued to provide economic assistance to the West African nation. As Herman Cohen stated back then:

> "All of the U.S. development assistance money for Africa, which is about $550 million and will be the same next year (1990), is concentrated in those countries which are making an effort. So, if you look down the list of countries that are making the greatest effort, you'll see the U.S.'s biggest allocations of funds. And this includes countries which are not necessarily friendly to the United States, like for example, Ghana. We've had big differences with Ghana over the years, but since they are the best performing country, it shows that our highest priority is in rewarding countries."[237]

Ten years later, Ghana was still one of the best performing countries, second only to Uganda. But the problems of infrastructure and lack of sufficient capital from foreign investors continue to plague Ghana just like

[235] S. Buckley, ibid.

[236] *1986 Reader's Digest Almanac*, ibid.

[237] Herman Cohen, in *Africa's Report*, op. cit., p. 19.

they do the rest of the African countries. For example, in terms of communications, there are only 3.5 telephones for every 1,000 Ghanaians. The entire sub-Saharan region has an average of only 4 telephones for every 1,000 people. Now contrast that with 4 telephones per 100 in Asia and 6 per 100 in Latin America,[238] which are developing regions themselves. In fact, New York alone has more telephones than all the countries of sub-Saharan Africa combined.[239]

In terms of transportation, Ghana has about 26,000 passenger cars, and 28,000 commercial vehicles.[240] That is in a country of about 18 million people.[241] Therefore in spite of the great progress Ghana has made, especially since the late 1980s, she still has a long way to go. So do the rest of the countries in sub-Saharan Africa all of which agreed just like Ghana, however reluctantly, to implement structural adjustment programs and free-market policies recommended by the World bank and the IMF to achieve economic growth.

But such economic growth can be lopsided with only a relatively few people being the main beneficiaries. And that is where the state should step in to narrow the gap between the haves and the have-nots, although that is wishful thinking, to say the least, in most cases, since the state itself is corrupt. But it can be compelled to act if the people demand accountability; or toss the leaders out of office in the next general election, especially in the few African countries which now practice some democracy.

There has always been a huge disparity in income in African countries even before they adopted the new free-market policies during the eighties and nineties which have stimulated economic growth; unfortunately, only after they were pressured by the IMF and the World Bank instead of taking the initiative themselves. But it is also worth looking at the income disparities in other countries as well, which adopted free-market policies before African nations did, that should be seen as a warning of what could happen in Africa if the economic reforms recommended by the IMF and the World Bank lead

---

[238] S. Buckley, ibid.

[239] Ibid.

[240] *1992 World Almanac*, (New York: Pharos Books, 1991), p. 763.

[241] *1997 Almanac*, op. cit., p. 196.

to rapid economic growth or utter disillusionment. We are going to look at Mexico as an example.

In 1994, Mexico appeared set to become a showcase of how free trade and private investment can transform a developing country into a haven of prosperity and an economic powerhouse. Having opened its economy and welcomed in billions of dollars in investment capital, Mexico signed a landmark free trade agreement with the United States and Canada and waited for an economic takeoff. It never did. Instead, its currency collapsed, investors pulled out of the stock market, and the country slid into a deep recession. The only economic takeoff that took place was the flight of capital - out of the country, by investors, except in the northern part.

Mexico immediately became a warning, and a classic case study, for critics who contend that globalization – the wave of unprecedented vast expansion of international trade and foreign investments that has swept the globe, except Africa of course, during the 1990s - is proving to be not a reliable means to end or alleviate grinding poverty so prevalent in developing countries. The critics include liberal and socialist-oriented politicians and scholars as well as labor unions in both industrialized and Third World nations. They also include advocates for international aid agencies which have through the years funneled their assistance into the underdeveloped nations of Asia, Africa, and Latin America.

They all argue, and rightly so even according to this African writer who also supports the new economic reforms and austerity measures adopted by African countries, that the new wealth generated by free trade and foreign investments mostly from the industrialized nations - does not go to the poor majority in many Third World countries and encourages the exploitation of poor workers and children. They also contend that many poor developing countries have been left out of the global economy, which is an empirical fact. African countries are a perfect example. They have been almost totally left out, deliberately.

By a glaring contrast, many Latin American countries including all the major ones – Mexico, Brazil, Argentina, and Chile – have been able to attract billions of dollars in foreign investments and have dramatically increased trade with other nations, especially those in the industrialized world. They have also been able to control skyrocketing inflation and declining incomes which plagued the entire Latin American region during the 1980s.

But in spite of all that, the results have been mixed. The new economic reforms have worked, but they have also failed in a very destructive way. It is true that during the 1990s, the opening of the world's markets has reduced the percentage of the people living below the poverty level in many countries round the globe. But it is also true that the percentage of the poor has increased throughout Latin America and the Caribbean. Almost an entire quarter of the population of Latin America - 110 million people - live on less than $1.00 a day, according to the World Bank. That is 25 percent, compared with 40 percent - about 400 million people - of the entire population of Africa who also live on less than $1.00 a day.

There are, of course, exceptions. The new economic liberalization policies have not been a total failure in Latin America. Chile is one such example of a country which has achieved considerable success. It began opening up its markets during the 1970s, a decade before most of the other nations of Latin America opened up theirs during the 1980s. Chile now has a vibrant economy and a declining rate of poverty - despite the fact that its economy nose-dived in the early 1980s and suffered a crash that was more devastating than Mexico's.

Yet few other Latin American nations have been able to duplicate Chile's success; their economies have not even grown fast enough to keep up with population growth. And the people have responded with a backlash against market reformers who advocate free-market policies. For example in 1996 in Ecuador, the people elected a populist president; Argentina was rocked by mass strikes; and there has been a resurgence of guerrilla activity by leftist movements in Colombia, Mexico, and Peru, fighting for an equitable redistribution of wealth to the masses.

However, it is in Mexico where the biggest problems are. Critics of the global economic model as the blueprint for poor countries to fight poverty are quick to point out Mexico's plight as a compelling argument against globalization: Mexico shows what can go wrong when a developing nation tries to enter the global marketplace without economic or social policies tailored to handle the pressures created by a huge influx of foreign capital.

During the last 10 years since around 1986, billions of dollars in foreign investments have poured into Mexico as the government disposed of state assets for acquisition by private investors, liberalized the economy, offered lucrative tax-incentive packages to manufacturers producing export goods, and deregulated the banking industry and financial markets. But like many other Latin American countries, Mexico is divided into two societies, separated by geography, technology, and ethnicity - with the indigenous Indian population loaded at the bottom, and white Spanish Mexicans sitting on top of the "wretched heap." Almost none of the new wealth has trickled to the bottom.

Most of the foreign investments were poured into the cities in northern Mexico, which is also the most prosperous part of the country. That is also where most white Mexicans of Spanish origin live. The money went into building new factories, starting numerous other businesses, erecting modern high-rise buildings, and produced "a new upper middle class whose members sip wine at fancy restaurants and industrial parks that churn out televisions, designer jeans and electronics. The money also helped create 15 Mexican billionaires; only four other countries in the world have more."[242]

Yet the southern part of Mexico received hardly anything. It is a region inhabited mostly by the native people, so-called Indians, who live in poor remote villages, scratching out a bare living on rented farms owned by white Spanish Mexicans who conquered them and destroyed their indigenous societies. In much of the south, the roads are not paved, sanitary conditions are appalling, and poverty is simply a way of life. But that is not all. Schools are no more than simple shacks that are falling apart, teachers hardly show up, and those who do are paid hardly anything if they are paid at all; and the illiteracy rate is four times the national average. There is another appalling statistic which reminds one of Africa: At least one of every three households in southern Mexico lacks running water. In Africa it is even worse than that: Only one in every four Africans has access to clean water.

In spite of the billions of dollars in foreign investments and the expansion of trade as well as rising incomes, thanks to globalization, the vast majority of Mexicans are still trapped in poverty. Where did all the money go? Africans are probably asking the same question.

The question becomes even more urgent as Africa's economies continue to grow, especially in countries which vigorously pursue free-market policies.

---

[242] Molly Moore, "New Riches Yet to Trickle Down to Latin American Poor," in the *International Herald Tribune,* January 2, 1997, p. 4.

And let us just face it. Capitalism is heartless by nature. But it can be tamed and used for the benefit of society because of its dynamism and incentives to production. It is for the modern African state to inject it with a doze of humanism to curb its predatory instincts.

AFRICA'S ECONOMIC SUCCESS

Despite dire predictions by some pundits, Africa's economies have, on average, performed well considering the odds against them. In some respects, Africa has in fact done even better than some of the best in other parts of the world. Africa's economies grew by an impressive average of 5 percent during the mid- and late 1990s, a growth rate unmatched even by Asian "tigers" many of whom went into a tailspin: during the late 1990s South Korea, Thailand, Malaysia and Indonesia faced serious economic and financial crises - while Africa's economies were doing very well - and had to be bailed out by the World Bank and other financial institutions as well as by the United States to avoid total collapse. This was a period when African countries were not only enjoying economic growth; it was a time when some of them were doing spectacularly well, a commendable performance which did not fit the stereotype of Africa as a perpetual loser. As *The Economist* states:

> "Little noticed by the rest of the world, much of sub-Saharan Africa is in the midst of an upturn... And the averages (of economic growth) hide some stunning performances: Uganda has been growing at more than 8 percent a year since 1992."[243]

And there have been even more stunning performances. According to the World Bank, Uganda's economy grew by 9.4 percent in 1996, a brilliant achievement by a country which only a decade before was devastated by war, and before then by Idi Amin's reign of terror. During the late 1990s when Uganda was doing extremely well, war was still going on against insurgency movements in the northern and western parts of the country.

---

[243] "Emerging Africa," in *The Economist*, June 14, 1997, p. 13.

Ethiopia, also ravaged by war for decades, is another country on the move. In fact its performance was even more stunning. In 1996, Ethiopia's economy grew by 11.9 percent.[244] Yet only a few years earlier, from 1991-95, Ethiopia registered a negative growth rate. Its average GDP (Gross Domestic Product) growth rate during that period was -0.4 percent.[245] Ethiopia and Uganda are the two countries which had the highest growth rate in East Africa during that year.

Malawi, which like Mozambique is in East Africa geographically but is also considered to be part of southern Africa, led the south with a stunning 16.1 percent GDP growth rate in 1996, followed by Zimbabwe with a highly impressive 8.1 percent, and Mozambique with an equally commendable 6.4 percent.[246] Few other countries around the world could claim such credit. Yet all this is coming out of Africa, a continent which has always been considered to be a hopeless case, an image aptly described by *The Economist*:

> "Africa does not shed its stereotypes easily. Just as it seemed time to drop the old clichés about the continent's corrupt dictators and political chaos, soldiers from America and France have had in the past fortnight (the first two weeks of June 1997) to fly into western and central Africa to rescue their nationals from eruptions of violence (in Sierra Leone and Congo-Brazzaville following military coups in May and June, respectively)... Out of Africa, it is tempting to conclude, there is never much that is really new.
>
> Tempting but wrong. Events such as the coup against the elected government of Sierra Leone are gradually becoming aberrations in today's Africa. Indeed, sub-Saharan Africa is in better shape than it has been for a generation. A new sort of African leader is trying to break the addiction to foreign aid, and to the idea that Africa's woes can be blamed forever on the legacy of colonialism. They are beginning to see their countries not as victims but as emerging

---

[244] Lynne Duke, "Africa: A Sign of Hope Amid the Turbulence: Economic Growth Catches Attention," in the *International Herald Tribune,* August 16, 1997, p. 1.

[245] "Hope for Africa," in *The Washington Post,* National Weekly Edition, September 1, 1997, p. 15.

[246] L. Duke, "Africa: A Sign of Hope Amid the Turbulence," ibid.

markets, capable by dint of their own efforts of profiting from the freer flow of trade in the global economy. It is high time that foreigners began to see Africa that way too...

The idea that lasting prosperity demands stable government and the rule of law has taken hold almost everywhere - the coup in Sierra Leone was condemned across the continent. Most African governments, moreover, have adopted promising economic policies: sound money, fiscal rectitude and the encouragement of private business as their mantras... inflation is being tamed and budget deficits are falling in much of the continent. And most important, Africa's leaders recognize that however great the problems, Africa can - and must - forge its own future."[247]

There is no question that most of those leaders remain corrupt. But there is also a new attitude among many of them towards accountability. And with the implementation of the new economic policies, efforts of the people to build their economies are beginning to bear fruit in different parts of the continent. Where statistics have been discouraging in the past, they are now a sign of hope and evidence of spectacular achievement, as we have seen from the stunning performances by Uganda, Ethiopia, Malawi, Zimbabwe, and Mozambique. But that is not all.

In West Africa, the tiny republic of Equatorial Guinea broke the record on the entire continent. In 1996, its economy grew by an astonishing 37.3 percent.[248] That is more than three times the growth rate of China's economy, the fastest growing in the world, which grew by about 12 percent during the same period,[249] a percentage that was still lower than that of two other African countries: Malawi's 16.1 percent, and even that of war-ravaged Rwanda, whose economy grew by 13.3 percent. Yet only a few years before, between 1991 and 1995, Rwanda's average GDP growth rate was negative, a frightening -11.4 percent.[250]

---

[247] "Emerging Africa," in *The Economist,* ibid.

[248] "Hope for Africa," in *The Washington Post,* ibid.

[249] "1997 Almanac," op. cit., p. 167.

[250] "Hope for Africa," in *The Washington Post,* ibid.; and *1997 Almanac,* op. cit., p. 256.

In addition to Equatorial Guinea, the other West African countries which achieved spectacular economic growth were Togo, whose economy grew by 10 percent,[251] and Ivory Coast, which registered a 6.8 percent GDP growth rate during the same period.[252] Such economic performance has become a continental phenomenon. As President Sam Nujoma of Namibia stated at an international economic conference in Harare, Zimbabwe's capital, in 1997:

> "We cannot afford to fail at the point where our continent is at the threshold of success."[253]

In spite of such stunning economic performance, it is worth remembering that an overwhelming majority of Africans still live in poverty - 40 percent of them live on the equivalent of less than $1.00 a day, barely surviving; and rampant corruption and political instability could erode all those gains within a relatively short period of time if the countries making spectacular progress don't stay the course.

But still, the continent has caught the attention of a number of foreign investors who believe Africa is on the way up. And they are getting support from a number of highly influential groups of scholars and analysts. For example the Council of Foreign Relations, an American group which has great influence on national policy, has urged the United States government, congressmen and senators to take advantage of what it calls "the most promising period since the onset of African independence 40 years ago."[254]

The Council pointed out that the United States exports more to Africa than it does to Eastern Europe and the former Soviet republics combined. It also said that Africa will become a major market for American products because more than a third of America's economic growth comes from exports, a lot of which will be increasingly sold to African countries as their

---

[251] Callisto Madavo and Jean-Louis Sarbib, "A New Africa Is Generating Success and Hope," in the *International Herald Tribune,* June 21, 1997, p. 6.
[252] L. Duke, *Africa: A Sign of Hope Amid The Turbulence*, ibid.
[253] Sam Nujoma, quoted by L. Duke, ibid.
[254] Lynne Duke, "The Long, Slow Road to Economic Renewal: For All the Continent's Problems, the Trends Are in the Right Direction," in *The Washington Post,* National Weekly Edition, September 1, 1997, p. 15.

economies and domestic markets continue to grow. As Lynne Duke reported from Africa in "The Washington Post":

> "Africa's new openness to investment and the news of its apparent upturn have attracted heightened attention from U.S. investors, who have crammed the ballrooms and wood-paneled chambers of Washington, New York and some African capitals during a series of investment summits held in recent months, including one this spring (1997) that attracted 700 people."[255]

Africa's spectacular economic performance can also be looked at from another perspective. According to Flemings Research, an arm of Flemings international bank, Africa is now the second-fastest-growing region in the developing world, after Asia.[256] Africa has thus surpassed Latin America, as a region, in terms of economic growth; a notable achievement considering the fact that Latin America has a better infrastructure and has attracted more foreign investments through the years than Africa has, and has been independent for almost 200 years while most African countries won independence only a generation ago, mainly between 1960 and 1968.

But the young and poverty-stricken African nations need sustained economic growth of at least 7 percent per year,[257] according to many economists, in order to offset an average population growth rate of 3 percent and to begin to generate enough locally created wealth to drastically reduce poverty. The good news is that most of the 40 black African countries which constitute sub-Saharan Africa already have an economic growth rate that exceeds population growth.[258] And the remaining few have the potential to reach the same kind of economic growth because of the new economic policies being pursued across the continent, and also because of Africa's abundant wealth of minerals and agricultural products which are found virtually in every African country. By contrast, East Asia hardly has any

---

[255] Ibid.

[256] Ibid.

[257] Ibid.

[258] Ibid. See also C. Madavo and J.L. Sarbib, *A New Africa Is Generating Success and Hope*, op. cit.

natural resources. Yet in spite of such poverty, the region has achieved the greatest economic growth rate in the entire history of mankind and has produced what have come to be known as Asian "tigers" renowned for their brilliant economic performance. So why not Africa which is even well-endowed with an abundance of natural resources? As Nicholas Kristof reported from the diamond-rich city of Kisangani, Democratic Republic of Congo, in *The New York Times*:

> "The area around this river port city in eastern Congo (on the Congo River), is dilapidated and impoverished yet (fertile and) studded with diamonds, like a billionaire on Skid Row. Back in the 1950's, when this country and several others in Africa were at the same income level as South Korea and while blessed with far more natural resources, it might have seemed reasonable that Africa would soon leave Asia in the dust. Now (resource-poor) South Korea has a per capita income of about $10,000 a year, and (mineral-rich) Congo stands at $150 per person."[259]

But Africa is now waking up, as we have learned from the stunning economic growth rates of several countries across the continent. Add to the list Angola and Lesotho: "At last count (in mid-1997), four countries - Uganda, Angola, Lesotho and Malawi - were enjoying growth rates of 10 percent. That is about as fast as the peak growth rates for the Asian 'tigers,' Hong Kong, Taiwan, Singapore and South Korea."[260] Now Africa's main task is to sustain growth over the next several decades, not just for a year or two. And that will require more than just economic reforms and free-market policies, but also great investment in education and health by the African governments themselves in order to have an educated workforce free from debilitating diseases which sap the energy of millions of Africans - and kill just as many - making it impossible for them to compete in the world market.

---

[259] Nicholas D. Kristof, "Tiger Tales: Why Africa Can Thrive Like Asia," in *The New York Times,* May 25, 1997, p. E-1; and N.D. Kristof, "From Asia's 'Tigers,' a Lesson for Impoverished Africa: How to Turn Poor Into Rich: It's More Than Economics," in the *International Herald Tribune,* May 27, 1997, p. 1.

[260] Ibid.

This is a long-term investment, and it will take years before African countries start to reap benefits. You cannot educate and teach people technical skills overnight, and you cannot build clinics and hospitals, train medical personnel, and improve health services tonight. Therefore in the meantime, African nations must vigorously pursue free-market policies to attract foreign investments in order to be able to sustain economic growth and, in turn, invest the wealth generated to improve education and health services to produce human capital - without which development is impossible. And there is hope for Africa's long-term economic growth. As Salih Booker, a senior fellow at the Council on Foreign Relations, states:

> "There's an emerging consensus that Africa is not hopeless, and that in fact there is an emerging renaissance going on in Africa."[261]

Yet developing human capital which Africa desperately needs to make what has been called "African Renaissance" a meaningful concept is a herculean task because of the lack of money in most African countries needed for initial investment - to set things in motion - in order to build schools and clinics, and train and pay enough teachers and health workers. Therefore African nations are forced into a situation in which they have to rely on foreign aid, although to a limited extent, to carry on those tasks. Africa's predicament in those two areas - of health and education - is exemplified by this case in what is now the Democratic Republic of Congo:

> "In the little village of Lalia, in eastern Congo, the principal of the mud-brick elementary school throws up his hands at the challenges he faces educating barefoot children who swarm around him. 'We have no notebooks and no teaching materials, and some teachers don't come because we cannot pay salaries,' said the principal, Bib Masakama, an energetic 32-year-old, as he showed a visitor around the school. The mud wall leaned ominously, and light came from holes in the walls that functioned as windows. Lizards ran about on the walls and on the rough wooden planks that served as desks and

[261] Salih Booker, quoted ibid.

benches. 'None of these kids has ever been vaccinated against any disease,' Mr. Masakama added. 'None has ever had a medical examination.'"[262]

But why has Africa lagged so far behind other continents? It has nothing to do with genetic differences among races, contrary to what Charles Murray and the late Richard Herrnstein state in their best-selling book "The Bell Curve"[263] published in 1994 in which they contend that black people are less intelligent than whites and Asians because of genetic differences; and that blacks in Africa have, on average, the lowest IQ in the world: an IQ of 65-70, which is considered retarded. That is an incendiary thesis.

Yet they are unable to explain why there are blacks - in fact millions of them by the authors' own admission - who have higher IQs than millions of whites and Asians. If black people are genetically inferior to members of other races, it should be impossible for any black person to score higher than any white person or any Asian on an IQ test - since the latter two are genetically "superior" beings - just as it is impossible for a duck to soar as high as an eagle because of obvious genetic differences between those two birds. Therefore genes - "it's all in the genes" - are not the reason why black Africans lag behind other people - or even why their kith-and-kin in America- African-Americans (black Americans) - lag behind whites and others. Whites themselves have not been ahead of other people all the time in human history; nor have Asians. Simple common sense says they should have been, since they are more "intelligent" than anybody else. "The Bell Curve" is the "Mein Kampf" of the twentieth-first century; and its twisted logic and doctrine of racial supremacy does not, and cannot, answer the question why black African countries lag behind others - for the same reason it cannot answer why black Africans, the very embodiment of failure who are supposed to be congenital idiots because of their genetic "inferiority" have surpassed whites - and the "invincible" Asians - in Britain and become the most successful group in terms of academic achievement. According to the "Sunday Times,"

---

[262] N.D. Kristof, ibid.

[263] Richard J. Herrnstein and Charles Murray, *The Bell Curve: Intelligence and Class Structure in American Life* (New York: Free Press, 1994).

London, January 23, 1994 (coincidentally the same year "The Bell Curve" was published, only months later):

> "Black Africans have emerged as the most highly educated members of British Society and are twice as likely to hold jobs in the professions as white people. The findings, which challenge popular stereotypes about black underachievement, are revealed in a new analysis of the official census that for the first time, details the social class, educational achievement and aspirations of Britain's three million ethnic minorities. More than a quarter of the 130,000 adult black Africans in Britain hold qualifications higher than A-levels (Advanced levels), compared with one in eight whites. They are now just ahead of the Chinese, the most academically successful ethnic minority in previous studies."[264]

Therefore there are other explanations, excluding genes, why African countries have not forged ahead like their Asian counterparts who were also once colonized. Several explanations have been given. Some people blame colonialism, the standard villain of course, contending that it inflicted far more damage on Africa than it did on Asia or anywhere else. Obviously, it is a sentiment that was shared by one of the world's most prominent and influential leaders, from Asia, Indian Prime Minister Jawaharlal Nehru, although the context in which he articulated that feeling spanned a much longer period during which Africa was drawn into the orbit of foreign influence which led to the conquest of the continent. As he stated in 1961:

> "Reading throughout history I think the agony of the African continent... has not been equaled anywhere."[265]

---

[264] "Africans Move to the Top of Britain's Education Ladder," in the *Sunday Times*, London, January 23, 1994. See also Christopher Stringer and Robin McKie, *African Exodus: The Origins of Modern Humanity* (New York: Henry Holt and Co., 1996), p. 190.

[265] Jawaharlal Nehru, "Portuguese Colonialism: An Anachronism," in *African Quarterly*, Vol. 1, No. 3, October-December, 1961, p. 9. See also Nehru, "Emergent Africa," in *African Quarterly*, Vol. 1, No. 1, April-June, 1961, pp. 7-9.

Other explanations for Africa's slow progress include the partition of the continent and its ethnic and linguistic diversity. There are those who say colonial boundaries, which were arbitrarily drawn, and the forced amalgamation of different tribal groups - divided by language and culture - into nations that were brought under colonial tutelage caused a lot of confusion in the newly formed countries which surfaced after the imperial rulers left. Based on this argument, hardly any of the African countries which exist today can legitimately claim to be united by a national ethos because - there is none.

Yet others contend that climate and culture are the main reasons why Africa lags behind other continents. Jeffrey Sachs, professor of international trade at Harvard University and an adviser to several African governments on economic development, is among those who contend that Africa's geography - hence climate as well - has played a critical role in impeding progress on the continent; therefore it is not entirely the Africans' fault that their countries are underdeveloped. Africa has been dealt a weak hand by geography, he contends. As he states in "Nature, Nurture and Growth":

> "Adam Smith attributed England's relatively high productivity to the advantages of natural geography and policy. England, he pointed out, had fertile soil, a long coastline and many navigable rivers. It also had secure property rights and the rule of law. Since Smith's time, economic development has continued to reflect the interplay between the two mutually reinforcing factors...
>
> Throughout history, coastal states, with their long engagements in international trade, have been more supportive of market institutions than landlocked states, which have tended to organize themselves as hierarchical - and often militarized - societies. Mountainous states, as a result of physical isolation, have often neglected market-based trade. Temperate climes have generally supported higher densities of population and thus a more extensive division of labour than tropical regions. Until this century, the burden of disease and low agricultural productivity in sub-Saharan Africa kept population density among the lowest in the world, with the exception of coastal trading regions and a few mountainous areas - such as the Ethiopian highlands and the

> Great Lakes region - where high elevations reduced the incidence of infectious disease."[266]

This is not an excuse for corruption and bad economic policies which have contributed substantially to Africa's economic retardation. But even if there were no corruption, and even if African countries had adopted free-market policies soon after independence to attract foreign investments, they would still be burdened with serious economic problems because of the continent's geography and climate. It is true that economic growth would have been faster than it was under state-controlled economies. Because of free-market policies which encourage business, investments from the private sector would have improved transportation and communications, thus influencing geography. But the influence on geography exercised by the new infrastructure of roads and railways, bridges and communications and storage facilities, would not have changed the climate; nor would it have moved mountains, or eliminated the kind of diseases which thrive in the tropical climate but are not found in countries that are in the temperate zone.

But that does not mean that Africa cannot develop. It does, however, mean that because of her geography, Africa is burdened with problems other continent's don't have, just as, of course, they face problems which Africa doesn't: winter and extreme cold temperatures, for example. And it also means that development will therefore be much harder to achieve than it would have been had Africa's geography been different and more conducive to international trade:

> "Smith understood that the physical isolation of the interior of Africa placed profound burdens on the region's development. Living a century before Pasteur and Koch, however, he could not fully appreciate the toll of infectious disease in the tropics. Malaria, schistosomiasis, filariasis, onchocerciasis, and a plethora of other lethal and debilitating maladies are restricted to tropical and sub-tropical climates. Pests and diseases wreak havoc with crops and herds. Other special features of tropical ecology also hinder

[266] Jeffrey Sachs, "Nature, Nurture and Growth," in *The Economist*, June 14, 1997, p. 19.

agricultural development. Torrential rains in equatorial regions tend to leach the soils of nutritions. Exceptional cases, such as Java (Indonesia's most populous island), usually reflect exceptional circumstances - in Java's case, a highly fertile volcanic soil...
In recent studies carried out by the Harvard Institute for International Development (HIID), global patterns of growth during 1965-90 were shown to depend on four factors: initial conditions; physical geography; government policy; and demographic change... Landlocked countries grew more slowly than coastal economies... And tropical countries grew 1.3 percentage points more slowly each year than those in the temperate zone, even after allowing for other differences. This seems to reflect the cost of poor health and unproductive farming."[267]

In terms of landlocked status, there are 15 African countries whose economic growth is partly affected by their geographical position. They have no direct access to the sea. They are: Mali, Burkina Faso, Niger, Chad, Central African Republic, Ethiopia, Uganda, Rwanda, Burundi, Zambia, Malawi, Zimbabwe, Botswana, Lesotho, and Swaziland.

However, in terms of tropical climate, all the countries in sub-Saharan Africa are affected. They suffer stunted economic growth because of poor health due to tropical diseases and also because of unproductive farming. But landlocked nations can gradually overcome their obstacles by improving their infrastructure - especially roads and railways to neighboring countries which have access to the sea. Tropical countries can also improve their farming. However, improving their health by combating disease is a much more difficult task because there are so many tropical infections. The tropical climate sustains a wide range of microbes which would not have been able to survive in a temperate climate where cold temperatures and harsh winters function as a defensive barrier against the spread of a number of diseases - not all of them - by killing deadly bacteria and other micro-organisms. Therefore geography plays a critical role in the fate of nations. And that includes defense of course.

---

[267] Ibid.

Another analyst who says geography has played a critical role in retarding Africa's economic growth is black American scholar Dr. Thomas Sowell of the Hoover Institution at Stanford University in California. Dr. Sowell, an economist, says culture - in addition to geography - has also been a retarding factor in the development of Africa and other societies around the world, as much as it has been a catalyst in others, an argument which is the central thesis of his books, "Race and Culture: A World View," and "Migrations and Cultures: A World View."[268]

Both - the role of culture and geography - are compelling arguments. But they are not equally applicable in the African context. The negative impact of geography has been more widespread than that of culture. Whereas geography has obstructed progress almost everywhere across the continent, culture has not. There are dynamic cultures in Africa which have facilitated progress as the record of achievement by different ethnic groups clearly shows: for example the Ibo and the Yoruba in Nigeria, the Baganda in Uganda, the Ashanti in Ghana, and the Kikuyu in Kenya whose people are among the most educated and most successful in business on the entire continent. And there are several others.

Their cultures have not retarded progress, as Sowell himself concedes in both of his books when he cites the Ibos as an example of a dynamic African ethnic group with a strong entrepreneurial spirit. Unfortunately, their success - because of their dynamism and business acumen - cost them tens of thousands of lives in Northern Nigeria in 1966, pogroms which led to their secession in Eastern Nigeria from the rest of the federation the following year, and consequent civil war at an even greater cost of more than 500,000 lives, most of them Ibo. Still, this horrendous tragedy was not able to dampen their spirit and they remain as dynamic as ever.

And as we just saw earlier, in Britain today Black Africans - who are supposed to be the most mentally deficient people in the whole world, according to conventional wisdom - have earned the enviable distinction as the most highly educated group, far ahead of everybody including the native British themselves. Yet they have been able to achieve all that only within the

[268] Thomas Sowell, *Race and Culture: A World View* (New York: Basic Books, Harper Collins, 1994); and Sowell, *Migrations and Cultures: A World View* (New York: Basic Books, Harper Collins, 1996).

past 30 years or so when they started migrating to Britain after their countries won independence during the sixties, except for Ghana which won hers in 1957. And they all come from different tribes across the continent, showing that no single African tribe has a monopoly on academic achievement and economic development. All their cultures are dynamic and conducive to progress.

However, the impact of geography on Africa's economic growth is acknowledged even by some Africans, although from a different perspective: not because the climate is hostile to economic growth but because it is too good to galvanize people into action and force them to fend for themselves; and not because the geographical features in different - although not all - parts of the continent present serious obstacles to transportation and the building of other infrastructure but because the scenic and majestic beauty of Africa's landscape and topography is such a compelling sight and so relaxing that some people would rather appreciate its beauty than destroy it in the name of development based on some alien ideas imported from Europe. Once basic needs are met, there is nothing much to worry about. Eat and take a nap. This is the climatic theory of underdevelopment from one African perspective, although not all Africans share this glossy assessment about an easy meal accompanied by a languorous siesta in Africa's garden of Eden. As the mayor of Congo's third largest city of Kisangani, Alauwa Lobela who seems to articulate this perspective, stated in 1997:

> "In Africa the climate is such that there's always fruit around, in the back of the house, and you just reach up and pick it when you're hungry. But in Europe and Asia, the climate forced people to get food, to protect themselves from the cold in the winter, to develop a spirit of battle."[269]

Such climatic explanations are in fact common, and many researchers including Professor Jeffrey Sachs and Dr. Thomas Sowell, to give only two examples, have empirically demonstrated that the economies of tropical countries do indeed grow at a slower pace than those of America and Europe

---

[269] Alauwa Lobela, quoted by N.D. Kristof, *Why Africa Can Thrive Like Asia*, ibid., p. 4.

and other parts of the world in the temperate zone for climatic reasons. But the statistical relationship is very small. In fact one study concluded that climatic differences accounted for only one-twentieth of the gap in economic growth between Africa and East Asia since 1965.[270]

There are, of course, glaring contrasts in terms of economic performance within each of those two regions themselves. For example, Southeast Asia includes North Korea which for decades before famine struck during the 1980s and 1990s due to economic failure under the communist system had a healthy population and a well-educated workforce; it still has a relatively well-educated population compared with African countries. Yet North Korea today is an economic disaster. That contrasts sharply with African countries such as Botswana, Ivory Coast, and Swaziland which also have had prosperous economies through the decades since independence during the 1960s.

But in spite of such African success stories, it still remains an indisputable fact that collectively sub-Saharan Africa has, in fact, performed very poorly, compared to Southeast Asia. Since 1965, the per capita incomes of Southeast Asia grew 11 times faster than those of sub-Saharan Africa. The question is why such a huge gap in economic performance between the two regions, both of which emerged from colonial rule roughly around the same time: during the post-World War II era.

There are several reasons. Economists point to a conjunction of factors associated with rapid economic growth in East Asia during the post-war period: countries like Japan, China, Taiwan and South Korea underwent land redistribution after World War II and became relatively egalitarian nations. That is one prime factor in the acceleration of their economic growth.

An egalitarian disposition does indeed seem to play a role in fueling progress, as the experience of some African societies clearly demonstrates. It is an empirical observation which seems to vindicate these economists who

---

[270] N.D. Kristof, ibid. See also Dinesh D'Souza, *The End of Racism: Principles for a Multicultural Society* (New York: Free Press, 1995), esp. chap. 11, pp. 431-476: *The Content of Our Chromosomes: Race and the IQ Debate*, in which the author discusses several genetic and climatic theories advanced by different people to explain the IQ differences between blacks and members of other races, and also the economic as well as the technological underdevelopment of Africa. Most of the theories are patently racist.

cite the egalitarian factor as a determinant of economic growth. For example the Ibos in Nigeria, and this is just one example among several, are a highly egalitarian people who have also been receptive to European ideas. Within only a few years - in less than three decades - they ended up being some of the most highly educated people in Africa. Yet when the British first arrived in the region, they found them to be among the most backward people in West Africa; at least that was the colonial perception applicable practically everywhere else on the continent with only slight variations. Even as late as the 1930s, the Ibos were not organized into larger groupings than the clan. And geography - the physical isolation - was also a critical factor in slowing down their economic development. As Margery Perham who knew Nigeria first-hand for decades states:

> "The tribes encountered along the coast... east of the Niger... numbered some which had become sophisticated as a result of their contacts with the outside world through the trade in slaves, palm-oil and other products. But, as the British presence was drawn irresistibly further inland, it met the more isolated groups, and above all the numerous Ibo people. The physical conditions of Africa have made possible the virtual isolation from fully effective contacts with other peoples of large populations with resulting sharp contrasts in civilization.
>
> The wet forests east of the Niger hindered the entry of peoples, especially the warlike, slave-raiding, horse and cattle people of the north (mostly the Hausa-Fulani), but the dividing forests also prevented the Ibo developing any political organization above the limited family or clan groupings. To the British officials they seemed at once the most backward and the most intractable group of any size they had met in West Africa, and all attempts failed to find or create any form of chieftainship through which the (colonial) administration could effectively administer these millions.
>
> The Niger Coast Protectorate was proclaimed in 1891. Yet, when I studied the Ibo administration 40 years later (during the 1930s), the British officials were still groping for some structure through which to advance a group regarded as the most difficult and backward in Nigeria. Yet all who knew the Ibo recognized their immense vitality

> and their readiness to embrace all the new influences brought to them, including the Christian faith. As a result, without losing their native vigour, the Ibo forged ahead in the 'forties and 'fifties to become the most active and westernized group in Nigeria and they streamed out of their poor and overcrowded land to employ their energies and their newly-gained skills and education in other parts of the Protectorate. They also showed a capacity, very obvious in today's crisis (the Nigerian civil war), to win the devotion of Europeans, official and unofficial, who worked with them. Add to this that their lack of chiefs and cities gave them an equalitarian unity."[271]

This case of the Ibos shows that, like many other African tribes, they share many characteristics with the people of East Asia which helped both groups to achieve rapid progress in telescoped time within a single generation - just as the Black Africans in Britain have.

The other factors - besides land redistribution after World War II in Japan, China, Taiwan and South Korea which helped to transform them into egalitarian societies - economists cite to explain East Asian economic success include a well-educated and healthy population, a dramatic decline in birth rates, and open free-market policies emphasizing exports which East Asian nations adopted relatively early, contrasted with Africa. A conjunction of all those factors proved critical to East Asia's economic growth.

East Asian countries also had something else in common African countries like Uganda and Ghana have implemented successfully since the late 1980s. They emphasized fiscal responsibility, contained inflation, vigorously promoted export trade, and kept their currencies undervalued. The Asian nations are still following the same combined strategy. African countries did exactly the opposite in the past. Most of the time, they did nothing to reduce skyrocketing inflation. They squandered money - and many are still doing it today. They discouraged production of export commodities by peasants and farmers by controlling the economy and imposing very high taxes. And they did not devalue their currencies, a critical step towards strengthening weak economies. Failure to do all that paralyzed African

[271] Margery Perham, "Nigeria's Civil War," in *Africa Contemporary Record,* op. cit., p. 2-3.

economies and made it impossible for their exports to compete on the world market.

Then there was socialism. Almost all African countries adopted some socialist policies in one way or another, and a number of them - for example Ghana under Dr. Nkrumah, Guinea and Tanzania - were virulently anti-capitalist. Capitalism was, and for good reason, identified with colonialism and the colonial powers - all of them capitalist - from whom they had just won independence, and was therefore seen as a system of exploitation whose continuation by the new African nations would only perpetuate their colonial bondage in a new form: neo-colonialism. By contrast, East Asian nations, especially the most successful ones, avoided socialism. Through the decades, socialism proved to be disastrous round the globe, and African countries were among those who suffered the most.

Savings is another factor which has played a vital role in the rapid economic growth of East Asian nations. Savings are needed to finance new factories and provide capital for investments that stimulate economic growth. Partly because of market incentives and government initiatives, national savings rates have been much higher in Asia, averaging more than 30 percent of the gross domestic product, than in Africa whose savings rate on average is only about 12 percent. For example from 1981-90, according to the World Bank, sub-Saharan Africa's savings rate was 12.6 percent compared with 33.2 for South Korea, Hong Kong, Singapore and Taiwan, and compared with 31.9 percent for Thailand, Indonesia and Malaysia.[272] And many Africans are well aware of the problem. As Professor Samuel Ndomba at the University of Kisangani in Congo states:

> "Our problem is that we don't save. When people get a bit of money, they just spend it to buy a beer."[273]

Besides the profligacy of some individuals, one of the main reasons why many Africans don't save is inflation and political instability compounded by corruption. Money saved ends up being stolen or is simply confiscated in

---

[272] World Bank Reports, East Asia: Savings Rates and Foreign Investment Data, 1981-1990, cited by N.D. Kristof, *Why Africa Can Thrive Like Asia*, ibid.

[273] Samuel Ndomba, quoted by N.D. Kristof, ibid.

many cases in a number of countries. There is no one to take to court because government officials and the courts themselves are corrupt, and they work together. The judges themselves are appointed by corrupt politicians; and politicians cannot be locked up by the judges whom they appointed. It is a vicious cycle. And the police who are supposed to be making the arrests are just as corrupt. Therefore they are not going to arrest the culprits who bribe them on regular basis; another vicious cycle. And they all work together. It is an interlocking mechanism.

If a lot of money was saved, it would help fuel Africa's economic growth. And it can be done. For example, during the nineteenth century, Japan had very low savings rates. But they went up dramatically because of government campaigns encouraging people to save, and also because of the establishment of savings institutions in different parts of the country where people could save their money. Eventually, the large national savings were used to finance Japan's industrialization, one of the most successful in the history of mankind.

Japan also invested a lot in education to train a sufficiently large number of people who then went on to play a critical role in the country's industrialization and rapid economic growth. Without a strong educational foundation, no country can develop on firm basis regardless of how much foreign investment is poured into it. A country first needs manpower. Then it can plan what to do next, including absorbing technical information from abroad because there is already a scientific community in the country to digest and use that information for national development. Many developing countries demand transfer of technology from industrialized nations to them. But where are the people who are going to apply it? There aren't even enough people who understand the technical journals which come from abroad. As Michael J. Moravcsik and J.M. Ziman, professors of physics at the University of Oregon and the University of Bristol respectively, stated in their article "Paradisia and Dominatia: Science and the Developing World" in "Foreign Affairs," July 1975:

> "There are still those who seem unconvinced of the urgency of the need for an indigenous scientific community in a country such as Paradisia. With scientific knowledge and technological know-how available for all on the world market, would it not be easier to import

and use whatever is needed, without building 'local production facilities' in these commodities? This commercial metaphor is appropriate, since the essence of this argument is an appeal to the principles of classical liberal economics - the open market, free trade, economies of scale, and the division of labor. Let the great knowledge factories of the advanced countries export their great surpluses of information, fact and theory, in exchange for industrial products manufactured in the newly developed nations.
At the most elementary level, this analogy is entirely fallacious. Scientific knowledge lacks many of the necessary attributes of a commercial commodity, and cannot be fairly bartered for material goods and services. It is not possible simply to 'import' science and technology in the absence of an indigenous scientific and technical community... (In) Japan, the large-scale importation of scientific techniques in recent times was preceded by decades of development of an indigenous scientific and technological community... Japan's industrial power is now matched by the intellectual resources of a first-class scientific community."[274]

In addition to Japan, each of the other East Asian nations also has a scientific community which is bigger and better trained than any found in black African countries, with the exception of South Africa which inherited a lily-white first-class establishment built by the apartheid regime to perpetuate white supremacy. But East Asia also has had another big advantage over Africa in terms of manpower in general, besides the large number of scientists and technicians. And that is something African countries cannot achieve within a relatively few years, not even in a generation, as demonstrated by Africa's slow progress through the decades; almost 40 years since, African countries won their independence. Countries like South Korea started out on the road towards economic development with citizens who were already more educated, and also more healthy, than those in Africa and other developing

[274] Michael Moravcsik and J.M. Ziman, "Paradisia and Dominatia: Science and the Developing World," in *Foreign Affairs*, July 1975, pp. 704-705, and 702. For a more direct attack on the attempt to represent knowledge as a quantifiable economic category, see J.M. Ziman, Book Review, *Minerva*, July 1974, p. 384.

regions of the world. And they continued to improve their educational and health services through the decades when African countries were taking their first step on a parallel road towards the same destination.

Most Asian nations were also homogeneous societies already for hundreds of years - in the case of China for thousands - before they came into contact with European conquerors. Therefore it was easier for them to function as nation-states in the modern world where the nation-state is the primary institution in the international community. By contrast, almost all the African countries today are relatively new, created by the colonial powers only about 100 years ago. There was no Nigeria before the British came; they are the ones who created it. There was no Senegal before the French came; no Belgian Congo and so forth. There were only different tribes living independent of each other in most cases. And they are still struggling to keep their countries intact and adjust to the realities of living under the modern African state which demands allegiance from all its citizens that supersedes tribal loyalties. And that has seriously interfered with economic progress through the years. It is not easy to build and develop a nation at the same time. And it is not easy to develop a country when there is conflict within. East Asia already had nations, which was one giant leap over Africa into the future.

And there are, of course, health problems which are much more serious in Africa than in the Asian countries which have achieved rapid economic growth. Parasites found in Africa destroy people - and the economy. As Nicholas Kristof reported from Africa:

> "Health problems have also been a greater economic burden on Africa than is often realized. Most Africans, for example, have stomach worms, and as a result millions of people cannot study or work energetically, and some children have their intelligence permanently impaired because of anemia caused by parasites. 'From the age of two, most people here have worms,' shrugged Bakondagama Barandala, a 24-year-old nurse at a shabby clinic in Mambasa, in northeastern Congo. The clinic is a metaphor for public health in Congo: it is the only clinic in the region, yet it has no doctor,

no electricity, no drinking water, no instruments and no medicines."[275]

Mobutu and his cronies stole all the money. His personal fortune alone, in the billions of dollars, equaled his country's national debt, at the very least.

But in spite of the huge gap in economic performance, there are still some similarities between Africa and East Asia. And that partly explains why many people believe African countries can duplicate Asia's success. Much like Asia before its unprecedented economic growth, hundreds of millions of Africans don't differ very much in wealth. One of the main reasons for such egalitarianism is that land in Africa is not owned by a few people as it is in Latin America. In fact in many traditional African societies, land cannot be sold; it can only be held in trust, by the user, because it belongs to the people.

Because Africa is relatively egalitarian in wealth, income gaps on the continent among the vast majority of the people will be smaller than they are in Latin America when African countries achieve substantial economic growth. But what is critical today is that, like in Asia, Africans are able use the land to develop their countries because they enjoy much latitude in deciding what to do with it; which is not the case in Latin America, a continent dominated by landlords versus the landless. Another hopeful sign that Africa can duplicate Asia's success is the decline in birth rates and an increase in literacy which have been recorded in several countries across the continent. Both of those are great achievements for African countries.

But even good economic policies, improved health care, low birth rates, and high literacy won't mean much if corruption remains rampant. There is corruption is Asia, no doubt about it; in fact on a very large scale. But Asians do get things done even when they steal, as shown by their country's spectacular economic growth through the decades. In Africa it is exactly the opposite. Many of those who steal - just steal. They do nothing to develop their countries:

[275] N.D. Kristof, ibid.

> "For the most part graft there (in Asia) is just another cost of doing business; in Africa it often prevents business from being done at all. A joke heard in business circles makes the point:
> An African visited an Asian friend, a Government official, and admired the official's spectacular home and opulent life style. The Asian explained his wealth with a wink toward his 'cut': 'You see that highway out there? Fifteen percent!'
> Then the Asian visited the African, also a government official, and found that he was living just as lavishly. Asked how he had prospered, the African pointed outside, saying: 'You see that highway out there?'
> 'No,' the Asian said, peering helplessly out the window. 'What highway?'
> 'That's just it. One hundred percent.'"[276]

Corruption is going to continue unless the leaders are held accountable for their actions. Africa's commendable performance in the economic arena should encourage the people to question their leaders even more on how they spend their tax money and all the other financial resources intended for national development. But Africa has a long way to go. Long-term development - for decades to come - is possible only if the money needed to sustain such growth comes from locally generated wealth accumulated from national savings and domestic investments, not from foreign investments.

Foreign investments are needed to fuel initial growth due to lack of capital in the poverty-stricken nations of Africa. But the ultimate responsibility for Africa's redemption from the vicious cycle of poverty is Africa's. The amount of foreign investments going to Africa will largely depend on what Africans themselves do to develop their economies. Uganda, and this is only one example, has been able to attract a large number of foreign investors precisely for that reason: It has recovered from economic ruin after making a lot of sacrifices, and is today a model for economic

[276] Ibid. Keith B. Richburg relates the same story in his book *Out of America: A Black Man Confronts Africa* (New York: Basic Books, Harper Collins, 1997), pp. 174-175.

development throughout the entire Third World. It is the leading African "tiger." As *The Economist* states:

> "The European Union (is interested in Africa)... in the hope of finding a few African tigers which the EU can coach and coax into the global economy. Without a success story or two, Africa will be left to its fate - even more than it is already."[277]

The United States is also interested in Africa, but trade between the two is still severely limited, although it is growing. As United States Deputy Treasury Secretary Lawrence Summers said during a visit to Africa in May 1997:

> "There is perhaps more room for well-grounded optimism about economic development in sub-Saharan Africa than at any time in a generation."[278]

Many people have written off the continent as a perpetual loser. But the spectacular economic performance by several African countries in recent years - and it is still going on - may change that perception. In addition to the countries we named earlier, Benin, formerly Dahomey, is another excellent performer. And the list continues to grow. But trade with the world's most powerful and richest country, the United States, will increase only after the majority of African countries have undergone fundamental economic reform and achieved substantial progress. Right now trade between the two is heavily biased against Africa despite some increase of American imports from Africa. According to *The Wall Street Journal*:

> "U.S. imports from sub-Saharan Africa jumped more than 20 percent last year (1996) to $15.2 billion. The European Union, with its many colonial ties, controls the lion's share of African trade. Though the

---

[277] "The EU and the Third World: Wanted - Some African Tigers," in *The Economist*, November 30, 1996, p. 41.

[278] Lawrence H. Summers, quoted by Michael M. Phillips, "U.S. Is Seeking to Build Its Trade With Africa," in *The Wall Street Journal*, June 2, 1997, p. A-1.

U.S. is the single largest national market for African exports, Africa accounts for just 1 percent of U.S. trade. 'The most important determinant of our trade with Africa is the success of African economic reform,' Mr. Summers says."[279]

Africa's exports to the United States consist mainly of oil and minerals from Nigeria, Angola, Gabon and South Africa. According to the United States Commerce Department, Nigeria accounts for the largest share of American imports from sub-Saharan Africa. In 1996, it accounted for 38 percent; Angola was next with 18 percent; South Africa 15 percent; Gabon 13 percent; and the rest of sub-Saharan Africa 16 percent.[280] Oil accounts for the largest share of the imports from Nigeria, Angola and Gabon. In fact Nigeria is the second-biggest supplier of oil to the United States after Saudi Arabia; and Angola is the second-biggest producer of oil in sub-Saharan Africa after Nigeria.

The road towards long-term economic development for Africa will not be easy, especially for much poorer countries. But for countries which don't have a lot of mineral wealth, textiles and other light manufactured goods such as footwear and other products as well as other items such as baskets and a variety of weaved material and wood products - and a host of other items from the cottage industry - can offer a well-tested path to development before they industrialize. Industrialization is a long-term goal which requires large investment and a well-educated and healthy workforce. As Benjamin Kipkorir, Kenya's ambassador to the United States, said on the prospects for light industry as the road towards industrialization for Africa:

"Every country that has industrialized, starting from England in the eighteenth-century, began with textiles. We'd like to do the same thing."[281]

Kenya's garment industry collapsed after the United States imposed an import quota in 1994.[282] Intra-African trade is probably the best alternative to

[279] Michael M. Phillips, ibid.
[280] United States Department of Commerce data, cited ibid.
[281] Benjamin Kipkorir, quoted ibid.

overseas trade which can save many African industries from collapsing. But an African economic union, which will create an African common market, is still a distant goal, although African leaders say they are already laying the foundation for it by forming regional economic blocs. There are two major ones so far on the entire continent, and both are in sub-Saharan Africa. The biggest is the Economic Community of West African States (ECOWAS) comprising 16 members:

Nigeria, Ivory Coast, Ghana, Senegal, Gambia, Cape Verde, Guinea, Liberia, Guinea-Bissau, Sierra Leone, Mali, Mauritania, Burkina Faso, Niger, Togo, and Benin.

The South African Development Community (SADC), whose members we named in the previous chapter, is Africa's strongest economic bloc because of South Africa's membership. It became even much more powerful when mineral-rich Congo, the former Zaire, joined the Community in 1997.

At the Organization of African Unity (OAU) summit in Zimbabwe in June 1997, the continent's leaders held the first meeting of the African Economic Community, 17 years after the plan for a continental economic union was first formulated in 1980; however, it had its genesis in the first meeting of African heads of state and government further back in May 1963 when the OAU was founded in Addis Adaba, Ethiopia. The plan is ambitious: it calls for the creation of an African common market on a continental scale embracing all the 53 African countries. But the time table is not: Africans hope to establish a common market by 2030, which is an entire generation from today.

The African Economic Community is intended to merge regional blocs into a single entity, similar to the European Union. It may even institute a common currency for the entire continent to facilitate commerce. But as Kenneth Kotelo, an economist at the Africa Institute in Pretoria, capital of South Africa, said about this ambitious goal:

> "In the 1980s, some countries were socialist, and policy divided us. For the first time now, Africa is pursuing a common economic policy, and market reforms have been embraced. But I don't see a single

[282] M.M. Phillips, ibid.

> economic community materializing by 2030. You would need to have the regional economic forums functioning first, but at the moment they are not."[283]

More than half a dozen such groups exist, with differing aims and limited success. But they are all headed in the right direction because their goals are Pan-African in intent. Besides ECOWAS and SADC, the other groups include the West African Economic Community (CEAO) comprising Ivory Coast, Senegal, Mali, Mauritania, Burkina Faso, and Niger, all of which are former French colonies, while ECOWAS is both Francophone and Anglophone with five English-speaking members - Nigeria, Ghana, Liberia, Sierra Leone, and Gambia - out of a total of 16. Four West African French-speaking countries are not members of CEAO. They are Guinea, Togo, Benin and Cameroon, although Cameroon is also identified as a central African nation.

Another group is the Central African Customs and Economic Union (UDEAC) whose members are: Cameroon, Central African Republic, Gabon, Congo-Brazzaville, and Equatorial Guinea - the only former Spanish colony in black Africa which joined UDEAC in 1983, and the FAC franc zone in 1985. The rest of the UDEAC members are former French colonies.

Then there is the Preferential Trade Area for Eastern and Southern Africa (PTA) comprising Ethiopia, Eritrea, Somalia, Djibouti, Kenya, Uganda and all the SADC member countries. There is also the Inter-Governmental Authority on Development (IGAD) whose members are Uganda, Ethiopia, and Eritrea who are also involved as a trio in the Sudan conflict supporting the Sudenese People's Liberation Army (SPLA) in its struggle for autonomy in southern Sudan. As the *New African* states:

> "The SPLA is on a roll. Its leader John Garang... has external support. He has friends in Uganda, Ethiopia, Eritrea, in effect all the states of the Inter-Governmental Authority on Development (IGAD) which, belying (its) development name, spends most of its time trying to resolve the Sudan conflict. IGAD's efforts at mediation have been

---

[283] Kenneth Kotelo, quoted in "African Union? A Bit Closer," in the *International Herald Tribune,* August 12, 1997, p. 13.

met with total intransigence by the Islamic regime and most of its members are actively supporting Khartoum's opponents. The SPLA has been directly assisted by Uganda and indirectly by the US that last year (1996) poured $20 million of arms into the countries that oppose the Islamic regime in Khartoum. Garang is supported by all Sudanese who want to restore democracy in their country. They are grouped under the umbrella of the National Democratic Alliance, which now coordinates all Sudanese opposition forces from its external headquarters in Asmara, Eritrea."[284]

Besides the conflict in the Sudan, the three countries involved - Uganda, Ethiopia, and Eritrea - also want to promote regional cooperation with other African countries to achieve economic integration. And the economic groups which exist today are the best institutional structures Africa has, so far, to pursue this goal. As President Robert Mugabe, chairman of the Organization of African Unity (OAU), stated at the OAU summit he hosted in his country's capital Harare, Zimbabwe:

> "In these institutions lies the embryonic form of community Africa seeks to achieve via political and economic integration."[285]

In the past it has been cheaper and easier for most African countries, whose economies are still based mostly on raw materials and commodities, to trade with their former colonial masters than with their neighbors. This is what they want change. And it is encouraging to note that African economic growth rose from less than 1 percent in 1992 to more than 5.5 percent in 1996,[286] an upward trend which is expected to continue. But population growth, at about 3 percent per year, is still a burden on a continent whose population is going to reach 1 billion by the year 2000. Unfortunately, market reforms and privatization have yet to be matched by an increase in foreign investments despite considerable inflows from Asia, led by Malaysia. However, Africa's impressive economic growth, like its ability in many cases

---

[284] "SPLA Opens Second Front," in the *New African,* op. cit., p. 21.

[285] Robert Mugabe, quoted in "African Union? A Bit Closer," ibid.

[286] "African Union? A Bit Closer," ibid.

to find markets for its export commodities, makes a strong case for the need to establish a common market on a continental scale. As President Yoweri Museveni, who has turned Uganda into an economic model, states:

> "Now that African economies are beginning to grow, basing themselves on private enterprise, we must think of one additional factor - the size of the market."[287]

And he has the credibility and credentials to talk about the imperative need for such a market because of what he has achieved in Uganda. When he assumed power, he started with virtually nothing in terms of financial resources, infrastructure, and institutions for effective administration. Uganda was a total wreck, pulverized from within. As Lara Santoro reported from Uganda in "The Christian Science Monitor":

> "The Ugandan president inherited a wasteland, a 'ground zero' of human devastation, and turned it into an economic powerhouse that sustained 6.3 percent growth over a decade. Between 1985 and 1995, Uganda growth ranked 15th in the world (out of a total of 186 countries)... By the time he took over in 1986, 16 million Ugandans had been collectively scarred by the rule of Idi Amin... During Mr. Amin's rule, more than half a million people were killed over the course of eight years. Museveni took over a country pockmarked with mass graves. The state was bankrupt, revenue from taxation was virtually nonexistent, and Uganda's economy was stagnant.
>
> Today, downtown Kampala (the capital) is a vibrant place. Like New York, this city never sleeps. Market vendors peddle their merchandise well past midnight in a swirl of smoke from nearby bonfires. All around them, people with pocket calculators settle deals, exchange wads of bank notes, and negotiate partnerships by the quivering light of candles. 'You don't know what Uganda was like before Museveni,' says a doctor who spent several months working for the Red Cross during Amin's reign (of terror). 'It was madness. This is good, very

[287] Yoweri Museveni, quoted in "African Union? A Bit Closer," ibid.

> good.' It took vision for such a transformation to take place. It took suspending protective tariffs, abolishing price controls, lifting restrictions on capital flows, and privatizing state-controlled businesses."[288]

Uganda is only one example, although probably the best besides Ghana and Botswana. Chances are good that Africa, with hundreds of millions of people and robust economies, could become the world's most lucrative market during the twentieth-first century. For decades, bad news had been coming out of Africa. Today good news is, a fact acknowledged by the World Bank as well. For example in February 1997, the Bank's Group President James Wolfensohn toured Senegal, Ghana, Mozambique, and South Africa and acknowledged that everywhere he was "getting good news out of Africa."[289] In supporting literature, at the time of Wolfensohn's trip, the Bank also conceded:

> "Africa is becoming a good business address... most African countries have turned their economies round in the last two years. Economic performance has improved considerably with 24 countries posting growth figures of over 4 percent - above the rate of population growth. This success has given grounds for cautious optimism about the continent."[290]

Things began to improve dramatically in 1994 on a continent where there had been negative growth - with populations increasing faster than production - in the 1980s and even in the early 1990s. But from 1994 the economies began to grow due to a number of factors including liberalization of foreign exchange, removal of restrictions on imports and foreign investments, and elimination of price controls for agricultural products which discouraged

---

[288] Lara Santoro, *West Cheers Uganda's One-Man Show*, op. cit. See also Yoweri Museveni's autobiography, *Sowing the Mustard Seed: The Struggle for Freedom and Democracy in Uganda.*

[289] James Wolfensohn, quoted by Alan Rake, "Good News Out of Africa," in the *New African*, op. cit., p. 30.

[290] World bank report, cited by A. Rake, ibid.

farmers from increasing production. For example in West Africa, the economies grew by an average of 1.4 percent in 1994, 4 percent in 1994, and over 5 percent in 1996.[291]

In French-speaking Africa, the change was even more dramatic. Not only did the economies improve; their common currency, the CFA which was instituted and is underwritten by France to perpetuate neocolonial control over her former colonies, was devalued in January 1994, a move which fueled economic growth. All the former French colonies in Africa, except Guinea, use the FCA franc. Guinea, since the days of its fiercely independent leader President Sekou Toure who died in November 1984, uses its own currency, the Guinean franc. In 1985 the CFA club got another member when Equatorial Guinea joined the franc zone. The former Spanish colony is the only member of the CFA franc zone which was not a French colony.

At first, devaluation of the CFA franc triggered skyrocketing inflation and led to a sharp increase in the price of imports. But it gave genuine value to the currency, leading to a dramatic increase in exports, the inflow of foreign investments, easier trade with neighboring countries, and more local cash to pay farmers for their crops. Immediately after the devaluation, trade increased. With the true value of the currency reflected in prices, farmers from landlocked countries increased their livestock exports to coastal countries such as Ivory Coast, Guinea, Togo and Benin. Factories which had been running at a fraction of capacity were able to compete with foreign imports and find export markets. Textiles and cement were particularly successful. Those are also some of the most common products African countries are able to produce, along with leather and wood products.

With the boom in the import/export trade came investments. Foreign investors invested a considerable amount of money in all the countries which were doing spectacularly well. Oil companies were among the biggest investors in several African countries: Congo-Brazzaville, Equatorial Guinea, Ivory Coast, Chad, and Cameroon which is building a $3 billion oil pipeline to export Chad's oil. Mining companies from America, Europe, and Australia also took great interest in Africa's growing economies and invested in gold

---

291 A. Rake, "Good News Out of Africa," ibid.

mines and others in all parts of the continent, from Ghana to Tanzania, Zimbabwe to Ivory Coast.

Agriculture, the mainstay of African economies, also enjoyed considerable growth during the 1990s across the continent, although still not enough to feed all its people and end food imports. But agricultural production is expected to increase. Agricultural commodities account for 30 to 35 percent of the gross domestic product (GDP) of African countries and up to 90 percent of their exports. It is also the largest employer with about 70 percent of the workforce. In the past overvalued exchange rates, government price controls, restrictions on private investment and lack of adequate infrastructure and markets, severely retarded economic growth. But fundamental economic reforms which led to almost a complete overhaul of the socialist system across the continent and the adoption of austerity measures have rejuvenated African economies. For example, devaluations in many other African countries besides those in the CFA franc zone have given governments more local currency to pay their farmers. And that has served as a big incentive to increased agricultural production.

According to the World Bank, Benin, Botswana, Burkina Faso, Mali, Uganda, and Tanzania have "experienced a turnaround in agriculture in the past few years." In the Ivory Coast, Ghana, Malawi, and Zambia, the agricultural sector is "improving," and Kenya has had steady growth of 3-4 percent during the past 25 since 1972.[292] The Bank attributes this to stable exchange rates, decreased budget deficits, high-quality public investment, reduced role of the state in production, processing and marketing; and investment in rural infrastructure, health and education. It is going to take a number of years before conditions improve dramatically for the vast majority of the people on the continent, but it is not going to take forever. For example, Alan Friedman of the *International Herald Tribune* asked J. Brian Atwood, administrator of the US Agency for International Development (USAID), the following question:

---

[292] Ibid. See also World Bank reports: "A Vote of Confidence in Emerging Africa"; "Regionalization: Forging Economic Links Inside Africa"; "Sub-Saharan Africa: An Overview"; and "Restoring Competitiveness: Successful Devaluation in the CFA Zone." All these are 1990s reports.

"Most people think it could take 50 years before much of Africa truly emerges in economic and market terms. How much can be done realistically?"[293]

He responded:

"I don't doubt that it will take a generation to exploit the great potential of Africa. It took about that long in Asia and Latin America, and we are now seeing the benefits of investments made 30 years ago. Africa has seen an enormous increase in growth in recent years and yet Africa still attracts only 1.2 percent of $200 billion of annual global private investment... There are pockets of rapid growth in places such as Uganda, Ghana and Botswana. These are some of the fastest-growing economies in the world... This is an indication of (Africa's) potential... It is a matter of the African nations accepting the need for reform, going through two or three years of pain as they deregulate, as they leave unprotected some of their internal productive capacity...
I think Uganda and Botswana are probably the best... models in Africa today that are embracing reform... Uganda has been highly disciplined in its economic reform over the last five years. They have opened up their economy, they have created an enabling environment that gives investors confidence by working to establish a good banking system and having a government that doesn't intervene in the economy. They are encouraging the private sector. And they have (more than) doubled the percentage of foreign investment as a percentage of their gross national product, from 7 to 16 percent. Botswana, meanwhile, is a very stable democracy and very fast-moving."[294]

It may take a generation for Africa to get where some of the Southeast Asian countries such as Thailand are today. And that is a realistic scenario,

[293] Alan Friedman, "Helping Africa Go the Way of Reforms," in the *International Herald Tribune,* May 20, 1997, p. 6.
[294] J. Brian Atwood, ibid.

just as Thailand is probably the best example that might be easier to match, since it is less developed than the other Southeast Asian nations - South Korea, Singapore, Indonesia, and Malaysia. But Africa must also do something else that Southeast Asia never did to achieve that goal. Starting with a less-educated workforce and in poorer health than the Asian nations did, African countries must conduct more inter-territorial trade and integrate their economies to fuel rapid economic growth. Otherwise all talk of African "tigers" emerging on the horizon a generation hence is no more than empty rhetoric.

Foreign aid has not worked. Africa is still underdeveloped. As long as Africa remains disunited, with each of the dozens of economies on the continent going its own way, and as long as corruption continues, any money given to Africa to help develop the continent is money wasted. Even the money given to implement free-market reforms has not always worked. As Michael Chege, a Kenyan professor at Harvard University, stated in "The Times Literary Supplement":

> "In the ostensible effort to kick-start self-sustaining and 'open' - as opposed to protectionist - capitalist economies in Africa, no region in the world has received as much external aid over the past two decades: $36 per capita in 1993, compared to $8 in Latin America and just $4 in South Asia. On average, some 16 per cent of that gradually disappearing global share of the African gross domestic product was made up of concessional financial infusions from Western governments and multilateral organizations like the World Bank and the European Commission. In equally poor Asia, economic recovery is already under way, even though foreign donations as a share of GDP were running at about a third of those of Africa up until the early 1990s."[295]

[295] Michael Chege, "Africa Is Not One Country: Time to Put Away the Heroic Stereotypes," in *The Times Literary Supplement*, London, January 3, 1997, p. 14. See also Merilee S. Grindle, *Challenging the State; Crisis and Innovation in Latin America and Africa* (Cambridge: Cambridge University Press, 1997); Benno Ndulu and Nicolas van de Walle, editors, *Agenda for Africa's Economic Renewal* (Brunswick, New Jersey: Transaction, 1997); and Mamadou

But in spite of Africa's enormous problems, there are many encouraging signs that the continent is moving in the right direction as shown by the increasing economic growth in different countries across the continent. Probably the most encouraging sign of what South African President Thabo Mbeki calls the "African Renaissance" is not only the fact that African economies are growing as never before, but the fact that they are growing at rates much higher than population growth which is climbing up at 3 percent per year. Yet there is reason not to be overly optimistic. As World Bank vice presidents Callisto Madavo and Jean-Louis Sarbib state in their assessment of Africa's economic performance and prospects:

> "Effective development in the region will require a hefty 8 to 10 percent annual GDP growth."[296]

Several African countries are already within that range. Some have even surpassed the 10 percent annual GDP growth rate recommended by the two World Bank chiefs, as we showed earlier in this chapter; while the average growth rate for the entire sub-Saharan region was more than 5.5 percent in 1996,[297] a very impressive performance by a continent facing so many problems. In fact Ivory Coast, Ghana, Uganda, South Africa and Botswana are now almost in the same league with Thailand, Malaysia, and the Philippines as prime markets for new foreign investments. Another country which has benefited enormously from the liberalization of exchange rates and other reforms is Mali where the new economic policies have improved export competitiveness without significant inflation. Yet this is a country which for years has depended on international relief efforts just to feed its people. If the present trend continues, it is going to be a different story within a few years. Mali is already destined to become one of the most prosperous countries in Africa, as we showed in the previous chapter. And as Madavo and Sarbib point out:

Dia, editor, *Africa's Management in the 1990s and Beyond* (Washington, DC: World Bank, 1997).

[296] C. Madavo and J.L. Sarbib, *A New Africa Is Generating Success and Hope*, op cit.

[297] "African Union? A Bit Closer," in the *International Herald Tribune*, op. cit.

"Togo, Lesotho and Uganda have averaged 10 percent growth in the last two years. Policy reforms in the CFA franc zone countries have led to export expansion from negative 3 percent (1991 to 1993) to positive 6.6 percent (1994 to 1996). Private capital is increasingly flowing to Africa, and seeing healthy returns. Private investment has increased more than 10-fold since the early 1990s, to $11.7 billion in 1996. From 1990 to 1994, rates of return on foreign direct investment in Africa averaged between 24 and 30 percent, compared with 16 to 18 percent for all developing countries."[298]

The rates of return would probably be even higher if foreigners increased their investments in Africa. However, that requires a complementary strategy involving foreigners on the one hand, and African countries on the other, working together. First, conditions must be suitable for investment in Africa, and must also be constantly improved. And foreigners must have confidence in Africa's economic prospects before they risk their investments. And now that the days of foreign aid - at least in substantial amounts - are virtually over, it is for Africans to make sure that they get their fair share of foreign private capital to help fuel their economies. The money is there, but it is not always guaranteed and can be reduced sharply or be completely withdrawn by foreign - and even by local - investors if it is in their best interest to do so.

Private investors have poured hundreds of billions of dollars into developing countries since 1990. They have overtaken public aid agencies such as the United States Agency for International Development (USAID) and others, as the main source of development finance. For example, in 1990 less than half of the international capital going to developing nations came from private sources. But by 1996, this share of foreign private investment had risen dramatically to 86 percent.[299] As they look around the world for places

[298] C. Madavo and J.L. Sarbib, "A New Africa Is Generating Success and Hope," ibid. See also "Economic Reform in Africa: The Rulers, The Ruled and African Reality," in *The Economist*, September 20, 1997, p. 49.

[299] Hilary F. French, *Investing in the Future: Harnessing Private Capital Flows for Environmentally Sustainable Development*, No. 139, World Watch paper, Washington DC, February 1998, p. 8. Development assistance spending decline and aid versus private flows

to invest from which they can get the highest return, foreign private investors naturally choose countries which have an abundance of natural resources. Africa is one of those places suitable for investment because of the continent's vast amount of natural resources. African countries are also among those which have seen the vital role foreign investments have played in fueling economic growth around the world.

According to the World Bank, the amount of private capital flowing into the "emerging markets" of the Third World exploded in the early 1990s, rising from $44 billion at the beginning of the decade to $244 billion in 1996.[300] The inflows of foreign capital accelerated a record-breaking economic boom in many countries, China being the best example. The world's biggest economy attracted the largest amount of foreign investments which helped it to expand at double-digit annual rates in the first half of the 1990s. But the inflow of such capital is determined by local conditions. Therefore, in order to be able to get a fair amount of this foreign capital to help fuel their economies, African countries must create conditions favorable to foreign investment especially under which investors earn high returns and are able to take those earnings out of the country. However, they must also be aware that the inflow of such capital can stop suddenly and throw their economies into a tailspin. As Hilary French states in "Investing in the Future; Harnessing Private Capital Flows for Environmentally Sustainable Development":

> "Nineteen ninety-seven was a rough year for the global economy. As a wave of currency depreciations, stock market collapses, and bank closures swept through East Asia, economists who just months earlier were singing the praises of the 'Asian miracle' were suddenly

based on World Bank, *Global Development Finance 1997: Volume I* (Washington, DC: 1997). Reasons for aid's decline from the Organization for Economic Co-Operation and Development (OECD), *Development Cooperation: 1996 Report*, (Paris: 1997).

[300] H.F. French, ibid., p. 5. See also United Nations Conference on Trade and Development (UNCTAD), *World Investment Report 1997* (New York: United Nations, 1997). Economic growth rates from the International Monetary Fund (IMF), *World Economic Outlook*, October 1996 (Washington, DC: 1996); private capital flows in 1997 a preliminary estimate from IMF, *World Economic Outlook*, Interim Assessment (Washington, DC: December 1997); and *Global Development Finance*, op. cit.

decrying the region's weak underpinnings... In the wake of the Asian crisis, the international capital that had been pouring into that region since the beginning of the decade suddenly reversed course as investors raced for the exit. This turnaround brought total private capital flows to emerging markets down to $175 billion in 1997, according to preliminary estimates by the International Monetary Fund (IMF)."[301]

Therefore the primary emphasis by African countries should be on capital accumulation from national savings and domestic investments which is the only way they can fuel economic growth on long-term basis for decades to come. Foreign investments do help, when they are available, and in amounts African countries deem necessary to finance economic development. But that is not always the case and they are no substitute for locally created wealth as the best source of capital for sustained economic growth. Just as important to remember is the fact that developing countries still receive only a relatively small share of total international private capital flows, for example only 37 percent of all foreign direct investment (FDI) inflows in 1996.[302]

Most of the international private capital comes from imperial corporations - tentacles of neocolonial powers - whose primary interest is to make money for themselves, not to develop African countries or any other Third World nations. Therefore they are going to invest where they expect the highest return; which means they cannot be depended upon to fuel economic growth in poverty-stricken nations because they don't expect to earn much when they invest in those countries. For example in Africa, they would rather invest in Angola than in Ethiopia, or in Congo (former Zaire) than in Burundi.[303]

And every country is stronger - or more attractive as a potential financial market - in some areas of investment than others, thus drawing in different kinds of investors in varying numbers. Private capital flows to the developing

---

[301] H.F. French, ibid., pp. 5 and 6.

[302] UNCTAD, *World Investment Report 1997*, op. cit.

[303] See, for example, "Battle for Strategic Positions in Zaire," in the *Financial Times*, London, April 23, 1997; Howard W. French, "The Great Gold Rush in Zaire," in *The New York Times*, April 18, 1997; and "Review of African Stock Markets," in *African Business*, No. 229, London, February 1998.

world take three principal forms: foreign direct investment (FDI) by companies, often through joint ventures with local firms; portfolio investment in which stocks and bonds are purchased on local capital markets by individuals and large institutional investors such as insurance companies, mutual funds, and pension plans; and commercial bank loans. But it is foreign direct investment (FDI) which is the largest source of private capital going to Africa and other developing regions of the world. It added up to $110 billion in 1996 - 45 percent of the total private flows - having more than quadrupled since 1990. In general, investment from domestic sources is still 10 times as large - $1.2 trillion in 1995 - but the share of foreign capital in the Third World is growing at a phenomenal rate.[304]

However, because domestic investments are the largest source of capital, there is cause for optimism among African countries, since it means they have the potential to mobilize substantial amounts of financial resources within, complemented by foreign capital, to fuel economic growth. And they have the capacity, the means, and the resources to do so, as shown by the great interest among foreigners to invest in those countries all of which remain highly dependent on direct natural resource extraction - farming, fishing, logging, mining and drilling for oil. For example in Botswana, diamond mining alone attracts most of the foreign direct investment (FDI).

The next biggest source of foreign private capital going to developing countries is portfolio investment. It accounts for just under 40 percent of the total share, a percentage which is not very far behind FDI's share of 45 percent. Portfolio investment includes stocks, in which investors own shares in companies; and bonds, in which private investors make long-term loans to governments or businesses at fixed interest rates. By 1997, 16 stock markets had already opened up in African countries including Zimbabwe, Ghana, Ivory Coast, Nigeria, Uganda and Kenya. Tanzania was scheduled to open hers in 1998, having completed the groundwork in 1997 for the establishment of such a market. Only a few years earlier, before African countries opened up their economies to the capitalist onslaught masterminded by the corporate elite and other financial moghuls, only South Africa had a strong stock

---

[304] World Bank, *Global Development Finance*, op. cit, and H.F. French, *Investing in the Future*, ibid., p. 11.

market. Popular sectors for portfolio investment include finance, infrastructure, manufacturing, mining, telecommunications, transportation, and utilities; the same sectors, among others such as construction and farming and fishing, which attract foreign direct investment (FDI).

But portfolio investment is also the most unreliable among all sources of private capital. Therefore it cannot be relied upon to finance long-term development projects especially in African countries which are politically unstable. Investors may withdraw their funds quickly if they lose confidence in a country's political stability and economic prospects. For example, when Kenya was rocked by political upheaval - ethnic violence, political demonstrations and murders many of which were instigated by the government itself and its security forces - for several months in 1997 before the general election in December, many investors pulled out and several loans by international lenders including the World Bank were suspended. The capital flight threatened to plunge Kenya deeper into chaos which could have degenerated into anarchy had the government not implemented some of the political reforms demanded by the opposition to liberalize the political process. However, the incumbent president, Daniel arap Moi, went on to win a rigged election, leaving the country in a state of uncertainty of where it was headed. Other African countries have suffered similar fate, only in varying degrees. But the lesson is clear: dependence on foreign investments to develop a country is suicidal.

The other source of foreign capital flowing into African countries and other Third World nations is commercial bank lending. In 1996, it accounted for 14 percent - or $34 billion - of the total foreign private investments in those countries. That was a substantial increase from the total at the beginning of the decade, which was $3 billion. However, the dramatic rise may have been a temporary phenomenon. Because of the economic and financial problems in Asian countries in 1997, the amount of commercial loans going into Third World countries dropped dramatically.[305]

Private capital from major world banks such as Citibank began to flow rapidly into developing nations during the 1970s, when petrodollars filling up major banks in the United States, Europe and Japan forced international

[305] Ibid.

bankers to find more customers in Third World nations. Unfortunately for those countries, high interest rates and questionable investment policies led to an astronomical increase in debt for them, leading to the debt crisis of the 1980s and stagnation in the disbursement of more loans.[306]

When international lending again went up in the mid-1990s, the loan recipients were mainly private businesses rather than governments. Much of the money was short-term loans to national banks - for example from Citibank to Tanzania's National Bank of Commerce (NBC) - which they in turn lent to local borrowers for a variety of business ventures. However, in many of the developing countries, the money was not well-spent. A substantial amount went into questionable ventures including real investment schemes in Asia, which were uncovered later on. A lot of the money also went into meaningful projects such as highways and power plants, although in those areas also like everywhere else, some of the money ended up in the pockets of corrupt individuals and officials.[307]

After looking at all the three major sources of international private capital going into African countries and other developing parts of the world, we see that none of them can be entirely relied upon to finance development projects and help fuel economic growth in the Third World on long-term basis. The money can come to an abrupt end at any time, and for any reason. However, because of Africa's vast natural resources, foreigners will continue to invest in different countries across the continent as long as the political and economic conditions are conducive to investment. So far, the mineral sector is the most attractive; and almost every African country has plenty of those, as we learned in the previous chapter. But countries endowed with an abundance of other natural resources are an excellent prospect as well. Investors are drawn to those countries in even larger numbers because they also have a dazzling array of minerals besides forest products, for example. Unfortunately, they don't control their own resources as much as they should when foreigners invest in those countries. Dependence on foreign capital and technology puts them in a compromising position despite the abundance of

---

[306] H.F. French, ibi., p. 18. See also World Bank, *Private Capital Flows to Developing Countries* (New York: Oxford University Press, 1997).

[307] H.F. French, ibid., p. 19.

resources they have at their disposal on their own soil. As Hilary French points out:

> "The growing flow of funds into natural resources extraction in developing countries is particularly pronounced within the mining industry. From 1991 to 1997, international spending on exploration for nonferrous metals... doubled in Africa... Spending on exploration for gold (worldwide) has been growing particularly fast, accounting for nearly two thirds of total spending on metals exploration in recent years...
>
> More than 90 percent of known oil and gas reserves are now in the developing world... (And in terms of logging), European firms, for instance have long been active in Africa: in the early 1980s, some 90 percent of logging operations in Gabon were foreign-owned, as were some 77 percent of those in Congo (Brazzaville), nearly 90 percent of those in Cameroon, and virtually all those in Liberia. At least 17 European companies were operating in Cote d'Ivoire (Ivory Coast) alone in 1990, and they have shown no sign of letting up in recent years...
>
> With their own forests greatly reduced, logging companies from Indonesia, Malaysia, and elsewhere in Asia are vying for vast timber concessions in Africa... Congo (Brazzaville), (and) the Democratic Republic of Congo (formerly Zaire)... are among the countries that have given or are on the brink of giving away the rights to log large tracts of primary forests - often at prices that do not reflect their marketplace value let alone their ecological worth. Some of the companies involved have a long history of catastrophic environmental destruction, tax evasion, and corruption - a fact that does not augur well for their new hosts."[308]

Such foreign control of Africa's resources does not augur well for the continent's future. Africans need to control their own resources. But they are

[308] Ibid., pp. 19, 20, 21 and 22. *African Business*, 1997-1998, and *New African Yearbook: 53 African Countries, 1997/98*, London, 1998.

severely handicapped in that area because they have to depend on foreign capital and expertise to extract those resources. So foreign investment and technical know-how will continue to come in from abroad until African countries industrialize and take over the operations from foreigners who don't even pay Africans what they are duly entitled to. Partnership between the two is for mutual benefit. But it is an asymmetrical relationship to the detriment of Africans who will continue to be exploited by foreigners - who don't care about the well-being of Africans and their environment - until they team up on regional and continental basis to achieve rapid economic growth without which industrialization is impossible.

But even the most dynamic economic reforms and policies leading to rapid growth are not going to end ethnic conflicts and overcome regional loyalties which have threatened the very existence of African countries since independence. They may, in fact, exacerbate conflict because of the inequity of power and wealth among different ethnic and regional groups many of which feel they have been locked out because of what they are. So far, the modern African state which has been almost a total failure through the decades as a fundamental dynamic in Africa's economic performance, has demonstrated the ability to maintain the integrity of African nations. However, it has been able to do so only by invoking authoritarian measures. But it has not resolved the underlying cause of the conflict, which is one of Africa's most intractable problems: tribalism versus nationalism. The two contending forces are irreconcilable, therefore mutually exclusive. How to resolve the conflict between the two is the subject of another book in which we focus on what was one of Africa's most violent explosions, the Nigerian civil war, and its implications for Africa today.

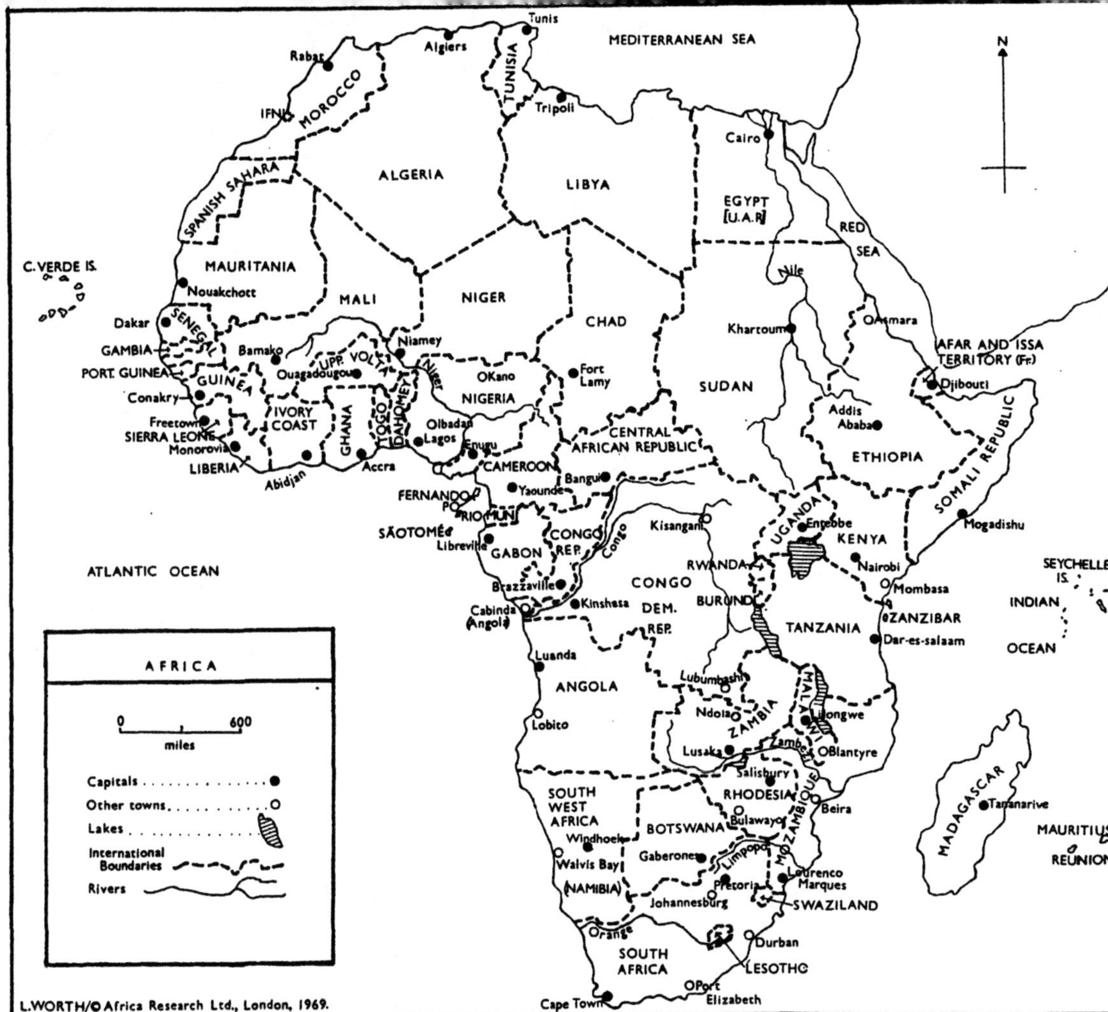

L. WORTH/© Africa Research Ltd., London, 1969.

ABOUT THE MAP OF AFRICA

Fernando Po (renamed Bioko) and Rio Muni, which constituted the colony of Spanish Guinea, won independence as Equatorial Guinea on October 12, 1968. Portuguese Guinea became independent as Guinea-Bissau on September 10, 1974. Dahomey was renamed Benin on November 30, 1975.

Spain turned over its colony of Spanish Sahara in northwest Africa to Morocco and Mauritania on February 26, 1976, and the territory was renamed Western Sahara. On the following day, the Sahara nationalists of the Polisario Front guerilla group declared independence as the Sahara Arab Democratic Republic. On April 14, 1976, Morocco and Mauritania agreed to partition the territory. Morocco annexed the northern two-thirds and Mauritania the southern third.

On August 5, 1979, Mauritania signed a peace agreement with the Polisario guerrillas and renounced its claim to the southern third of Western Sahara. Morocco went on to claim the whole territory, invoking history to justify its claim that the area had always been part of Morocco. But Western Saharans resisted the encroachment. Western Sahara remained contested territory at the end of 1999, awaiting a UN-supervised referendum – which Morocco has blocked through the years – to determine whether or not the people of this former Spanish colony want independence or incorporation into Morocco.

The French Territory of Afars and Issas became independent as Djibouti on June 27, 1977. Rhodesia won independence as Zimbabwe on April 18, 1980. Upper Volta changed its name to Burkina Faso on August 4, 1984. South West Africa became independent as Namibia on March 21, 1990. And Eritrea separated from Ethiopia and won independence on May 3, 1993.

The names, and territorial integrity, of the rest of the African countries remain the same.

ABOUT THE AUTHOR

GODFREY MWAKIKAGILE was born in Kigoma, Tanganyika, which became Tanzania in 1964 after uniting with Zanzibar. He was a reporter of *The Standard*, which later became the *Daily News*, in the capital Dar es Salaam, where he also once worked as an information officer at the Ministry of Information and Broadcasting. He is a graduate of Wayne State University in Detroit, Michigan, USA, and the author of six books: *Africa and the West*, *Military Coups in Africa since the Sixties*, *Africa after Independence: Realities of Nationhood*, *The Modern African State: Quest for Transformation*, *Economic Development in Africa*, and *Ethnic Politics in Kenya and Nigeria: Including an In-depth Look at the Nigerian Civil War 1967-1970.*

INDEX

A

acceleration · 224
accountability · 70, 174, 183, 206, 212
African unity · 33, 38, 59, 98, 146
agricultural commodities · xi, 109
agricultural potential · 9, 12, 89, 99, 101, 109, 110, 138, 140, 154, 159, 160
agricultural products · 28, 77, 101, 103, 116, 130, 132, 136, 138, 154, 163, 199, 214, 239
agricultural sector · 14, 26, 76, 89, 100, 109, 112, 114, 129, 159, 162, 163, 185, 187, 241
Agriculture · 13, 88, 119, 132, 185, 241
Angola · x, 5, 106, 153, 162, 163, 164, 165, 166, 167, 168, 169, 170, 171, 191, 193, 201, 215, 234, 247
apartheid · 86, 156, 158, 159, 165, 196, 229
Asia · 2, 22, 35, 72, 129, 176, 177, 180, 199, 206, 207, 214, 215, 218, 223, 224, 226, 227, 229, 231, 232, 237, 242, 243, 250, 251
assassination · 201
Australia · 90, 198, 240
automobiles · 16
autonomy · 35, 48, 49, 50, 192, 236

B

balance of payments · 196
bankers · 250
banking services · 90
banking system · 242
banks, commercial · 194
base metals · 9
Bechuanaland · 11
Benin · ix, 5, 71, 114, 115, 116, 124, 171, 193, 233, 235, 236, 240, 241, 254
Biafra · 38, 40, 44, 105, 122
Botswana · 11, 12, 13, 14, 15, 16, 17, 18, 59, 71, 106, 121, 155, 156, 160, 164, 165, 171, 221, 224, 239, 241, 242, 244, 248
bourgeoisie · 81
Brazil · 113, 129, 172, 207
Britain · 2, 26, 32, 44, 65, 99, 111, 189, 217, 218, 222, 226
brothers · 111, 202
bureaucracy · 4, 67, 72, 73
Burkina Faso · 28, 108, 109, 124, 125, 171, 174, 221, 235, 236, 241, 254
Burundi · 51, 52, 141, 149, 150, 151, 152, 153, 171, 193, 195, 201, 202, 221, 247
business transactions · 80, 199

C

cabinet members · 49, 59
cadmium · 100
calculators · 125, 238
Cameroon · 31, 33, 104, 120, 121, 130, 131, 171, 193, 202, 236, 240, 251
Canada · 81, 90, 91, 122, 123, 190, 207
Capital · 76, 245, 246, 250
capital flows · 239, 247
capital shortage · 132
capitalism · xii, 1, 18, 19, 84, 85, 93, 141
Caribbean · 208
Central Africa · 107, 108, 122, 133, 171, 192, 193, 195, 221, 236
Chad · 106, 107, 116, 171, 191, 193, 201, 221, 240
chaos · 59, 99, 176, 177, 211, 249
cheap labor · 8, 181
Chile · 207, 208
China · 97, 98, 199, 212, 224, 226, 230, 246
Christians · 49, 50, 56
chromium · 189
Churchill, Winston · 140
citizenship · 39, 51, 52
civil war · 38, 44, 59, 102, 105, 106, 111, 113, 128, 144, 154, 164, 167, 168, 169, 170, 191, 201, 202, 203, 222, 226, 252
Civil War · 226
coal deposits · 12
cobalt · 8, 9, 78, 91, 92, 100, 122, 141, 153, 189
cocoa beans · 28
Cold War · 2, 44, 62, 200
colonial rule · 32, 33, 42, 59, 123, 126, 184, 196, 224
colonialism · 145, 174, 196, 211, 218, 227
Colorado · xii, 28
commercial banks · 194
commodities · xi, 20, 29, 72, 101, 120, 162, 183, 185, 189, 193, 197, 226, 229, 237, 241
common sense · 142, 148, 217
communism · ix, 94
communities · 70, 137
Community · 87, 118, 119, 122, 161, 164, 165, 166, 167, 172, 182, 195, 196, 235, 236
conflicts · 78, 93, 94, 191, 202
Congo · 51, 99, 100, 101, 102, 103, 147, 160, 163, 164, 165, 167, 168, 171, 177, 193, 195, 201, 215, 216, 223, 227, 230, 235, 247, 251
constitution · 7, 38, 43, 48, 49
constitutional authority · 166
consumer goods · 136, 181
consumption · 83, 114, 126, 155, 160, 161, 163, 169
cooperation · 119, 120, 122, 150, 192, 196, 237
copper · 4, 5, 6, 7, 8, 9, 10, 12, 16, 100, 102, 103, 106, 115, 122, 135, 138, 141, 153, 155, 159, 160, 162, 163, 170, 188
copper mines · 4
corruption · 3, 51, 67, 69, 70, 72, 73, 80, 81, 82, 89, 90, 99, 104, 105, 134, 140, 146, 147, 174, 175, 176, 203, 213, 220, 227, 231, 243, 251
Corruption · 51, 69, 108, 176, 232
cottage industry · 234
cotton · 8, 10, 36, 66, 89, 101, 107, 109, 114, 115, 117, 119, 124, 126, 130, 135, 137, 138, 141, 152, 153, 154, 156, 159, 164, 189
crop production · 136
crops · 8, 9, 12, 60, 66, 68, 77, 89, 101, 102, 104, 107, 109, 111, 114, 115, 116, 120, 124, 130, 135, 137, 138, 141, 151, 152, 153, 154, 156, 159, 161, 162, 163, 185, 197, 198, 220, 240
Currency · 194
currency exchange · 68

D

Debt · 189
decay · 103
decentralization · 14
decolonization · 122
democracy · xi, 35, 37, 41, 42, 45, 46, 47, 55, 56, 57, 63, 93, 94, 95, 97, 98, 106, 144, 145, 183, 184, 206, 237, 242
deregulation · 8
devaluation · 63, 240
Devaluation · 241
Developing Countries · 250
diamond mines · 12, 16, 169
diamonds · 12, 13, 15, 77, 78, 91, 100, 102, 103, 106, 108, 110, 111, 112, 122, 126, 147, 155, 157, 159, 160, 161, 162, 163, 169, 170, 189, 215
diet · 102
distribution of wealth · x, 29
diversification · 15, 117
domestic investments · 232, 247, 248
droughts · 108, 116, 131, 137, 138

E

earth · 68, 117, 153, 160
East Africa · 32, 34, 35, 36, 37, 39, 52, 62, 66, 72, 82, 87, 88, 93, 133, 138, 139, 143, 153, 166, 182, 191, 193, 194, 195, 196, 211
East Asia · 186, 214, 224, 226, 227, 229, 230, 231, 246
Eastern Europe · 213
ecology · 220
economic development · x, xii, 1, 2, 3, 12, 18, 20, 22, 44, 58, 74, 108, 112, 118, 119, 121, 122, 125, 127, 131, 136, 138, 139, 145, 149, 152, 153, 159, 161, 163, 172, 181, 183, 184, 185, 196, 219, 223, 225, 229, 233, 234, 247
economic growth · x, 3, 6, 8, 13, 19, 68, 71, 76, 83, 99, 108, 109, 110, 111, 113, 117, 119, 121, 123, 124, 127, 130, 131, 133, 134, 137, 138, 139, 140, 151, 157, 160, 162, 163, 164, 168, 172, 176, 180, 181, 183, 184, 186, 187, 188, 196, 203, 205, 206, 210, 213, 214, 215, 216, 220, 221, 222, 223, 224, 225, 226, 227, 228, 230, 231, 237, 240, 241, 243, 244, 246, 247, 248, 250, 252
economic model · 208, 238
economic performance · 6, 20, 25, 66, 69, 80, 83, 173, 181, 203, 213, 214, 215, 224, 231, 233, 244, 252
economic policies · 2, 6, 29, 46, 59, 60, 62, 63, 64, 66, 70, 75, 85, 87, 92, 99, 107, 176, 183, 212, 214, 220, 231, 244
economic policy · 5, 235
economic potential · 110, 113, 133, 136, 137, 153, 163, 164, 165, 167, 171
economic productivity · 124
economic recovery · 243
economic reform · 7, 51, 69, 70, 71, 80, 83, 85, 127, 206, 207, 208, 215, 233, 234, 241, 242, 252
economic transformation · ix, 22, 62, 82
Economists · 224
Ecuador · 208
education · 8, 13, 59, 60, 62, 70, 126, 127, 142, 176, 185, 215, 216, 226, 228, 241
egalitarianism · 46, 231
Egypt · 107, 120, 129, 137, 193
El Nino · 139
elections · 47, 53, 55, 57, 59, 139
electricity · 4, 67, 76, 87, 131, 166, 169, 231
Elf Aquitaine · 167
England · 194, 219, 234
enterprises, Private · 145
entrepreneurship · 2, 5, 181
environmental impact · 93
Eritrea · 32, 133, 134, 135, 138, 171, 193, 236, 237, 254
Ethiopia · x, 5, 8, 32, 71, 133, 135, 136, 137, 138, 147, 171, 193, 211, 212, 221, 235, 236, 237, 247, 254

ethnic conflict · 52, 59, 144, 152, 252
ethnic groups · 45, 56, 75, 222
ethnic minority · 218
ethnic relations · 52
ethos · 1, 46, 76, 94, 219
Europe · 14, 15, 22, 23, 74, 81, 101, 120, 126, 128, 142, 156, 189, 198, 223, 240, 249
Europe, Eastern · 213
European Union · 100, 134, 233, 235
exchange controls · 5, 8
exchange rates · 241, 244
excuse · 189, 220
exercise · 55
exploitation · 70, 77, 86, 107, 109, 116, 148, 153, 155, 163, 182, 190, 207, 227
export earnings · 7, 13, 112, 157, 162
exports · 6, 8, 14, 15, 16, 20, 26, 33, 46, 66, 83, 104, 108, 110, 111, 112, 113, 114, 116, 117, 118, 119, 120, 121, 122, 124, 126, 129, 130, 135, 137, 138, 139, 141, 151, 152, 153, 156, 161, 162, 164, 165, 167, 170, 183, 195, 197, 213, 226, 227, 234, 240, 241

F

failure · 4, 7, 21, 29, 40, 41, 44, 58, 62, 66, 69, 75, 81, 173, 181, 183, 185, 208, 217, 224, 252
family · 51, 61, 62, 81, 225
Far East · 24, 192
farming · 65, 82, 86, 89, 93, 112, 118, 149, 156, 159, 161, 186, 221, 248, 249
farmland · 114, 153
financial resources · 64, 91, 232, 238, 248
financial sector · 27, 90
Fishing · 101, 103, 109, 110, 111, 113, 117, 130, 139, 141, 155, 159, 163
Flows · 245, 246, 250
food shortages · 81
foreign aid · 2, 8, 61, 69, 83, 122, 134, 144, 145, 161, 172, 174, 181, 185, 188, 200, 203, 211, 216, 245
foreign capital · x, 15, 208, 246, 248, 249, 250, 252
foreign debt · 83
foreign direct investment · 83, 245, 247, 248, 249
foreign exchange · 10, 11, 13, 17, 29, 66, 68, 81, 83, 117, 128, 139, 152, 174, 197, 198, 239
foreign exchange reserve · 13, 83
foreign investment · x, 4, 5, 8, 9, 11, 14, 19, 22, 71, 77, 92, 119, 130, 132, 133, 140, 176, 178, 199, 200, 202, 203, 207, 208, 209, 214, 216, 220, 228, 232, 237, 239, 240, 242, 244, 246, 249, 252
foreign investments · 200, 202, 207, 208, 209, 214, 216, 220, 232, 237, 239, 240, 244, 246, 249
foreign investors · 2, 4, 11, 14, 15, 22, 35, 71, 76, 83, 89, 106, 109, 110, 122, 164, 176, 178, 188, 199, 203, 205, 213, 232
foreign markets · 14, 18, 149
Foreign Policy · 129
foreign trade · 133, 155
foreign workers · 133
France · 34, 103, 122, 189, 211, 240
free market · 86
free speech · 38
Freedom of speech · 184
free-market ideas · 44, 58
free-market policies · 3, 7, 26, 63, 142, 183, 184, 186, 206, 208, 209, 215, 216, 220, 226

G

Gabon · 36, 103, 104, 122, 123, 131, 156, 161, 171, 193, 234, 236, 251
Gambia · 32, 59, 117, 118, 119, 171, 174, 201, 235, 236
gasoline · 74

GDP · 3, 9, 10, 61, 69, 129, 157, 165, 167, 172, 173, 203, 211, 212, 213, 241, 243, 244
geography · 209, 219, 220, 221, 222, 223, 225
Georgia · 45
Germany · 26, 65, 189
Ghana · x, 3, 5, 8, 18, 19, 22, 23, 24, 25, 26, 27, 28, 31, 43, 68, 71, 82, 90, 98, 99, 106, 108, 109, 113, 114, 116, 120, 121, 124, 125, 126, 127, 171, 174, 176, 178, 180, 186, 187, 193, 204, 205, 206, 222, 223, 226, 227, 235, 236, 239, 241, 242, 244, 248
global economy · 5, 11, 29, 58, 176, 178, 199, 207, 212, 233, 246
global market · 18, 182, 208
globalization · 207, 208, 209
Globalization · 170, 186, 199, 204
gold and silver · 9
gold mines · 90, 91, 241
good reputation · 28
goods and services · 83, 229
Government · 18, 39, 48, 64, 71, 72, 82, 195, 232
government policy · 47, 65, 221
gratitude · vii
Great Britain · 194
Gross Domestic Product · 3, 61, 211
gross national product · 12, 116, 159, 161, 180, 183, 242
Guinea · x, 5, 7, 18, 28, 33, 34, 35, 98, 109, 110, 112, 118, 119, 124, 125, 131, 132, 133, 171, 190, 193, 212, 213, 227, 235, 236, 240, 254

H

health care · 231
health services · 176, 185, 216, 230
Hong Kong · 215, 227
House of Representatives · 48
Housing · 24
human capital · 203, 216
Hutus · 52, 151, 152, 153
hydrocarbon resources · 190

I

illiteracy · 59, 209
imperialism · 174
import duties · 87, 136
import substitution · 196
import tariffs · 166
import/export · 152, 240
imports · 13, 14, 29, 37, 63, 67, 74, 104, 108, 111, 117, 118, 129, 136, 141, 153, 161, 164, 165, 183, 195, 196, 233, 234, 239, 240, 241
Income · 186
independence · ix, xi, 2, 3, 4, 5, 6, 7, 8, 10, 12, 17, 18, 19, 20, 31, 32, 33, 34, 35, 38, 40, 42, 43, 45, 51, 58, 78, 97, 99, 100, 111, 114, 118, 121, 122, 125, 126, 127, 129, 131, 133, 134, 138, 154, 166, 167, 169, 170, 172, 173, 174, 176, 177, 180, 181, 182, 183, 184, 185, 186, 194, 196, 197, 200, 201, 213, 214, 220, 223, 224, 227, 229, 252, 254
India · 26, 42, 59, 98, 128
Indian Ocean · 34, 72, 76, 77, 88, 139, 155
indirect taxes · 195
Indonesia · 3, 97, 99, 129, 172, 173, 174, 210, 221, 227, 243, 251
industrial output · 8
industrial policy · 15
industrial sector · 187
industrialization · 66, 77, 110, 121, 126, 131, 138, 181, 187, 188, 197, 199, 228, 234, 252
industrialized nations · 2, 17, 180, 181, 182, 183, 189, 193, 197, 207, 228
inflation · 23, 70, 83, 203, 204, 205, 207, 212, 226, 227, 240, 244
infrastructure · 4, 8, 23, 65, 67, 72, 90, 92, 112, 117, 133, 137, 147, 152, 154, 164,

176, 185, 187, 188, 190, 200, 203, 205, 214, 220, 221, 223, 238, 241, 249
Infrastructure · 199, 204
intelligence · 230
International Monetary Fund · 19, 63, 186, 205, 246, 247
international trade · 29, 176, 207, 219, 220
intervention · 167
interview · 60, 63, 66, 142, 145, 176, 184, 196
intimidation · 65, 175
investment · x, 2, 3, 4, 12, 14, 18, 19, 21, 22, 23, 72, 83, 84, 87, 89, 91, 92, 137, 142, 145, 155, 164, 168, 176, 188, 197, 199, 200, 203, 207, 214, 215, 216, 234, 241, 242, 245, 246, 247, 248, 249, 250
investment opportunities · 22
investment promotion · 142
IQ · 217, 224
Iran · 37, 129
iron ore · 71, 77, 92, 100, 103, 106, 109, 110, 111, 112, 114, 115, 116, 117, 121, 122, 129, 138, 170
irrigation · 115, 126, 156, 160
Islamic fundamentalism · 36
Islamism · 53
Israel · 115, 158
Italy · 32, 178
Ivory Coast · 8, 18, 28, 59, 103, 106, 108, 109, 120, 121, 122, 123, 124, 125, 156, 163, 171, 187, 193, 200, 205, 213, 224, 235, 236, 240, 241, 244, 248, 251

J

Japan · 110, 224, 226, 228, 229, 249
joint ventures · 15, 110, 248
Julius Nyerere · xi, 19, 28, 38, 40, 43, 44, 45, 46, 58, 84, 142, 146, 149, 150

K

Kaunda, Kenneth · 6, 7
Kenya · 8, 18, 26, 36, 57, 70, 74, 81, 88, 93, 138, 139, 140, 160, 166, 171, 174, 187, 194, 195, 196, 222, 234, 236, 241, 248, 249
Kenyatta, Jomo · 140
know-how · 228, 252
knowledge · 228, 229
Korea · 3, 97, 99, 174, 210, 215, 224, 226, 227, 229, 243
Kwame Nkrumah · x, 19, 28, 43, 98, 114, 126, 147

L

labor force · 108, 132
labor restrictions · 9
Latin America · 176, 177, 180, 190, 199, 206, 207, 208, 209, 214, 231, 242, 243
leadership · ix, 3, 19, 28, 38, 46, 50, 53, 58, 59, 60, 63, 78, 101, 104, 107, 128, 131, 144, 145, 146, 147, 148, 175, 203, 204
least developed countries · 113
Leninism · 18
Lesotho · 153, 160, 161, 165, 166, 171, 215, 221, 245
liberalization · 3, 53, 63, 67, 73, 142, 208, 239, 244
Liberia · 36, 112, 113, 124, 129, 147, 171, 202, 235, 236, 251
Libya · 104, 156, 161, 193
life style · 232
lifestyle · 51
light industry · 110, 234
literacy rate · 59, 104, 161
literacy rates · 104, 161
loans · 5, 74, 122, 134, 145, 174, 248, 249, 250
local economy · 11
long-term loans · 248

loyalty · 39

M

mainland · 33, 36, 37, 38, 40, 48, 49, 50, 51, 53, 54, 56, 93, 94, 104, 118, 131, 132, 156, 161, 171, 194
Malawi · 123, 153, 154, 155, 165, 171, 195, 200, 211, 212, 215, 221, 241
Malaysia · 97, 174, 175, 210, 227, 237, 243, 244, 251
Mali · x, 5, 18, 32, 71, 106, 107, 121, 124, 171, 200, 221, 235, 236, 241, 244
manganese · 12, 100, 103, 104, 106, 109, 122, 126, 132, 160, 162, 163, 170, 188, 189
manufactured goods · 29, 181, 182, 183, 187, 199, 234
manufacturing · 9, 16, 60, 82, 86, 89, 101, 112, 126, 157, 159, 187, 200, 249
marketplace · 251
Marx, Karl · 21
Marxism-Leninism · 1, 18
Maryland · xii, 43
Massachusetts · 36, 75, 129
Mauritania · 202, 235, 236, 254
Mauritius · 165
mediation · 236
Mexico · 207, 208, 209
Middle East · 129
military conflict · 202
military power · 129
minerals · 8, 9, 11, 12, 13, 16, 17, 77, 78, 86, 88, 90, 91, 92, 99, 100, 101, 102, 104, 106, 107, 109, 110, 111, 112, 113, 114, 115, 116, 117, 119, 121, 126, 129, 135, 136, 138, 141, 147, 151, 152, 153, 154, 155, 159, 160, 162, 163, 164, 169, 170, 189, 193, 214, 234, 250
mining · 9, 15, 24, 25, 27, 78, 82, 86, 89, 90, 91, 92, 93, 108, 109, 110, 111, 112, 127, 154, 159, 161, 162, 163, 170, 248, 249, 251
mining companies · 78, 82, 86, 90
modernization · 42
momentum · 126, 184
Money · 227
morality · 36
Morocco · 132, 161, 193, 254
Mozambique · x, 5, 16, 79, 153, 154, 155, 156, 165, 171, 181, 186, 192, 193, 195, 211, 212, 239
multiparty system · 42, 46, 57, 84, 85, 94
multi-party system · 35, 37, 41
Muslims · 50, 51, 56

N

Namibia · 16, 106, 153, 156, 161, 162, 165, 171, 201, 213, 254
national elections · 44, 47, 55
national interest · x, 46
national leader · 50
national policy · 120, 213
national savings · x, 89, 227, 228, 232, 247
national unity · 1, 41, 47, 48, 52, 54, 55, 94, 95, 183, 184, 185
nationalism · 11, 94, 149, 252
Nationalism · 42, 43
nationalization · 4, 75, 181
nation-state · 185, 230
natural gas · 76, 103, 129, 130, 138, 151, 155, 169, 171, 189, 190, 191, 192, 193
natural resources · 2, 6, 9, 78, 99, 102, 103, 106, 110, 111, 114, 115, 119, 122, 123, 130, 131, 132, 133, 136, 137, 138, 152, 154, 159, 161, 163, 189, 191, 199, 215, 246, 250, 251
Nelson Mandela · 143, 158
neocolonial powers · 247
neo-colonialism · 227
New Jersey · 243
nickel · 9, 12, 16, 78, 89, 91, 92, 109, 152, 160

Niger · 105, 109, 116, 117, 124, 171, 181, 221, 225, 235, 236
Nigeria · 3, 8, 18, 31, 38, 39, 44, 45, 99, 104, 105, 106, 114, 116, 120, 121, 123, 124, 125, 127, 128, 129, 130, 132, 133, 137, 152, 157, 163, 166, 167, 171, 172, 173, 174, 187, 191, 193, 201, 202, 203, 205, 222, 225, 226, 230, 234, 235, 236, 248
Nile River · 141
North Africa · 193
North Korea · 148, 224
North Sea · 190
nuclear bomb · 128, 158
nuclear weapons · 158, 159

O

OECD · 246
oil exploration · 168
oil industry · 167, 168, 170, 192
Oil Industry · 190, 191
oil prices · 66, 129
oil resources · 190
Oman · 54
one-party system · xii, 6, 7, 41, 42, 43, 44, 46, 47, 55, 56, 57, 59, 84, 93, 183
OPEC · 128
opposition parties · 53
oppression · 50, 94
Oregon · 228
Organization of African Unity (OAU) · 123, 235, 237

P

Pacific · 98
palladium · 9
Papua · 98
Paris Club · 83
partisanship · 94
peacekeeping · 129, 166
Pemba · 35, 37, 38, 48, 53, 54, 55, 56, 88
Persian Gulf · 54, 192
personality · 42
Peru · 208
petroleum products · 10, 130
Philippines · 244
pipeline project · 76
platinum · 9, 12, 138, 153, 160, 188, 189
pluralist democracy · 47
police · 64, 228
political class · 67
political environment · 17
political instability · 34, 203, 213, 227
political movement · 57
political parties · 35, 44, 47, 56, 144, 145
political process · 41, 44, 46, 59, 249
political reform · 249
political space · 150
political stability · 249
pollution · 127
population density · 152, 219
population growth · 186, 208, 214, 237, 239, 244
population growth rate · 214
Portugal · 154
poultry · 8, 77, 101, 102, 109, 116, 130, 138, 141, 153
poverty · ix, 34, 67, 72, 99, 104, 107, 108, 114, 115, 116, 117, 118, 131, 135, 149, 151, 152, 154, 161, 172, 174, 176, 179, 181, 207, 208, 209, 213, 214, 232
precious metals · 9, 90, 189
Pretoria · 235
price controls · 8, 239, 241
prime minister · 48, 51, 111
private business · 10, 212, 250
private capital · 70, 90, 245, 246, 247, 248, 249, 250
private enterprise · 20, 145, 238
private ownership · 35, 58, 61, 76
private property · 203
privatization · 5, 6, 7, 8, 11, 14, 18, 19, 21, 22, 23, 24, 25, 26, 27, 71, 73, 74, 75, 76, 79, 80, 84, 86, 89, 142, 237

productivity · x, 1, 60, 61, 79, 219
property rights · 219
public opinion · 41, 85
public sector · 35, 68

R

race relations · 69
rate, birth · 226, 231
rate, economic growth · 3, 71, 121, 186, 205, 214, 215
raw materials · 64, 175, 181, 182, 188, 189, 197, 198, 237
reasoning · 18
recession · 68, 207
Red Cross · 238
reforms, economic · 7, 69, 70, 71, 80, 83, 127, 206, 207, 208, 215, 241, 252
refugees · 51, 52
regional powers · 129
regionalism · 145
reliability · 28
Renaissance · 22, 216, 244
repatriation · 205
rhetoric · 19, 56, 243
rhodium · 9
ruling elite · 204
ruling party · 35, 37, 40, 41, 50, 55, 183
rural areas · 2, 14, 65
Russian Revolution · ix
Rwanda · 51, 52, 141, 143, 149, 150, 151, 152, 153, 171, 195, 201, 202, 212, 221

S

sales tax · 87
Saudi Arabia · 127, 234
science and technology · 229
Security Council · 128
security forces · 34, 59, 184, 249
self-interest · 21
Senegal · 8, 18, 32, 42, 118, 119, 120, 121, 124, 171, 193, 201, 202, 230, 235, 236, 239
Separatism · 33
Seychelles · 165
Singapore · 97, 110, 117, 136, 174, 215, 227, 243
skilled labor · 137, 176
slave trade · 36, 118
social change · 173
social justice · 18, 43
social services · 61, 62, 68, 70, 126
social transformation · 145
socialism · ix, x, xi, xii, 1, 18, 19, 43, 44, 58, 60, 65, 66, 73, 74, 75, 76, 84, 85, 93, 142, 146, 227
socialist countries · 44
socialist society · 21
socioeconomic status · 178
soil erosion · 149
Somalia · 1, 5, 135, 136, 137, 171, 193, 202, 236
Somaliland · 135
South Africa · 8, 9, 14, 15, 16, 17, 22, 23, 25, 27, 71, 78, 79, 82, 84, 85, 86, 88, 90, 91, 97, 99, 105, 106, 112, 123, 127, 128, 129, 148, 149, 153, 155, 156, 157, 158, 159, 160, 161, 162, 164, 165, 166, 167, 171, 173, 196, 200, 229, 234, 235, 239, 244, 248
Southeast Asia · 97, 99, 164, 224, 242
sovereignty · 40, 94, 119, 150
Soviet Union · ix, 59, 188, 189, 200
Soyinka, Wole · 105, 106
Spain · 132, 254
standard of living · 11, 70, 79, 80, 102, 115
state enterprises · 27, 75, 185
state intervention · 27
state ownership · 10, 21
stock exchange · 11, 25, 27, 84
stock market · 7, 76, 207, 246, 248
sub-Saharan Africa · 14, 33, 36, 71, 127, 141, 145, 153, 157, 165, 167, 171, 178,

201, 206, 210, 211, 214, 219, 221, 224, 227, 233, 234, 235
subsistence crops · 12, 130
Sudan · 36, 143, 201, 236, 237
Suez Canal · 135
superpower · ix
Swaziland · 59, 153, 155, 156, 157, 160, 161, 164, 165, 171, 221, 224
Switzerland · 111, 156, 157, 177
sympathy · 175

T

Taiwan · 72, 215, 224, 226, 227
Tanganyika · xi, 31, 32, 33, 40, 43, 45, 50, 51, 52, 56, 59, 62, 77, 82, 88, 152, 194, 195
tariff barriers · 183
tariffs · 14, 37, 38, 68, 239
tax burden · 89
tax evasion · 251
tea plantations · 10
telecommunications · 22, 24, 84, 87, 194, 249
territorial claims · 202
territorial integrity · 33, 35, 53, 254
textiles · 10, 15, 130, 137, 164, 234
Textiles · 240
Thailand · 3, 97, 99, 174, 210, 227, 242, 244
Third World · 13, 46, 63, 64, 97, 102, 128, 140, 157, 171, 176, 180, 181, 182, 183, 190, 199, 203, 207, 233, 246, 247, 248, 249, 250
Third World countries · 129, 181, 183, 207, 249
Togoland · 31, 113
tourism · 12, 17, 82, 88, 89, 92, 93, 115, 133, 139
trade union · 6
transportation · 4, 16, 27, 59, 67, 101, 106, 107, 108, 109, 110, 112, 116, 117, 119, 121, 126, 127, 132, 138, 139, 141, 151, 152, 153, 154, 161, 162, 172, 176, 194, 195, 206, 220, 223, 249
tribalism · 45, 46, 47, 95, 145, 147, 252
troops · 33, 52, 103, 131, 191, 201
Tunisia · 193
Tutsis · 52, 151, 152, 153

U

Uganda · 3, 8, 18, 41, 42, 45, 52, 56, 71, 81, 99, 140, 141, 142, 143, 144, 146, 147, 148, 149, 152, 166, 171, 184, 186, 194, 196, 201, 205, 210, 211, 212, 215, 221, 222, 226, 232, 236, 237, 238, 239, 241, 242, 244, 245, 248
unemployment · 23, 34, 205
unions · 33, 80, 81, 207
UNITA · 167, 169, 170
United Kingdom · 113
United Nations · 32, 129, 179, 182, 199, 246
United States · 11, 19, 20, 36, 59, 64, 79, 87, 97, 107, 111, 123, 127, 146, 158, 188, 189, 200, 205, 207, 210, 213, 233, 234, 245, 249
uranium · 100, 103, 104, 106, 108, 109, 116, 117, 132, 136, 153, 154, 159, 160, 162, 188
urbanization · 186

V

violence · 46, 53, 59, 65, 93, 139, 211, 249
voting · 55, 56, 57

W

water resources · 100
weapons of mass destruction · 158
work force · 8, 17, 179

workers, migrant · 133
World Bank · 7, 19, 20, 61, 63, 69, 74, 83, 87, 107, 134, 179, 203, 205, 206, 208, 210, 227, 239, 241, 243, 244, 246, 248, 249, 250
world economy · 182, 193, 199
world peace · 159
World War II · 224, 226

Y

Yugoslavia · 94

Z

Zaire · 51, 99, 100, 101, 141, 143, 147, 160, 163, 164, 168, 169, 171, 174, 175, 201, 203, 235, 247, 251
Zambia · 3, 4, 5, 6, 7, 8, 59, 71, 88, 99, 151, 153, 155, 160, 165, 171, 195, 221, 241
Zanzibar · 31, 32, 33, 35, 36, 37, 38, 39, 40, 48, 49, 50, 53, 54, 55, 56, 59, 62, 70, 88, 93, 94
Zimbabwe · 8, 9, 10, 11, 14, 23, 25, 71, 106, 153, 154, 155, 160, 164, 165, 166, 171, 195, 201, 211, 212, 213, 221, 235, 237, 241, 248, 254
zinc · 8, 100, 102, 103, 109, 162, 170